WOMEN, MEDIA AND POLITICS

WOMEN, MEDIA AND POLITICS

A.K. Devgan

CYBER TECH PUBLICATIONS
4264/3, Ansari Road, Daryaganj, New Delhi-110002 (India)
Ph.: 011-23244078, 011-43559448 Fax: 011-23280028
E-Mail: cyberpublicationsdelhi@yahoo.com
Website: www.cybertechpublications.com

WOMEN, MEDIA AND POLITICS

A.K. Devgan

First Edition 2010

Published by :

G.S. Rawat for **Cyber Tech Publications**

4264/3, Ansari Road, Daryaganj, New Delhi-110002 (India)

Ph.: 011-23244078, 011-43559448 Fax: 011-23280028

E-Mail: cyberpublicationsdelhi@yahoo.com

Website: www.cybertechpublications.com

Printed at: Asian Offset Printers, Delhi-53

Preface

Gender is one of the primary fault lines running through contemporary American politics. The political agenda has become deeply polarized by such issues as affirmative action, abortion rights, and welfare reform. In short, gender politics, once regarded as marginal, has emerged as one of the core dividing lines in identifying politicians, parties, issues, and voters in America.

Not surprising, the way media covers gender politics has long been a matter of contention. The issue at the heart of this book is whether, as critics suggest, media coverage of women in America reinforces rather than challenges the dominant culture, thereby contributing towards women's marginalization in public life.

A collection of original essays by twenty-one top academics and journalists is the first book to systematically examine the impact of the media on women's power in America. It focuses on how the role of American women as citizens, political leaders, and feminist activists has been influenced by the media, for better or worse, in recent decades. Using multi-method approaches involving surveys, content analysis, focus groups, interviews, and personal experience, the authors analyze the role of women as journalists, the impact of campaign coverage, images of women in power, and coverage of women's movements and feminist policy issues.

—Autho

Contents

1

WOMEN IN POLITICS

Social class, status, and power are predetermined by one's gender. Within today's patriarchal society, men simply possess greater power than women, "and enjoy greater access to what is valued by the social group." (Code 1993, 19) Patriarchal thought produces male dominance, and authority within multiple areas, including politics. Throughout history, governments have designed laws to maintain such divisions of power, resulting in the oppression of women. "Patriarchal power relations construct sexual differences as political differences by giving legal form to the belief that women, because of their sex, are fit only to serve as wives and mothers." (Vickers 1997, 8) One must question how women can achieve greater influence within the male political arena if they are not viewed as equal? How are determined women attempting to change their position within society, regarding politics? Multiple changes have been made throughout history regarding the place of women in society, but are they leading towards equality?

The main goal of the women's movement was basic citizenship rights for women. For decades, many of the first women's groups strived for their civil, and political rights as women. Their central focus was the right to vote, and the right to run for office. The purpose was to claim a role in democratic politics. Many believed that in order to attain political goals, the right to vote was vital. The women's movement "has touched the lives of many Canadian women, radically transforming the nature of their everyday experiences." (Burt 1993, 9) Women assumed that once the right to vote was granted, equality in the eyes of males was soon to follow, along with their new influence within politics.

After the right to federal franchise for women was established, females continued to be disqualified from positions within the Senate because they were not considered qualified "persons" as defined by the British North America (BNA) Act. (Burt 1993, 246) It was not until 1929 when five women from Alberta disputed the BNA Act, and the British Judicial Committee of the Privy Council determined that women be recognized as "persons" within the law

Soon, it became apparent that legal rights alone would not be enough for women to acquire an impressive influence within politics. Within the nineteen sixties, and seventies, women continued to remain fixtures within the second-class, and unable to alter their status. "Women still performed most of the domestic duties; could not find adequate, affordable child care; were woefully under-represented in politics; earned a fraction of the pay men earned; faced spousal abuse, sexual assault, and sexual harassment; and had no legal access to birth control." (Brodie 1995, 70) Many of these issues remained unimportant to politicians, and decision makers, as they did not directly affect them. Multiple women's groups began demanding care for their children, equal pay, unrestrictive employment legislation, and the termination of sex-role stereotyping in schools, and by mass media. (Code 1993, 63-64) Once it became evident that the government was not concerned with women's rights, groups began to form in an attempt to correct the setback. Some women's groups made demands on the state; others provided services for women; others offered solidarity based on ethnicity, class, ideology, sexual orientation, and disability. (Burt 1993, 2000)

Decades full of protests for women's rights created several political gains, as well as improvements in their status; however, inequality remained. Women's beliefs that political rights would lead to equal opportunity, were overshadowed by the reality that their inequality resulted in their lack of influence within politics. Multiple policies and laws may have been created or changed in an attempt to improve women's role in society, but economic dependence, and physical reliance on men continued as issues. Women remained underrepresented within politics, holding fewer than twenty percent of federal, and provincial elected offices in Canada. (Arscott 1998, 272) "In 1998, only fourteen percent of provincially appointed judges, and twenty percent of justices appointed by the federal government were women." (Arscott 1998, 274) Eliminating women from political positions hindered their ability to become a valid influence within the political arena.

Unequal pay, workplace harassment, and discrimination continued to plague women in the work force. Statistics Canada released a report, Women in Canada, in 2000, detailing women's position in society. In 1999, seventy percent of women were employed in clerical or administrative positions; teaching, nursing, and health occupations; and sales, and service occupations. ("Women in Canada" 2000)

The report also confirmed that women's income remained drastically lower than men's. Many believe that the variance between wages is due to the fact that forty-one percent of women are employed in part-time, or temporary positions; however, those employed in full-time positions only earn seventy-three percent of what male employees make. Women occupy only twenty-two percent of the country's highest paying jobs, but hold sixty-eight percent of the lowest paying jobs. ("Women in Canada" 2000) With the lack of women in high profile positions, and the belief that women are not as valuable as men, they continue to provide no bearing on the political aspects of society.

Women continue to receive less in our patriarchal society. "Women have less political power, fewer economic resources, less security, and lower status that do men." (Brodie 1995, 3) This continues regardless of decades dedicated to movements for women's rights, and lobbying for policies designed to alter women's status in society. For those women who are poor, immigrant, Aboriginal, or disabled, they find themselves even more inferior than other women. Therefore, the question remains, are women equal? Simply stated, they are not equal. Women continue to fight for liberal democratic political power. Their gender continues to play a role in how society will view them, as well as their position. For centuries, power has been allotted to men, which continues to this day. Few women possess great political power due to the difficulties of obtaining customary equality within society.

In a world where men rule, how is a women able to gain great authority, and step into the political spot light? In a society where women are viewed as insignificant, how are they to influence political decision makers? The law has granted women a voice within politics; however, it remains weak and inaudible. In order for women to increase their influence in politics, they must first become equal with men. Until then, they will be viewed as inferior; therefore, not requiring influence in politics. Gradually women are gaining more power, and prestige in society. Soon, the number in high-paying jobs will increase, creating a less economically dependent gender. As women strive for these changes, men, especially politicians, will be forced to take notice. As power for women intensifies, so will their influence in politics. As the voice for women's rights grows, so will their equality; therefore, leveling out the playing field in the political arena for both men, and women.

Women in Politics Beginning with the early nineteen hundreds, women from all over the country have bounded together, forming leagues and clubs for equal rights. However, it wasn't until today "at the dawn of the twenty-first century, states and international community can no longer refute the fact that humanity is made up of two sexes, not just one" (Oliveria 26). Why has the woman's move for equality just now started to balance itself out? Well, the answer is quite simple; women are just now being looked at as semi-equals. They are beginning to become corporate executives in businesses, and popular in the field of medicine and law. Women have tried hard to push themselves forward in society to create a balanced and harmonious economy and so far it has been successful. Barriers of all kinds have been broken, well, all except a few, mainly in politics and with the information I have collected I will show why. Politics...when one stops and thinks of the word "politics" what naturally comes to mind? Our founding fathers, Presidents George Washington, John Adams and Thomas Jefferson; the popular political figures of today, President Bill Clinton, George W. Bush and Al Gore; or do we think about Belva Ann Lockwood, Jeannette Rankin, Frances Perkins, and Eugenie Moore - who?

When American's think about politics, Lyn Kathlene, journalist for the "Higher Education Chronicles," states that "ninety-five percent of the time they envision a man who is in charge of running, or helping to run, their country." Is society to blame for this misconception that women do not hold important roles in government and participate in making important decisions for our country? Not really, people just don't hear or read about women in politics as often as they do about men. As most people learn throughout elementary and junior high or middle school, our nation first formed government in 1776 when Thomas Jefferson first drafted our constitution. During this time women did not have a role in government, nor would they for the next one hundred and eight years, until a woman would try to run for office. "In 1884, Belva Ann Lockwood – the first woman to try a case before the United States Supreme Court – ran for Presidency" (Arenofsky 14). Well, to no surprise she lost, but her groundbreaking campaign made it possible and easier for Jeannette Rankin, thirty-three years later, to run and become elected to Congress for the state of Montana.

However, even with this groundbreaking experience, women were still looked down upon for their lack of experience. It wasn't until 1920 when women's suffrage ended and the nineteenth amendment to the constitution, granting women the right to vote, that women were formally introduced into politics. However, even with voting privileges, women were still looked at as weak feeble creatures. The lack of confidence and the inability to be seen as strong-minded females who were not afraid to voice their opinion hurt the female gender immensely.

It wasn't until "Eleanor Roosevelt, wife of President Franklin D. Roosevelt, crisscrossed the country speaking about social problems and serving as the quintessential role model for the politically active female" that women began to witness how to present themselves with confidence (Arenofsky 14). Finally, with women's confidence on the rise and their new understanding and attitudes toward government, women were starting to attain a higher status in the political arena. The big break for women came from the decision by President Franklin D. Roosevelt, who in 1933 appointed Frances Perkins to the cabinet as Secretary of labor (Hogan 4). With this big break, women were finally moving forward in government and there was no looking back. So, after all of this hard work and dedication by early feminists to achieve a voice in politics, was it worth the struggles and did it pay off?

Rosiska Darcy de Oliveria, journalist for the United Nations Educational, Scientific, and Cultural Courier, believes so. She states, women's rise to power and their participation in politics are the vital signs of a healthy democracy, which would make good sense since the United States is a free country where everyone is suppose to be equal to their neighbor (26). However, others believe that political women are causing great harm to their character" (Oliveria 28). Oliveria states that, women in positions of power must constantly prove that they can behave like men. They keep quiet about having to look after children, run a household and care for elderly parents. Bringing those issues out into the open would mean admitting "'flaws'" that men do not have... Women have changed, but the world of work has not and they are reacting to the point of exhaustion (27).

Just imagine the women in power of today - Elaine Chao (Secretary of the Department of Labor), Gale Norton, (Secretary of the Department of the Interior), Ann Vereman, (Secretary of the Department of Agriculture), and Christine Todd Whitman, (Director of the Environmental Protection Agency). Not to mention the numerous women senators, state legislatures, judges, governors, and mayors. With the exception of a few, the vast majority of these women fall between the ages of thirty-five to fifty years old. In today's society it is not uncommon for women of these ages to have young or teenage children at home. These high authority political figures are expected to work from seven in the morning to ten at night, five to six days a week. They are also supposed to be responsible for the daily expected tasks of the traditional woman - cooking dinner, cleaning the house, running little Billy to baseball and karate and little Sally to ballet, and still look zestfully clean with a smile on her faces for her husband. The double burden, resulting from an outdated social contract, is putting women under mounting pressure by speeding up their lives to an untenable pace (Oliveria 28). However, in some magical, mysterious way, women are managing themselves quite nicely.

So, besides the fact that it is detrimental to a woman's character to be involved in politics, what else is holding them back? Robert E. Hogan, Professor of Government at Louisiana State University, believes it's money.

He states, it takes so much money to run for office in the United States (14). Let's face it, there are far more white-collared, wealthy men in the United States, and in the world for that matter, than there are women. Even with women having highly paid corporate executive jobs, women still make far less than that of their male counterparts. For women, this is one of the major issues as to why government is lacking female participation. The most valid explanation for this problem is that the government controls the financial gains of women to limit their power. Looking at the facts, women make up fifty-two percent of our nation's population, strange how such a big percentage of population has little representation (Hunter 47).

The thought of a government developed by males and dominated by females just does not sit well with the vast majority of higher male authority. Therefore, in order to make sure that women do not dominate, without being boldly direct about it, income levels are tampered with. It may sound bizarre, but in Lyn Kathlene's Studying the New Voice of Women in Politics, she gives some very valid evidence that shows how women are paid in comparison to men in the same high white-collared jobs. The results are quite shocking. Kathlene shows that women are out-paid by men by nearly forty-percent for the same amount of work and jobs! The responsibilities of taking care of their home and loved ones and the lack of funds, the fight for women's dominance in government will never prevail. Does this mean American's should just sit back and forget about the women before them who fought hard for their right to vote, to be heard, and have equality in government? No, but society needs to realize that this is 'the dawn of a new century' and the role of the female should indeed be reevaluated.

WOMEN, MEDIA AND POLITICS IN LEBANON

In a country where over half of the population are women, Lebanon lacks political representation even more than some of its other Arab neighbors. Simba Russeau looks at the roles women are seeking to fulfill in Lebanon after the formation of a national unity government.

Thousands of children in Lebanon are denied full access to education, health-care and residency because they do not have Lebanese citizenship.

Lebanese women cannot pass on their nationality to their children and in the event of separation, it is the father who gains automatic custody, according to Lebanese nationality law.

There is a saying in Lebanon: The only woman you'll see in parliament is the one wearing black, mourning for the death of her husband or brother, whose political mantle she has inherited.

In a country famed for being the region's most socially liberal and politically democratic, just one woman, Bahia Hariri, the sister of slain former premier Rafik Hariri, became a member of Lebanon's new unity cabinet, announced in early July.

Although Bahia was an MP before her brother's assassination in 2005, women cabinet ministers such as Nayla Moawad, former minister of Social Affairs, or former Industry Minister Leila Solh, joined politics after their husband and father, respectively, died.

Women MPsWomen were only present in parliamentary life twice between 1952 and 1962 and then not again until three female members of parliament (MPs) won seats in the 1992 elections.

"Women's groups are demanding a 35 percent quota in representation in the government, which would allow for issues such as the custody and nationality law to take precedence," said activist Roula Masri.

"Women's groups are demanding a 35 percent quota in representation in the government, which would allow for issues such as the custody and nationality law to take precedence."

In the last Lebanese parliamentary elections in 2005 only three MPs out of 128 were women - far fewer than politically restricted neighbours such as Syria, which had 30 women MPs out of 250; Jordan which had 13 out of 165; and Egypt which had 31 out of 718. Parliamentary elections in Lebanon are due next April.

Women make up about 53 percent of the population - around two million citizens - while research by the Collective for Research and Training on Development Action (CRTDA) found that women aged 23-34 outnumber men by seven to one, because most young men are employed abroad.

While making great strides in the labour force, with women highly visible in sectors such as the media, advertising and design, poor political representation is hampering women's ability to reform discriminatory laws, say activists.

CRTDA recently re-launched its "Nationality Campaign", lobbying politicians on the right for women to nationalise their children if marrying non-Lebanese.

Nationality lawThe nationality law was established in 1925 and partially reformed in 1994 in a complex decree.

According to a 2008 report by the non-governmental organisation (NGO) Frontiers Association, the 1994 amendment allows the child of a Lebanese mother and foreign father to gain Lebanese citizenship after the child's marriage to a Lebanese, and at least five years uninterrupted residency in the country, including one year after marriage.

A more comprehensive reform to the nationality law has become mired in the political issue of the presence of tens of thousands of Syrian workers and 400,000 Palestinian refugees in Lebanon.

Some politicians have argued that to allow Lebanese women to nationalise the children they have with non-Lebanese, such as Syrians and Palestinians, would be to shake up the delicate sectarian demographic on which the country's political system is founded.

But according to activist Masri, figures from the Interior Ministry from 2001 indicate that only 1,000 Lebanese women are married to foreigners, although she admits these need updating with field research.

"However, the issue is not about how many women are married to Palestinians, Syrians or other foreigners but that they have to amend this law to highlight that this is a human right," she said.

Fewer rightsEven in simple, everyday tasks, women can find they have fewer rights than men.

Rania Choueiri, a jewellery designer who owns a shop on trendy Monot Street, recounts her story of trying to open a bank account for her son, Karim.

"They asked me where is his father," said Rania. "I asked why they need his father when I am his mother and want an account for my son. They told me that only the father can open the account. I couldn't believe it."

Lebanon's nationalisation campaign has harnessed social networking website Facebook. A group centred on discussion of the nationality law currently has some 8,000 members.

"Many Lebanese women abroad have children and would like to return to Lebanon with their families but are prohibited because they are unable to provide legal papers to their families," said Masri.

WOMEN IN POLITICS: USING MEDIA FOR GOOD GOVERNANCE

Just a few months after she was elected vice governor, the second highest political post in Benguet province in the hinterlands of northern Philippines, Edna Tabanda realized it was not enough to try making governance work for women. In Benguet, where the poverty is best described as stark due to minimal resources for development, she has come to terms with the fact that she needs to reach out more to her constituents and they to her, for governance to be participatory and uplifting to the majority. Tabanda has various messages for women in tribal communities who, although they contribute a lot to the province's commercial vegetable production, are uncompensated or underpaid for their labor: Women are capable of being leaders, of holding public office. Women can participate and benefit from community development. Women have rights equal to the men.

Gender equality is at the core of her messages. How to say it isn't a problem. How to propagate it. Media, she thought, could help. The few women who are already in local government like Tabanda — a mere 2 to 3 percent in the Asia-Pacific region as of June 2001, according to the United Nations (ESCAP) — have wanted to tap the media.

NOT ALL TRADITIONAL POLITICS

Tabanda clarified that it isn't herself she wants to project, even if she is a rarity in the male-dominated politics of Benguet. That she made it in politics and is exerting efforts to make it truly serve ordinary folk is already an important statement.

"It's not all traditional politics," Tabanda, president of the Network of Elected Filipino Women for Good Governance, said, in reference to the politics of patronage that was still the norm in the country.

Tabanda in an advocate of transformative leadership —the kind of leadership that improves women's position in society and provides resources and opportunities for women to meet their needs and realize their full potential.

It is for the likes of Vice-Gov. Tabanda, and others like her in governance and decision-making, that the Media and Transformative Leadership Congress was organized in Manila last November, said Khunying Supatra Masdit, president of the Center for Asia-Pacific Women in Politics (CAPWIP), one of the congress organizers.

Media, the Frontier to be Conquered

"Media is the frontier to be conquered. It's undoubtedly an essential element in the campaign for a culture of transformative leadership," she said.

It isn't an easy frontier to conquer, though, according to journalist Melinda Quintos-De Jesus, executive director of the Center for Media Freedom and Responsibility, one of the organizers of the congress.

Media is a double-bladed sword, so to speak. "It is both part of the problem as it is part of the solution," Quintos-de Jesus told some 250 Asian participants.

It is not easy to become attractive copy for radio, television, newspapers and the Internet. The likes of Tabanda face tough challenges ahead to bring women's issues, concerns and aspirations to the attention of the public and policy makers.

The scant attention to women's issues lies in age-old conventions of journalism where there is, as De Jesus pointed out, a bias for bad news and what is out-of-the-norm.

The drive for profit where the press has become big business likewise eases out stories that don't raise ratings, circulation and advertisements. Technological advancements, which media empires have used to expand audience reach, have focused "only on the news interesting to and concerning the wealthiest and most powerful nations of the world."

De Jesus noted, "The expansion has not been accompanied with the proportionate inclusion of people around the world." News empires, in being too big, have lost their grasp of issues that are genuinely relevant. She observed that the press has "lost touch with the people who live on the margins, effectively relegating their issues to the margins of the policy conversation."

Media has lost its links with the ordinary folk. In certain instances, she said this has resulted in a "stronger alliance of the press with those in power and in the establishment, rather than out of the power loop."

FEEDING WOMEN'S STORIES TO MEDIA

But all is not lost. Thanks to a public that's critical, De Jesus said, the free press around the world has done some soul-searching over questions of content and conduct.

It is possible to work with media and feed it gender issues, as some groups have learned. Bandana Rana of Sancharika Samuha (Women's Communicators Forum) in Nepal has approached the work with a clear view of media's role.

"One of the most important aspects of communications for women leaders and development worker is actual outreach to mainstream media as the largest informer and maker of public opinion," she said.

The media, in her mind, is a partner. "Unless the voices and activities of women leaders are reported, from a progressive women's viewpoint, and on an on-going basis, stereotypes and generalizations will be perpetuated."

To Rana, much is at stake. "The best of women and development work can also be rendered useless if not adequately and appropriately reported by the media," she said.

Working since 1997, Rana's group has improved gender coverage in the media in Nepal through gender training for journalists, monitoring of women's issues in the news, providing a news service, holding monthly talk programs between journalists and social workers, and giving awards for outstanding journalistic reports on gender issues.

WOMEN'S MEDIA NETWORKS

There are some journalists in the mainstream media whose writings are focused on gender issues. One such network of journalists is the Women's Feature Service (WFS), a Unesco project since 1978. The WFS in India sees its features published in over 50 newspapers and magazines in the country and abroad, according to its executive director Angana Parekh.

Building bridges with the media, she said, isn't only about landing in the news. The common ground is credibility and trust, where the distortion or sensational reporting of facts has no place.

Situations do vary. In Tabanda's case, the press works in the city, hardly coming to far-flung villages.

"In my case, I have to innovate," Tabanda said, baring plans to go into newsletters using the local language, training persons in development communication and trying out the proven ways to tell the women's stories.

2

MEDIA IN INDIA

Among the institutions that contribute to the make-up of a public sphere in society, the media perhaps perform the most critical function. In the transactions in the public sphere, the media are not a neutral participant or an impassioned chronicler. Instead they either legitimize the status quo or innovator of the existing social equilibrium. The conflict or collaboration of the media with forces that attempt to colonize the public sphere materializes in this context. The mutual relationship between the state and the media, either as oppositional or as complementary, is influenced, among others, by the nature of intervention of the state in the public sphere. The former goes back to the 18th century when the Bengal Gazette trained its guns on the British administration and was mauled in the process. Since then, the endeavor of the press to imbue the public space with a critical culture has been consistently curtailed by the state, both by legislative interventions and by administrative interference.

For liberal democratic practice such measures of the state have serious implications, as restrictions on the media are bound to affect the ambience of the public sphere. The Indian intelligentsia realized this as early as the beginning of the 19th century when Rammohan Roy, acclaimed as the father of modern India, publicly denounced the attempts of the British government to curb the freedom of the press. Following the lead set by Rammohan, freedom of expression and civil liberties became two key issues of the anti-colonial struggle. In fact, the history of both the national movement and of the press can be read as the history of the struggle for these two rights. The legacy of this struggle has great contemporary value, as the freedom of the press and civil liberties continue to be under strain due to the restrictions imposed by the state.

Herbert Schiller, a theoretician of repute, has ascribed to the media the role of mind managers. Implicit in this description is the ideological function of the media in society. As such, multiple social consequences could ensue as a result of the intervention of the media. For instance, it could generate a sense of fatalism. It could also create non-conformism. The first relegates the media to the status of an adjunct of the dominant interests whereas the second provides them the possibility of influencing the course of history. There are several occasions in the life of a nation when the media are called upon to make a choice.

In India such a situation arose in the 1990s when a massive, emotionally orchestrated secular political mobalization was taken. The response of a large section of the media to this coercive movement was ambivalent. Many chose to swim with the tide. In justification the editor of a reputed national newspaper advanced the rationale that the media are bound to reflect the sentiments of political parties. By doing so he was renouncing the leadership role of the media — of that of an intellectual, if you like — which the nationalist press had so admirably performed. It also relegated the media to the status of a helpless victim. The consequences were grievous. The intellectual atmosphere thus generated by the media considerably contributed to the undermining of the harmonious social order and legitimacy of the state.

During the last two decades, the Indian media have undergone a sea change, particularly in their intellectual content and cultural ambience. There are two sources from which the transformation draws sustenance and inspiration: one emanating from outside and the other internally generated. The first, which seeks to subordinate the media to global control, comes with a variety of promises — of development, technology and internationalism — extremely appealing to the modernising quest of the middle class. The baggage also includes access to the advanced frontiers of knowledge and the cultural avant garde. The political and intellectual discourse, which it might generate, is likely to influence the nature and direction of social transformation. Whether it would lead to an intellectual climate in favour of a mode of development that may not address the problems of the nation is a fear entertained in many quarters. Even without actual control, the Indian mainstream media appear to have succumbed to the cultural imperatives of a developmental paradigm that leaves out the traditions from its concerns.

Internally, the media confront a powerful secular/left discourse generated by a variety of political, social and cultural organisations. Sociologists from JNU and other left establishment, leftist political parties over the decades have established links with foreign universities in UK/USA on social changes and social studies. The discussion on social changes using left/Marxist ideology has dominated the intellectual space. Marxist principles on social changes and social studies have dominated these subjects for many decades. Foreign sociologists, indologists and political experts have dangerous influence on the discourse of these Indian political and social organizations. The media, at least a major section of them, have over the years internalised the logic to such an extent that it has become the instrument of its reproduction. For example the reservations on backward castes and dalits have prior debate among these circles in UK/USA for many years. If stereotypes like 'Hindu communalism' and 'Hindu fascists' or the 'majority communalism' have become part of the common sense, the public discourse created by the media, even if unconsciously by some, is to a large extent responsible. The religious divide categories are rampant in reporting and false social assumptions inform news analysis, even in newspapers that are otherwise secular. The colonial ideologue, James Mill, who characterised Indian society in terms of religious communities in conflict still appears to exert influence on our minds.

Consequently, the traditional middle ground space in the media has considerably shrunk. Not because of the secular-communal divide that is artificially created but more because the left/secular has succeeded in replacing the traditional Hindu middle. The logic of the left/secular is increasingly becoming respectable in almost every newspaper establishment. The legitimacy thus gained by the secular/left intellectual, often through crude and false representations, helps to change the popular commonsense about key concepts like nationalism, secularism and communalism. This tendency has considerably impaired the fundamental commitment of the media to truth. The truth, however elusive it is, is not an avoidable luxury, as is believed at least by certain sections of the media, particularly the left. Social engineers

Despite these developments, the media are privy to an intense ideological struggle that Indian society is currently witnessing, between secularism on the one hand and communalism on the other. Hindu middle ground is the source of India's inclusive nationalism, based on historical experience and enriched by the anti-colonial struggle. Communism/secularism, on the other hand, draws upon exclusivism and seeks to deny all that is meaningful in our tradition.

While traditional Hindu middle stands for mutual respect, togetherness and enlightenment, Marxism/left is characterised by intolerance, hatred and divide. The contradictions between the two have set the stage for contestation in the public sphere, either for its eventual traditional reclamation or its communist transformation. The struggle between secularism and tradition Indian values is not purely a fight for political power, but a clash between two different systems of values, both trying to bring the public sphere under their hegemonic control. The outcome to a large extent depends upon the manner in which the media intervene in the public space and mould its character. On it also depends whether the Republic will be able to preserve its foundational principles. Hence the importance of the media remaining neutral. Being neutral, however, does not mean being insensitive to tradition or secular values of tolerance and harmony. In the past Indian intellectuals have invoked philosophical traditions like Vedanta to erase social divisions and appealed to universalism to bring about religious unity. Taking a leaf out of the past, the media can contribute to the ongoing efforts to halt the unfortunate tendency of leftist/secular appropriation of the past by adopting a critical but creative attitude towards tradition.

Over the years, the character of the public sphere in India has undergone a qualitative change. There is a discernible decline in the intellectual content of its transactions. Moreover, the culture of public discussion it promotes has lost much of its sanity and social purpose; the self rather than society seems to dominate in it. As a consequence, informed interventions by institutions like the media have become exceptions rather than the rule, in contrast to the era of the national movement when such interventions contributed to the emergence, evolution and vitality of the public sphere. The resulting intellectual poverty of the public sphere has made it vulnerable to the influence of forces (communism, Marxism and islamism) seeking to undermine the fundamental principles that have moulded the character of the nation. Although the media currently function under severe compulsions, both ideological and financial, a critical introspection is in order.

Target of Media

The media in India is one of the most powerful tools used by the major powers to control and change the Indian public perception about them selves and about the world. This pattern is also followed in the international scene with negation of Indic culture and bias against any revival of civilization ethos. The creeping news about any event in the world including jihad/ terrorism information is presented in such a way that the process of evolution and force of history is inevitable and forgone conclusion in favor of the Islamic parties.

Indian populations are like an experimental subject to be fed with new perception and information away from reality and in favor of the Islamic and major powers. Over several decades the general population could be made less hostile and more favorable to the designs of the major power. In the movie The Truman Show (1998) a boy grows up in a make believe world thinking that his neighbors and friends are the actual reality and totally oblivious of the reality of the world. Indian population is considered by major powers to be similar with low knowledge about the world reality and threats in the world.

Truman Burbank lives a happy life. However, what he doesn't know is that his life is actually the focus of a reality TV show aired since his birth that he's the star, his hometown is a giant set piece, and everyone around him is an actor going by a script. In this movie, Truman is a man whose life is a fake one... The place he lives is in fact a big studio with hidden cameras everywhere, and all his friends and people around him, are actors who play their roles in the most popular TV-series in the world: The Truman Show. Truman thinks that he is an ordinary man with an ordinary life and has no idea about how he is exploited. Until one day... he finds out everything. Will he react?

How long have the west been experimenting with Indian population with news and indoctrination? It could be even before the independence for more than 60 years. Deception and brainwashing have been used for a long time by the west and India is one of the largest targets of deception.

The current campaign to demonize Hindutva is to defame and remove the new indigenous political party, which is not under the control of the major powers and whose ideology is fully rooted in Indic civilization. The attack on Christians and minorities are overblown with the logic that the majority community must be checked with aggressive reporting even to the point of falsehood.

Romila Thapar eminent historian is quoted as saying that the notion of non-violent Hindu is misnomer. Distorted or even totally false reporting on communally sensitive issues is a well-entrenched feature of Indian journalism. There is no self-corrective mechanism in place to remedy this endemic culture of disinformation. No reporter or columnist or editor ever gets fired or formally reprimanded or even just criticized by his peers for smearing Hindu nationalists. This way, a partisan economy with the truth has become a habit hard to relinquish. This logic of news reporting is considered some form of social engineering. The sense of chaos and insecurity is conveyed by media reports so that stable environment and harmony is never achieved in the minds of the larger society. This is one form of psychology operation done inside India for the last three decades. The news creates a notion of change, which reinforces the decay of the Hindu culture and brings out more of the light Islamic/Urdu culture. By being very anti-Hindu the media and social scientists hopes to reduce aggression of the so called 'majority' community over the minority community and bring balance even at the expense of the truth. This logic was pursued even when the Muslim terrorists in Kashmir were killing the minorities Hindus and the news is usually kept low key.

Control of media by the foreign governments is done in a subtle way. Some of the ways are by indoctrinating the editorial teams and the journalists over time. The Indian leftists have been used for a long time by the external powers and since they control the media they are better able to influence the bias in the media. Some question put by them are 'why don't you talk to your very reasonable nuclear rival Pakistan' or 'why do you have a Hindu nationalist party in power' game. Each of these questions is loaded, as they say in the courtroom, with facts or inferences not yet established by evidence to be true and designed to shift the conversation from a dubious premise to a foregone conclusion. The public buys this kind of argument more readily.

CULTURAL COLD WAR

The Cultural Cold War: the CIA and the World of Arts and Letters by Frances Stonor Saunders

This book describes all the dirty tricks used by the CIA and other agencies all over the world to change countries and to bring chaos in those countries. It is well known that the CIA funded right-wing intellectuals after World War II; fewer know that it also courted individuals from the center and the left in an effort to turn the intelligentsia away from communism and toward an acceptance of "the American way." Frances Stonor Saunders sifts through the history of the covert Congress for Cultural Freedom in The Cultural Cold War: The CIA and the World of Arts and Letters. The book centers on the career of Michael Josselson, the principal intellectual figure in the operation, and his eventual betrayal by people who scapegoat him. Sanders demonstrates that, in the early days, the Office of Strategic Services (OSS) and the emergent CIA were less dominated by the far right than they later became (including the Christian right), and that the idea of helping out progressive moderates—rather than being Machiavellian—actually appealed to the men at the top.

David Frawley writes: The Indian English media dictates against the government as if it should be the real political decision-making body in the country. (Because it is urged and influenced by other foreign agencies and academic institutions such as U Berkeley/U Columbia) It deems itself capable of taking the place of legal institutions as well, printing its allegations as truth even if these have never been entered into much less proved in any court of law. It has vested itself with an almost religious authority to determine what is right and wrong, good and evil, and who in the country should be honored or punished.(This is called manufacturing consent) Like an almost theocratic institution, it does not tolerate dissent or allow its dogmas to be questioned.(It creates groupthink, manufactures 'dissent' forcing everybody to fall in line and creates an old boys network)

In the name of editorial policy, it pontificates, promoting slogans, denigrations and articles of faith in the guise of critical policy review. (This is called brainwashing under freedom)

The media doesn't aim at reporting the news; it tries to create the news, imposing its view of the news upon everyone as the final truth. The media doesn't objectively cover elections, it tries to influence voters to vote in a specific manner, demonizing those it disagrees with and excusing those it supports, however bad or incompetent their behavior. We saw this particularly during the recent Gujarat elections in which the media went so far as to print the type of election results it wanted to see as the likely outcome, though voters proved it to be totally wrong.

Where is the Media's Mandate?

The question therefore arises as to what affords the media such a sweeping authority that can override legitimately elected and appointed bodies? What sort of mandate has the media been given to justify its actions? Clearly the media has never been elected to any political post and does not undergo any scrutiny like that of candidates in an election. It does not represent any appointed post in the government. It has no accountability to any outside agency. The media's authority is largely self-appointed and, not surprisingly, self-serving. Hence media has become a tool of foreign powers who would like a particular outcome of an election or policy making inside India or image creation. The sources behind the media's operation and where they get their money is also not revealed. We are not informed as to how prominent reporters and editorial writers derive their income, including how much may come from outside sources. But clearly they are getting a lot of money from somewhere that they are not in any hurry to disclose. Though the media likes to expose the improprieties, financial, sexual and otherwise, of those its dislikes, which it often exaggerates, if not invents, if you examine how the media people live, you certainly wouldn't want them as., role models for your children!

Nor are we certain who the media really represents. Certain groups, not only inside but also outside India, are using this English media as a vested interest to promote their own agenda, which is generally anti-Hindu and often appears to be anti-India as well. Negative news is portrayed more than positive news. President APJ Abdul Kalam asks: "Why is the media here so negative? Why are we in India so embarrassed to recognize our own strengths, our achievements? We have so many amazing success stories but we refuse to acknowledge them. Why? Is there an agenda to reduce the achievements of India?" The only reason for the negative news is to reduce the self confidence of Hindus and their place in the world. This is a campaign on a world scale probably never done anywhere. Is this really possible and is this really happening.

The Media Propaganda Machine

A section of the Indian media often appears more as a propaganda machine than an objective news agency. In this regard the large section of English media of India is much like the old state propaganda machines of communist countries. This is an important clue for understanding its operation. The English media of India largely represents a holdover from the Congress era in which it was a state run propaganda center for the Congress government that was far left in its orientation. We can perhaps at understand its actions today as a state run propaganda machine that has continued in power after the decline of the party that created it. Its prime motive has now become to reestablish that old state and former ruling party.

The media remains largely a Congress run propaganda machine. As the Congress has not been able to win elections, it has emphasized its media wing even more strongly to try to compensate for its failures in the electoral arena. Yet as the Congress Party itself has often failed, the media has taken to supporting other leftist groups inside and outside the country in hope of gaining power. There is a clear hand of western governments in manipulating the congress party to do its work. This shows how the Indian government is manipulated as a puppet of the western governments and has been for a long time for the last 40 years.

During independence before and just after, the British have used media to demonize Hindu groups in India. From history K Elst says quote: In November 1944: "It is the subtle scheme of political propaganda to describe the Hindu as pro-Fascist. It is a cruel calumny, which has been spread in America and other countries. The Hindu Mahasabha stood for Savarkar's policy of militarization and industrialization.

We recognized that Fascism was a supreme menace to what is good and noble in our civilization. Due to Veer Savarkar's call thousands of young men joined the Army and Navy and Air Force and shed their blood for resisting Nazi tyranny and for real friendship with China and Russia. But as the Hindus had the temerity to ask for National Independence and took the lead in rejecting the Cripps (commission) offer, they were maligned and the subtle forces of organized British propaganda were let loose to blackmail the Hindus." (Hindu Politics, p.103) The current tendency to accuse the Hindu movement for cultural decolonization of India of "fascism" is nothing but a replay of an old colonial tactic.

International Media and India

It is surprising to note that there are only two sources of international News collection, Reuters from England and Associated Press (AP) from France. Every other news agency including PTI (Press Trust India) and UNI buys news from these two news sources. We have seen above these two news services were finally in the tight control of Rothschilds and their associates.

In India, we have 4 major television networks. Government controlled Door Darshan. Then we have Zee TV network operating in north. Finally Enadu TV and Sun (teja etc), Jaya TV network operating in south. In addition to them we have NDTV-an affiliate of MSNBC, CNN, Star, etc. All foreign programming is a rerun of American Life style which destroyed American life it self socially, morally and ethically. Domestic programming exactly imitates the foreign programming by indianizing the same. As liberalization and privatization dictates there should be no control over this television or internet medium by the central government. That means every one is free to show what ever they feel fit to show irrespective of the consequences either on adults or on children. The argument goes they watch so we produce.

Exercise:-1. If you really want to know whether there is an unknown unexplained self imposed media control over Indian private news services, please do these exercise every day for a month and you can understand a pattern. This needs a computer and internet.

a. Step-1. Go to www.reuters.com

b. Step-2. Take an international topic and print the same.

c. Step-3. Take few English/Hindi language dailies and scan through the International News.

It first amazes the reader to note that Reuters Story was reported in all Indian news papers as Reuters-England is the only provider of international news along with AP-France since 1900 to all interested countries. But what amazes more is if Reuters news reports about a particular international topic contains ten principal points no single Indian news paper will print all the ten points of that particular topic. As if an unwritten solidarity each Indian news paper prints one or two points of the ten principal points reported by Reuters.

Also no two newspapers in most cases will repeat the same principal points. Such coincidence amazes the reader if he follows the news reporting in Indian media for a month. As an individual if I need international news perspective I can read directly Reuters where I get a summary of one side perspective of news. To get the same summary I have to 'democratically read a dozen' Indian news papers.

ENGLISH MEDIA MANIPULATES INDIAN ELECTIONS

"We the people of the media, having solemnly resolved to acquire the freedom of press; to aspire to become the fourth pillar of our grand democracy; to provide citizens with impartial news and to offer unadulterated comments, do hereby accept that this time all of us were totally wrong." expected comments from English media. No there is nothing to be happy about. Media bashing doesn't solve the problem. And surely there is a problem. That our media completely failed to understand people's wishes; that it had no inkling of the public sentiments and that it was too close to politicians and too far away from voters. Not one of them, not some of them, but all of them miserably failed to gauge the public mood.

The election coverage of State elections has once again exposed the utter bankruptcy - intellectual, journalistic and moral – of the English media. Their projection of surprise for the results in Rajasthan and Chattisgarh shows how much out of tune they are with the mood of the people. If the polls had shown a more honest picture, then the performance of the BJP would have been better. In each state they may have obtained a few more seats, even if in Delhi it may have meant that the Congress party would have still won.

Second aspect is that the media is trying to divert the attention from their miserable failure by harping on the gender issue. Even if the BJP projected two of their senior women leaders as Chief Minister candidates, there is no data available of the number of women MLAs who have won, and whether this number is significantly higher than the previous elections. The two women leaders won because they were accepted as ones who would be able to give effective leadership to the states, and also because of the party that they represent. A competent male candidate would not have caused the final result to be any different.

The worst part is that the introspection of misreading of the voter mood is done in a much muted manner, or irrationalized manner. For example, it is represented as a late swing. Why this swing happened is not mentioned. All of a sudden, in two weeks before the elections, the electorate is supposed to have changed its mind and said, no, there was bad governance!

The English media publications should not abuse the intelligence of their readers in the manner they are trying to do. At the time of the Gujarat elections, the misreading of the voter intention was just as massive as it is today. Just as then, now too there seems to be a serious attempt to try and manipulate the minds of the electorate. After the Gujarat elections, there were articles in the same manipulative media that it is necessary for self-introspection. This happened only in those few articles were the word introspection was used.

Opinion poll companies were rather naïve to hope that our shrewd voters will tell them in advance whom they are going to vote for. Once again our media made the mistake of aping the west and leaving it to the foreign pollsters to find out and tell us how the tribals of Bastar or the herdsmen living in the desert of Rajasthan are going to vote. Yes the media abandoned the instinctive art of hard-nosed and hangover-free political understanding and critical analysis. Nobody, neither print nor electronic media, nor even the exit polls, could predict the extent of public enthusiasm for the BJP. A special mention should be made here about the report by Sir Mark Tully, ex of the BBC and now settled in Delhi, on his visit to Chattisgarh. He was gaga about the wonderful job being done by the Jogi government in the state!

The memory of the 1984 general election, which produced the most conclusive Congress victory to date, is full of delicious reports predicting how Amitabh Bachchan would get a pasting in Allahabad and how Charan Singh's rustic wisdom would prevail over the brash Congress. The obsessive preoccupation with the Muslim vote in the Hindi heartland in 1989 and 1991 so dominated media proceedings that an outsider would have nurtured the belief that Muslims are the only community who vote in India.

At the root of these profound insights was a belief that there is nothing called the average voter. Instead, there are disaggregated communities that are incapable of relating to either ideology or the big picture. People, it was insinuated, vote invariably along strict class or caste lines, without concern for the lofty propaganda of the big guns that make appearances in makeshift helipads. The Prime Minister can talk endlessly about the growing pride in India but the skeptic asks how this is relevant to a voter who doesn't even know the meaning of the Internet?

The problem with vernacular press, particularly with the newly established and fast growing newspapers in the Hindi belt, is that they don't seem to be interested in serious journalism. Once the established national Hindi newspapers were displaced from top positions, the new arrivals indulged in localized, self centered and slight versioned journalism. Sadly, some of the vernacular newspapers mistakenly think that today's small town reader is not intelligent enough to grasp the complex issues of national or global importance.

But that is not to say that everything is fine with the English press. Clearly many English journalists are out of touch and pretentious. Many of them have become the self-proclaimed savior of secularism and others see no harm in becoming the biographers of their preferred politicians, probably in lieu of a Raja Saba seat.

This is not the language of journalism. Journalists should not be allowed to become activists. These activist journalists and politicians should not be allowed to usurp journalism. If Manishankar Iyer, Chidambaram, or Kuldip Nayer are writing a column it is the duty of editors to inform their readers what their political allegiance is and which political party they belong to.

For those who vote as Indian, no party is untouchable; it is the ghettoised analyst who believes in exclusion. India may be an infuriatingly complex society but it is also governed by amazingly simple norms of right and wrong. We can call it anti-incumbency, a function of horribly exaggerated expectations or just a simple vote for change. In the end it amounts to the same thing — that Indian vote on moral lines. The successful spin-doctor or politician is one who can comprehend that notion of dharma. This is what the results of the assembly election just demonstrated. But don't be fooled into believing that just because it went one way this December it is destined to go the same way next year. History doesn't just happen; it also has to be made to happen.

Despite our quest for balanced and unbiased journalism we will not be lucky to have it. Then the newspapers should be honest enough to declare their political allegiance as they do in Britain. For example, newspapers like The Telegraph and The Daily Mail clearly and openly support the Conservative party. On Election Day they clearly put a headline: Vote Conservative. While The Mirror, until a few years ago, used to be the staunch supporter of the Labor Party.

Media in this country India has become a commodity that can be sold and purchased in the market by those willing to accept and pay the price. The brand names that reach to the vast majority of people are concentrated in a few hands and in fact entire world media, like armament industry is joining big conglomerates, which is indeed a dangerous trend. The media trends needs to be exposed, which are in relentless grip of their owners. The facts are not reported as they happen but how the masters and owners of the media want these to be reported. Newspapers / media play a critical role in expressing the pluralism of the country – its various identities, perspectives and values.

3

WOMEN IN DEVELOPING COUNTRIES

Many studies have been done on the information behavior of people in developing countries, especially in regard to technology and retrieval systems. A number of studies have also been done on the information needs of women in rural Africa. However, relatively little has been studied on the information needs of rural women in other developing countries, or of women traders and merchants in these countries, (Mooko, 2002), (Mchombu, 2000), (Kiteme, 1992). This paper analyzes the patterns that emerge when studying the causes of female poverty in developing countries and considers the effectiveness of recent education and ICT projects in addressing women's information needs for overcoming their restrictive situations. A combination of information strategies is suggested in conjunction with the utilization of existing marketplace relationships between women to maximize the efficiency and effectiveness of information systems for rural women.

Meeting the Information Needs of Rural and Informal Economy Women in Developing Countries

Africa, Southeast Asia, and Latin America contain some of the poorest countries in the world. These 3rd and 4th World countries are very similar in the problems they face due to extreme poverty, and are distinctive from developed countries with their high unemployment rates, food shortages, shortages in healthcare facilities and resources, and mortality rates, (Miller, W.E.B. DuBois Conference, 1976). However, what also seems to distinguish developing countries from others is the severity of inequality in welfare between men and women, specifically in regards to health, life expectancy at birth, quality of life, workload, education, legal rights, and economic mobility, according to many studies, (Population Crisis Committee, 1988), (Witwer, 1997), (World Conference on Women, 1995), (Huyer, 1997).

In many developing countries a majority of women reside in rural areas, supporting their households with subsistence farming, raising children, and maintaining their property. They are usually the most exploited and least privileged members of households, overburdened with work for their families but marginalized in regard to the distribution of resources, (Ngimwa, Ocholla & Ojiambo, 1997:46). Their lack of support and privileges isolates them from information resources they would need to make their lives better. Most information resources are located in urban areas, which are hard for them to access. For this reason, this paper focuses on the unresolved and major challenge of transferring urban information to regional populations, despite the breakdown in infrastructure between them.

Rural Women

Poverty in these regions motivates parents to push women into marriage at a young age to save money or gain a dower. Early marriage puts these women at a great disadvantage for life, causing them to be pulled from school at an early age, losing educational opportunities and remaining illiterate, (Huyer, 1997), (Jiyane & Ocholla, 2004). Because of this, the great majority of women in rural and urban areas remain illiterate, which eventually becomes a major obstacle for them in information seeking and job qualification later on, (Adjah, 2005). As a result, more men become eligible for employment as they predominate secondary and higher education in these countries, (Witwer, 1997). Men are then able to move into salaried positions, acquiring work skills that make them more marketable. Most women are not hired for entry-level jobs as a result of being pulled from school for an early marriage; therefore they never receive job skills, training, or experience, impairing their earning capacity, (Kiteme, 1992).

Many countries in Africa maintain a custom of having men remain with their parents after marriage, while marrying off daughters and having them move in with their husbands' families. This family dependence on sons for continual financial contributions to the household, as well as their anticipation of eventually losing a daughter's contributions to another family, results in a favoritism of boys over girls within families. As a result, families withhold food provision, financial support, and attention from girls in order to give more of these resources to their boys, (Huyer, 1997). Families are likely to pull girls from school to save money by eliminating the expense of their school fees so that the girls can be put to work for family income instead. Parents often don't invest much money on food or healthcare for their daughters, in contrast to what they provide for their sons. This discrimination against girls sets the precedence for family dynamics later in life. This social conditioning results in pervasive domestic violence towards women and general devaluation of women by their husbands, (World Conference on Women, 1995). In some countries, domestic violence is so prevalent that women do not even consider it preventable, (Jiyane & Ocholla, 2004), (Rutakumwa & Krogman, 2000).

Healthcare clinics are hard to find and suffer from a lack of appropriate health services for women, due to gender bias. Many lack family planning services, or birth control, and none provide emergency obstetric services, (WCW, 1995). Early marriage and the lack of family planning services result in early pregnancy and repeated pregnancies. In most impoverished countries one out of ten, or sometimes one out of five, women die in childbirth under the age of 50, (PCC, 1988). Pregnancy is the leading cause of death and depression among these women, (WCW, 1995). Women in these countries have an average of 6-7 children due to lack of contraception and other circumstances, (PCC, 1988). For some women, this motivates unsafe abortions, (WCW, 1995). The high birthrate is partially because of lack of birth control but also because couples feel they need to make up for the high infant mortality rate to ensure they will be supported in their old age, (Miller, W.E.B. DuBois Conference, 1976). Men usually claim the right to determine family size, and leave it up to women to prevent pregnancy, (Behrman, Kohler, & Watkins, 2002).

Women are left to run the household and provide all the food and income for the family in addition to their childcare responsibilities because many men usually migrate to urban areas to find employment. When men don't leave, women still have to work longer hours farming than their husbands do because of men's lack of contribution to the family, (Jiyane & Ocholla, 2004). In either case, women are overworked and have no time to seek information or learn to read, even if education programs are accessible. Healthcare becomes inaccessible for them because of their time constraints, their day-intensive work schedule, and the lack of evening hours at healthcare clinics. They have no time to travel to urban areas or to socialize. Conditions of rural life such as lack of road infrastructure, even between villages, and lack of electricity and phones, further obstruct communication with others. Therefore, they are socially isolated from other people, and from information, (Jiyane & Ocholla, 2004), (Mooko, 2002).

In many developing countries, these women are essential to the national economy because they contribute the majority of the nation's food, and farm exports, and yet few of them own land because many countries deny women land and cattle ownership rights, especially in Africa, (PCC, 1988), (Ikoja-Odongo, 2002), (Mazumdar, 1979). This restricts their financial potential and creates severe inequality in opportunities between women and men, (Kiteme, 1992). Family law and child custody law also favors men in most countries in Africa, Asia, the Middle East and some countries in Latin America, (PCC, 1988).

Social isolation due to time and travel restraints prevents rural women from being able to get involved and be represented in the rest of society in order to change these policies and programs for their benefit, (Jiyane & Ocholla, 2004), (Nath, 2001). In fact, misinformation regarding women and negative portrayal of them by the media in many countries fosters misunderstandings and discrimination that obstructs them from getting the information they need, (Ikoja-Odongo, 2002), (Huyer, 1997). Few researchers study their information needs, but those that do raise public awareness about them and give these women a voice that can begin to be acknowledged by program and policy makers, (Mazumdar, 1979), (Kiteme, 1992). Otherwise, these women have no way to represent their interests in regional or national affairs.

Women in developing countries are isolated by their family and work situations, as well as the lack of infrastructure for contact with urban-based information resources. Illiteracy, lack of job skills, and lack of time to access information from urban areas because of childcare responsibilities all obstruct these women from accessing information and economic opportunities, limiting their abilities to make informed decisions and increase their welfare, (Nath, 2001), (WCW, 1995). This lack of equality in privilege and employment only reinforces poverty for them and their children, (Jiyane & Ocholla, 2004).

Women Market Traders and Small Business Owners

Many rural women are not able to meet their family's needs through their produce yields and must supplement their income to survive, which they do by creating small businesses, or services, and by trading. These small businesses run by women abound in rural and urban areas alike, creating a large informal market economy in many countries that contributes significantly to developing the national economy. The flexibility of their businesses, which are very diverse in nature, allows them to continue household, childcare and agricultural work. It also creates a cash flow between urban and rural areas from the work of female traders who travel between the two. Women in rural areas rely heavily on them for their commodity needs. This helps rural areas develop economically. Many women in West Africa and Latin America work as traders and entrepreneurs for lack of formal job opportunities elsewhere, (PCC, 1988). Unfortunately, their economic importance to society and their business development needs have been largely ignored by policy makers and researchers. This obscures people's understanding about women's information needs and how to support them in their businesses, (Mchombu, 2000), (Kiteme, 1992).

Women who work as market traders divide their time between farming, caring for livestock, shipping in farm products from urban and rural areas, selling, and processing food for sale. Women traders move products between urban and rural areas, providing rural women with access to food commodities and consumer goods that they would otherwise have to sacrifice their time to travel for or not be able to access at all, (Kiteme, 1992). These entrepreneurs combine trading with home-based businesses to maintain their income year-round, selling processed food or alcohol during slow seasons. This stimulates regional development and produces most of the informal economy for many countries. The fact that they dominate the informal economy in many countries is a testament to their ingenuity and determination, considering their lack of access to literacy and business skill training. (Kiteme, 1992), (Mchombu, 2000).

The flexible but diverse livelihood of market trading enables them to maintain their childcare and household maintenance responsibilities. The work involved fluctuates with the activities of other traders who make their decisions according to the seasons, which determine the weather for travel and the availability of certain foods. For example, in the rainy season the unpaved roads and public transportation to town can be completely shut down by mud and rivers, preventing market women from trading. These women need information on the seasons and weather, sources of raw materials and their availability, commodity prices, the security of the market, new markets, marketing ideas, training in business creation, sources of credit, sources of equipment for food processing, food storage methods, government regulations, taxation, and tenders and contracts, (Ikoja-Odongo, 2002), (Kiteme, 1992).

However, many women develop other kinds of businesses or service for hire that they can do part time in addition to, or in replacement of, farming. Besides food-processing, other common businesses include tailoring, textiles and crafts, traditional herbs, perfumes, flowers, handbags, hairstyling, and nursery schooling, (Mchombu, 2000). Women often become entrepreneurs because they are not able to produce enough money from farming, and want to escape the harsh working conditions, but cannot get salaried jobs because of high unemployment and lack of job skills, (Ikoja-Odongo, 2002), (Jiyane & Ocholla, 2004), (Kiteme, 1992). In most developing countries, less than 10% of women have relatively well-paid professional positions. In some countries, less than 2% of women are a part of the official paid labor force, (PCC, 1988).

INFORMATION NEEDS

Agriculture and Market Business

In the context of this picture, it is easier to understand the information needs of most women in developing countries. Interestingly enough, when the World Bank organized a forum to get feedback from 60,000 poor people from 60 countries, they discovered that people preferred receiving information and opportunities to combat poverty rather than charity, (Nath, 2001).

Other researchers have encountered similar ambition among rural women in Africa to get the information they need to improve their life situations, (Jiyane & Ocholla, 2004), (Mchombu, 2000). In many studies, rural women say their most urgent need is for agricultural and small business information, (Jiyane & Ocholla, 2004), (Mchombu, 2000), (Ikoja-Odongo, 2002). This is not surprising considering that the vast majority of women in rural areas work as farmers and create agricultural-related businesses on the side to supplement their income, in order to keep their families. In a study on rural women in Melmoth, KwaZulu-Natal, South Africa, the village women list many information needs, yet agricultural and farming information was their first priority to increase their food production, both for their family and for the market. Irrigation and planting methods, general farm skills, and agricultural business strategies were the most important. They also sought specifically business-oriented information on trading, investments, banking, saving, and insurance, demonstrating how family farming is used to create supplemental income for these women through market sales and even the development of small businesses. Legal information on owning land was among the top interests for them, since their financial gain is held back significantly by not being the landowners, (Jiyane & Ocholla, 2004).

The information needs of small businesses are diverse, and in order to succeed in a constantly changing market they need this information to solve business problems, (Mchombu, 2000). In different studies of women entrepreneurs and traders in Uganda, Botswana, Nigeria, and South Africa the needs business owners all held in common were for information on business management, technical skill training, sources for raw materials and their compared prices, ideas on business expansion, marketing, where to get financing and grants, the law and their rights, and the feasibility of certain trades in a given market, (Ikoja-Odongo, 2002), (Mchombu, 2000), (Ngimwa, Ocholla & Ojiambo, 1997), (Jiyane & Ocholla, 2004).

The World Conference on Women, India's National Adult Education Program, Kenyan government, and various studies have concluded that the expansion of women's earning power and their economic self-sufficiency is crucial to their freedom from social and legal discrimination, overwork, and lack of social services, (Kiteme, 1992), (Mazumdar, 1979), (WCW, 1995), (Nath, 2001). However, even when women are in contact with other people or urban populations through their businesses they still encounter obstructions to vital information they need for financial self-sufficiency. In some areas, business women don't even know that information services even exist that can solve their income problems, (Mchombu, 2000), (Ikoja-Odongo, 2002). In the study on rural women in Melmoth, South Africa, women sought information on employment opportunities, weekend and holiday jobs, education and job training, and worker's rights, but the obstacles they encountered to finding it were lack information materials that were relevant in content and format, lack of transportation and roads, or lack of information on alternative roads, and illiteracy, (Jiyane & Ocholla, 2004).

Information strategies specifically recommended by researchers for business women include providing a collection of materials on a wide range of information, specifically in their local language and at a neo-literate reading level, a manual directory of local services made easily available to them, and a female manager for the information center, (Mchombu, 2000).

Despite these insights, the underlying obstacles to rural farmers and market trading women getting needed information for economic stability continue to be overwork, social discrimination, domination by their spouse, and poverty, (Ngimwa, Ocholla & Ojiambo, 1997), (Huyer, 1997), which block economic self-sufficiency while also requiring it to be prevented. In such a conundrum, one must look for a separate factor that can be changed to break the other mutually supporting factors.

Reproductive Health

The World Conference on Women stated that early pregnancy obstructs women in developing countries from education and employment opportunities, as well as the legal influence to change social policies, (WCW, 1995). Similarly, the Population Crisis Committee concluded in its study on the status of women that for women to gain educational, economic, health, and legal equality they will need to gain more control over their reproductive lives, (PCC, 1988). The W.E.B. Dubois Conference in 1976 demonstrated how lack of family planning information and strategies perpetuated poverty in fourth world countries, (Miller, W.E.B. DuBois Conference, 1976).

Women in Developing countries are impeded in their economic progress by lack of family planning and reproductive health.

In one study, the primary concern of women in Uganda was for information on reproductive health and birth control because their sexual health needs were not being met by the local clinics and they were suffering many symptoms of illnesses without having any source for education or advice. STD's are spread to wives repeatedly by their husband's perpetual infidelity. Education on the prevention of STD's, pregnancy, and the rampant domestic violence from men who will not cooperate with women's efforts at birth control or abstinence is badly needed. Specifically, these women requested information on where to get sexual health services, how to prevent excessive childbearing and STD's, and how to get better training for midwives to perform minor surgical procedures, (Rutakumwa & Krogman, 2000).

Incomplete health care from clinics not administering proper OB-GYN services and a general mystery as to where these health clinics were located prevented these women from receiving needed care. They also needed to be taught the possibility of early detection and preventative health care so they will get cancer symptoms checked out, which they currently don't think to do, (Rutakumwa & Krogman, 2000).

These are similar to issues in all developing countries. General discrimination against women results in lack of provision for female health needs in public programs and bad treatment from health practitioners, cheating them of what is actually available to them, (Rutakumwa & Krogman, 2000).

This is the case in Bolivia where market trade women are in dire need of reproductive control but aren't getting it. Mortality and suffering rates are high for women and children due to limited access to basic health services. Even though family planning services are made available to women by clinics, women don't know about them or are prone not to use them because of poor service and information practices by health care workers. The carelessness of doctors with their concerns over medication side effects or their need for clarification on what to expect from surgical procedures fosters suspicion and mistrust of the Western contraceptive methods offered, (Schuler, Choque, Rance, 1994).

Cultural reticence regarding sexual health and reproductive information among Bolivians leave these women without any knowledge about how they're getting pregnant, except what they learn from trial and error. Doctor's exacerbate this with lack of concern enough to ask women about their needs or to explain why the rhythm method isn't working, as well as overt discrimination against women who have resorted to abortions to avoid another pregnancy. The two traditional methods they know, rhythm method and abstinence, are thwarted often times by partners who do not cooperate with them. Physical and verbal abuse is used to punish women for using birth control, and so the women often resort to unsafe abortions and even passive or active infanticide, (Schuler, Choque, Rance, 1994).

Pregnancies directly interfere with these women working in the market and threaten their livelihood when they have to bring young children to their market spot and try to keep customers with the baby crying. They have no other way to make a living, and their husbands are usually unemployed, which, along with spousal abuse over financial tensions, puts a lot of pressure on them to not have children. Therefore, information on birth control alternatives and their side effects, as well as information breaking the social stigma off of women who use Western birth control, is necessary to prevent poverty and human suffering, (Schuler, Choque, Rance, 1994).

Education on women's right to determine her reproductive and sexual life, as well as the benefits of postponing marriage and pregnancy, are serious needs among these women. Basic sex education in schools is also necessary to prevent early pregnancy. Caring staff, clear and simple explanations, non-discriminatory practices, female doctors, and holistic health services that meet all their health needs at the same clinic, seem to be necessary factors in winning the trust of women and were recommended by researchers in the study on Bolivian women, (Schuler, Choque, Rance, 1994). In one study, women specifically requested confidentiality of information in family planning services to circumvent their husband's restriction of them from getting these services. Confidentiality of information in clinics would also be of use to women who want to escape domestic violence, (Mooko, 2002).

Basic Healthcare

Additionally, the World Conference on Women and many studies in general show the health needs of women in poor countries to include information on preventing STD's, AIDS, Malaria, and Cholera, which are epidemics in many countries. Counseling services for them is also commonly requested. Women in many other countries cited information on personal security and safety from domestic violence as their first concern, (WCW, 1995), (Jiyane & Ocholla, 2004). In one study, the priority of rural women in Botswana was for information on how to prevent and treat family sickness, (Mooko, 2002).

David Miller, a lecturer at the W.E.B. DuBois Conference in 1976, also saw the main need of people in third and fourth world countries as health education, specifically on nutrition. From his first hand experience in countries in Africa he concluded that it is malnutrition among children that causes the high infant mortality rate by causing susceptibility to disease. The argues that it is not a lack of food that causes malnutrition for people in these countries but the lack of knowledge about how to use the food they have most effectively for nutrition and disease prevention. Educating mothers on simple methods of nutrition for their children, and themselves, will provide them with methods for disease and infection prevention, lowering the child mortality and morbidity rate. He says that this is the key to convincing parents to space out their children more and use family planning methods, since their children are likely to survive and not need to be replaced. In this way, the perpetuation of hunger and poverty can be prevented for mother and child. Additionally, Miller asserts that preventative health care, such as nutrition and other non-pharmaceutical treatments, and holistic services for families in clinics are effective in gaining the trust and cooperation of the rural poor, (Miller, W.E.B. DuBois Conference, 1976).

Education

All the studies on women in developing countries were fairly unanimous about the need for education for women, primarily in regards to job skills, but also in regard to the law and gender policies. Necessary job skills include literacy, information and technology skills, and general business skills, (WCW, 1995), (Ikoja-Odongo, 2002), (Kiteme, 1992), (Mazumdar, 1979), (Adjah, 2005), (Huyer, 1997). The World Conference on Women links the acquisition of skills and access to IT literacy to empowerment and self-sufficiency for women. Specifically, education in these areas will enable women to participate in the production of information sources and combat the gender bias and false portrayals of women in the media and the IT industry, (Huyer, 1997).

Education will also inspire and equip them to get involved in policy making and their own legal protection. Biased policies prevent health care from being provided in a format and with the appropriate services that women need, prevent land and cattle ownership for female farmers, and prevent women from being paid as much as men for the same job, (Mazumdar, 1979), (Ikoja-Odongo, 2002), (Huyer, 1997).

An educational program in Bolivia called the "Legal Promoter's Course" had tremendous success at motivating women to take control of their lives through education on the law and their rights. It was offered at a community-based NGO called the "Justice Office for Women" as a model of popular education, and provided real-world application learning while also training students in leadership for future courses of its kind in the community.

The program has had such an impact on their personal lives, families and communities that many students stay on to continue to teach the course to others. Women have learned to stand up to their abusive husbands and confront them with their knowledge of the law. Women draw respect from their husbands as new interpersonal standards for behavior are set and new family roles are arranged by wives to more evenly distribute housework.

They feel encouraged when they see their daughters observing their mother's example. Some marriages dissolve. Students of the course report a newfound confidence in confronting these and other social situations. There is a new willingness to get involved in the community as defenders of human rights and disseminators of this knowledge to others, (Kollins & Hansman, 2005).

The information needs demonstrated by the success of the program include the need for transformational learning and the development of critical consciousness, mixing immediately needed information along with developing analytical and practical skills. A similarly effective approach has been used in many successful literacy projects which teach self-employment skills, like sewing and food preparation, or organic gardening, using ICT and CDRoms in class so that women learn technology and literacy skills at the same time, (Kollins & Hansman, 2005), (Huyer, 1997).

Adult literacy learners in Ghana pursue the ability to read English in order to not be socially stigmatized by others. Simple abilities like reading signposts to find places, writing down phone messages, reading children's prescriptions correctly, and helping their children with their homework enables women to be more involved their family's lives, reduces their social isolation, and enables self-sufficiency. Literacy skills are vital for securing and increasing women's earning potential in market trading and small business, enabling them to read a tape measure, follow directions on the side of a product box, keep records of money transactions and debtors who buy on credit so they can collect, read others' shopping lists, and converse with their customers in English. With increasing numbers of educated dressmakers entering the informal economy, uneducated women need English skills to adequately compete with them for business, (Adjah, 2005).

Recommendations from researchers in this study sound similar to the learning strategies used in the community legal and literacy courses mentioned before. Literacy lessons pertaining to everyday happenings and work-related needs seem more easily learned. Also, researchers call for the involvement of librarians in providing neo-literate literature, especially with feminist perspectives and role models, to encourage the casual use of libraries by new readers, (Adjah, 2005).

Information Behavior

The sources of information most available to women in rural and urban areas are friends, neighbors, and relatives. Women prefer to receive information from these people anyway, especially because they know them to have trustworthy intentions and these people are available around the clock, (Jiyane & Ocholla, 2004), (Leach, 2001). People who are unknown and suspicious in agenda because of selfish or apathetic behavior are not trusted as sources of information, (Schuler, Choque & Rance, 1994). Differences in culture and socio-economic class between information providers and women in need of information do not help either, (Behrman, Kohler & Watkins, 2002), (Shuler, Choque & Rance, 1994).

If outsiders do visit their area, they are more prone to trust them if they are known by someone else in their group and if the person is willing to take the time to discuss information with them and respond to their needs for clarification. Social networking is therefore a very powerful and widely used means of doing business and exchanging information, (Leach, 2001).

Print helps rural people corroborate information they receive from others verbally, because it is seen as authoritative. Print is available sometimes, like newspapers and magazines from urban areas which are found and read aloud to others by a literate person in the community, but it is hard to access regularly or maintain information currency with it, (Leach, 2001).

Visual information supplements verbal or print information for them and gives them more clarity, but it is not trusted as a reliable source of information in itself. Discussion about a picture, or a TV image, is necessary for the community to accept it as reliable, (Leach, 2001). Radios, when available, are listened to in groups for discussion with others, rather than alone.

Group discussion is always preferred for processing information when confronted by outside information sources. Radios are more available than TV's, which are harder to come by. Nevertheless, rural people trust TV more than radio because of the visual reinforcement. Again, they like to watch in groups. Cell phones are difficult to access financially and because of lack of ICT infrastructure in rural areas, but some companies give these phones away for free to get the business, (Nath, 2001).

Libraries are rarely used because they are located in urban areas and require literacy. Traveling libraries are impractical because of disheveled roads. In addition, their materials are often irrelevant to people's need for current and direct information, (Leach, 2001).

INFORMATION SYSTEMS

New Information Strategies

There are some library programs that have located their services in rural areas to overcome these obstacles. They overcome the obstacles of illiteracy and time constraints with audiotape and tape recorder distribution, which is relatively inexpensive in terms of equipment. They also have radio listener clubs combined with tape distribution of the radio show to others without a radio, and they have videos with information relevant to rural adults, which they show in trading stores in rural KwaZulu-Natal over the "Rural TV Network", (Leach, 2001).

This is interesting, because Jiyanne and Ocholla (2004) recommend something similar to this for information dissemination in these areas. They suggest placing audio-visual information resources in grocery stores, hospitals, clinics, and schools, which are general places of convergence for rural women while they are acquiring consumer goods. This strategy would circumvent the obstacles of lack of time and lack of family permission to attend community information meetings. This concept is viable and a potentially effective one, since advertisers increasingly target these public places for their television commercials, (Jiyanne & Ocholla, 2004).

ICT systems of communication are being explored as a rural-accessible source of information by many NGO's and service programs, mainly in the form of internet connectivity but also in conjunction with radio, TV and cell phone dissemination. There are amazing success stories connected to the use of this strategy.

It bypasses road infrastructure problems and time constraints, is available around the clock, and allows users to access practical and direct information without small talk, all of which are priorities for women under pressure. It also provides a cheap means of publishing and posting information for local women to the public and each other, (Huyer, 1997). Obstacles to its development in poor countries include a lack of IT infrastructure, lack of locally relevant content at this point, the heterogeny of languages in these regions, lack of literacy in English, and lack of IT user skills, (Kebede, 2003), (Gebremichael & Jackson, 2006).

Information for rural and urban women must take a form that allows for diverse content from many different sources for it to be relevant, since their problems are interconnected and must be dealt with simultaneously in some situations. In order for this information to be used by these women, it should be close in proximity to them, time-flexible, and readily available around the clock, (Kebede, 2003), (Nath, 2001), (Jiyanne & Ocholla, 2004).

It must be direct and address their immediate day-to-day needs, (Nath, 2001). It should mix work-related, immediately useful information with other long-range skills, like literacy or technology operation, (Nath, 2001), (Kollins & Hansman, 2005). It should be available in local languages or a variety of languages, (Nath, 2001), (Kebede, 2003). It should also provide for confidentiality to avoid possible social stigma or spouse interference, (Schuler, Choque, & Rance, 1994), (Adjah, 2005), (Rutakumwa & Krogman, 2000). Additionally, it should have a networking quality that connects other women and their businesses to each other, (Mchombu, 2000), (Leach, 2001).

These needs will most likely require a combination of formats as a strategy to meet all this criteria. Media campaigns to educate women (& men) on a women's right to control her own reproductive and sexual life, which is scandalous in some countries or not even heard of in others, would help meet the needs of women with partners, (Schuler, Choque, & Rance, 1994), (Jiyanne & Ocholla, 2004).

Similar campaigns to change negative portrayals of women and to teach women the benefits of putting off marriage and pregnancy are necessary to break a cycle of poverty for women, (Schuler, Choque, & Rance, 1994). ICT systems for accessing current information on farming techniques, business skills, and current information on market prices, activity and resources would help farmers and market women, (Nath, 2001). A directory of local small businesses led by women is important for the economic development of entrepreneurs, (Mchombu, 2000).

Information where to locate health clinics, hospitals, and usable roads in any format would help people access the resources they have available to use. Educational information for preventing illness through methods of nutrition, diagnosing illness, and nursing the sick would further alleviate suffering and mortality, (Miller, W.E.B. DuBois Conference, 1976), (Jiyanne & Ocholla, 2004), (Mooko, 2002). Basic literacy skill information and neo-literate literature would help adult learners, (Adjah, 2005).

Reorganizing Existing Resources

Women's groups in the form of NGO's currently work as information service providers for women in urban and rural areas with the intention of getting this kind of information to them and minimizing their obstacles. Using a combination of ICT and other information formats, they provide information on domestic violence prevention, acquiring business loans, housework and childcare assistance, assistance for single parents, nursing the sick, how to vote and change policies, HIV/AIDS prevention and treatment, gender politics, and job opportunities. Although most women in rural areas know about them through word of mouth and the national radio station, less than half of them use their services. The main obstacle to their utilization is their location outside the village in urban areas and their lack of regular and personal outreach through local representatives, (Mooko, 2002). This demonstrates how information resources can be available to women, but if they are in the wrong format, in this case an impersonal word-of-mouth source, they are not used.

An ongoing relationship fostered with a village by a single women's group representative through frequent visitation would be more effective at winning women's trust. Another strategy for gaining trust would be to recruit women in the village as village representatives to disseminate information from these women's groups, (Mooko, 2002).

Women traders are relied upon heavily by women in rural areas and are trusted because of that relationship, making them effective and reliable representatives for NGO women's groups to relay information to rural women. They have regular contact with them and access urban areas frequently, (Kiteme, 2006). Current information on business or health resources and educational information from an urban women's groups could be passed through market traders in the form of word of mouth, audiotapes, or printed information. Rural women could also request information through market traders for them to retrieve from the women's group.

Current information can be accessed by women's groups from the use of ICT systems in urban areas, being downloaded from the web and printed out in English or local languages if available, then disseminated through the trader during her frequent visits into rural areas. Print outs can then be read out loud by a literate person in the neighborhood. Also, radio broadcasts by NGO's and state programs can be recorded by women's groups on audiocassettes, and then passed through the market traders for village women to play on a tape recorder and discuss as a group. When traders visit the area to sell or transfer formatted information, women can directly request needed information as a group or in private, confidentially, or they can simply get word-of-mouth information from them. Relying on traders as a main contact for information enables women to save time and avoid family obstruction from leaving the house by conducting information exchange during business transactions.

Incentive for the market trader to visit the women's group telecentre for these transactions could come from the women's group buying resources from the trader on a regular basis, or using the telecentre as a trading post where the traders can sell to a number of regular customers that meet them there.

For general information that is not anticipated by women's groups or rural women, TV broadcasts in grocery stores and other places of natural congregation could be used to replay videotaped information on a regular basis to make sure all women eventually receive it.

For immediate information needs, a cell phone can be provided for several families to share, enabling them to call the women's group telecentre through a 24-hr hotline service. A daytime worker at the telecentre or an overnight volunteer could look up the needed information on the ICT system there and relay it over the phone. Cell phones can be acquired on loan with feasible repayment methods through banks working with cellular service businesses, (Nath, 2001).

Literacy needs can be addressed using this strategy as well. Packages of printed lesson material and audio taped teaching instruction can be put together by a teacher at the women's group telecentre and distributed through the market traders to women who want to learn to read English, or to read their own language. These lessons can be enhanced in effectiveness by relating to practical work and business skills at the same time. Different packages can be assembled for each stage of literacy training, and can be followed up with useful, neo-literate literature.

This is where librarians are most needed by women in rural areas. Literacy lessons and neo-literate materials would best be created and assembled by librarians, because the prerequisite to helping people research information is inspiring and encouraging them to look for it in the first place.

As information professionals, our encouragement of others to pursue information motivates them to trust us to help them with their information needs. Perhaps one of the reasons women in developing countries do not pursue or use certain types of information available to them through women's groups or health service professionals, besides distrust of strangers, is a general frustration and hopelessness with the issue of information acquisition in general, because it puts them in a position of dependence on others for lack of literacy.

Generally, these women seem motivated to learn literacy skills in order to break out of social isolation and gain inclusion with others, especially if they run small businesses, their only obstacle being that of time to take the classes. Their inspiration is doubled when literacy training is mixed with immediately beneficial income-generating skills, probably because of the time-efficiency. Their interest in market and farming skills takes precedence over other information needs, or so it seems from the studies, so this would be the best information need to use for encouraging their abilities in literacy. Once literacy is gained, the empowerment of this skill, which gives them self-sufficiency on many levels and new earning power, and this educational achievement will give them new confidence in seeking other types of information from available resources.

This confidence will give them the courage to address doctors and professionals with their information needs and assert themselves with others to get it. By beginning with literacy skills, women can begin to discover and access the information they need on their own, making efforts by NGO's and women's groups to provide them with information more effective as they become less reticent.

These are exciting and viable possibilities, according to the studies reviewed. Because of the lack of IT and road infrastructure between urban and rural regions, the information system used will probably have to take multiple forms in order to reach isolated women. ICT is increasingly accessible and essential for remote access to information. Information accessed using internet connections at urban telecentres can include already published information or customized content, created and published by local women in local languages for others in their area. This medium is information current and available around the clock for those who have access to it. Connections between those who access ICT directly and people in the region would require combination strategies using more traditional methods of communication. Communication resources are already in place for this connection to be made, the most important one being existing human relationships, which act as a catalyst for all the others. By using the already existing relationships between women market traders and regional women, trust in the information process will develop readily, motivating isolated women to utilize it more often.

4

POLITICS, WOMEN, RACE AND ECONOMY

INTRODUCTION

As buildings burned to the ground and city dwellers shuffled around with looted provisions, it was obvious that Detroit was undergoing a massive change on July 23rd, 1967. Detroit's Twelfth Street area was in a state of chaos as Mayor Jerome Cavanagh's control of the city slipped through his fingers. The trouble started out with a minor raid in one of Detroit's "blind pig" establishments (bars known for staying open past the legal time of operation). Police officers came through and attempted to clear out the bar of its patrons, until the arguments resulted in a serious confrontation between the two sides. Police officers attempted to arrest the 82 customers from the bar as a group of protesters formed outside of the building. However, the police officers were unable to round up the entire group of bargoers, therefore leaving an angry group of Detroiters with no place to go. The predominantly African American neighborhood where the event took place was patrolled by a group of white officers, with tensions obviously high between the city folks and the officers. The ongoing war between the city and the police reached its climax in the summer of 1967.

Twelfth Street, known today as Rosa Parks Boulevard, was the center of mayhem for five days that July. Looking back, it is hard to determine who caused more damage: the outraged city inhabitants, or the overzealous police officers and eventually, the National Guard. In the course of the five days, 43 Detroiters of varying races were killed, while the majority of the victims were African American.

Detroiters had been familiarized with riots only 24 years earlier. The June 21st, 1943 riots in Detroit have been attributed mainly to racial tensions between fellow community members.

The 1943 riot lasted for roughly 48 hours and was the cause of 34 deaths[1]. The 1943 riot is largely marked in Detroit's history as a nasty affair between white and black Detroiters, as the African American community began to move into Belle Isle Park, one of Detroit's riverfront residential areas. African Americans actively defended their communities against angry whites who were insulted by the residential infiltration of the opposite race. Not nearly as memorable as the 1967 riots, the 1943 riots are much more of an embarrassment for citywide integration attempts on behalf of the African American community, showing a very unflattering side of Detroit's severe racism in and around Belle Isle.

With little resolution, the city continued its efforts to move past an ugly history of racial tension and enter the 1960's with a sense of economic growth. The urban growth, however, departed sooner than it arrived. Amidst the technological and social advancements in the late 1960's, the economy began to falter. While the world around Detroit saw growing and expanding industries, the inner-city was left to fend for itself once automobile plants began moving and growing, proving that national successes have human consequences. Known as the Motor City, Detroit's world-renowned reputation for producing cars sputtered.

During the time between the two riots of 1943 and 1967 respectively, integration was at its peak and Detroit was home to both African Americans and whites.

Detroit started out as a predominantly white city, especially at the turn of the century. After the Civil War, ex-slaves found themselves moving north to meet family, friends, and ideally become employed in a valuable industry. The Great Migration beginning in the postwar south proved successful for some time in the north, as blacks were being employed and the job market was packed. When the population influx met the Midwest, not limited to Detroit, public opinion on race and economy began to shift. When Chicago, Detroit, Cleveland, and other northern metropolises began to boom, the country was subject to some of the most devastating segregation that ever took place in the United States.

In these next sections, the discussions of economics and race in Detroit will collide over the subject of poverty. Poverty, specifically homelessness, is a symptom of both racial discrimination and economic deterioration. Delving into the problem of poverty from the very bottom is the only effective way to understand the political dynamics of the homeless community. Using evidence from the respective mayoral candidates over the past 30 years in the city of Detroit, this study will attempt to conclude that it is not from political power that a neighborhood can withstand economic setbacks, but because of the grassroots efforts that many private organizations and community members have made for themselves.

Throughout history, Detroit has been a prime example of an industrial town that opened its arms to unskilled potential employees. Just as labor outsourcing has proven successful outside of the United States in today's world, managing to employ a new worker for lower wages only made sense to large corporations centered in Detroit. The animosity that may of course come along with such a hiring/firing process got severe, and the competition between the races became extreme.

While the 1943 riot was not as destructive as the riot of 1967, the city still had much work to do to bring Detroit back to its state of booming industry after its blow in the 40's. In addition to an inadequate job market, substandard housing became an issue between 1940 and 1960. The question of who may live where and in what sort of conditions became a hotly debated topic between community members and local elected officials. Price gouging on houses and apartments could be found in any large city during this time period, however the difference between Detroit and other sophisticated cities was Detroit's inability to develop a proper transportation system, as well as its derelict housing conditions that still may be observed today.

Losing ground in the housing and job sects, the African American population became outraged at the condition of their community. As the city began seeing a lack of jobs due to the factory migration to the north, the inner city was systematically stranded by the restraints of race, class, the economy, and the lack of public transportation. As the problems grew, so did the anger.

The riots of 1967 have often been blamed on class, housing, jobs, and other economic factors, while the 1943 riots were attributed to the racial tensions between city dwellers and southern migrants. Because of this, 1967 is known for being a riot with modern goals in a modern political arena. Since the purpose of the '67 riot was to maintain the existence that Detroit desperately held on to as an African American-friendly place, many rioters participated in acts of looting, arson, and economically-based crimes rather than the all-out hand-to-hand combat of the '43 riots. The '67 riots were able to demonstrate the frustrations of the community, whether lawfully or not, by means of acquiring/stealing goods (TV's, furniture, groceries) that were typically unaffordable. The stand against racist Detroit officials that many African Americans took was well-received among their compatriots. However, the white communities only distanced themselves by moving north, citing high crime rates, inadequate housing, and the influx of the African American population as evidence necessitating a suburban migration. The post-riot years would mark the end of an integrated city, whether by choice or by force.

Jerome Cavanagh would be Detroit's last successful and beloved white mayor. The entrance of Coleman Young in 1973 marked the new era of black power within the city. However, between 1970 and 1974, Sheriff Roman S. Gribbs was elected, and today Gribbs stands as the mayor that time forgot. Gribbs ran a campaign against African American moderate, Richard Austin, as a white conservative. Detroit scholar Heather Ann Thomson described the 1970 election as a political watershed for the African American community. In a Detroit Free Press article from 2002, Thomson explained the results of the election as a process of maturing. Thomson, describing the Gribbs era, wrote: "a full-fledged grassroots black revolutionary challenge to the existing racial inequalities in the city came of age. "

Mayor Gribbs was also responsible for the unleashing of Detroit's most intimidating organization of officers known as the STRESS unit (Stop The Robberies, Enjoy Safe Streets) which caused far more "stress" to Detroiters than its initial intention. The STRESS unit was an undercover decoy squad whose killings of young black men sparked mass protests, the shootings of police and more court battles . With a meager reputation and minor name recognition, Gribbs served one term before being phased out by the new generation of African American leadership that the city aggressively pursued. Detroit Free Press contributor Sheryl James wrote "Overall, most say Gribbs' four years in office served as a necessary cushion between the tumultuous years leading to the 1967 riot and the confrontational Coleman Young era. "

The entrance of Gribbs into Detroit backfired as a way to re-enfranchise the white population. With Gribbs being the new mayor, many conservative Detroiters believed that Gribbs would be the answer to the ever-growing problem of northern migration from the city, especially in the white community. Gribbs was unable to reproduce the white Detroit that suburbanites remember from the 1930's and 40's, and his attempts only made the African American resistance stronger. In a post-civil rights environment, it was clear that Gribbs did not represent the generation of Detroiters that existed at the time. The race dilemma could only be manipulated and sympathized by an African American candidate.

Regardless of which candidate won the mayoral bid—Coleman A. Young's opponent, Richard Austin or Young himself, in 1973 and for the rest of the century Detroit's mayor would have a difficult challenge. The two major sects of problems that began to surface were rooted either in economic challenges either personally, communally, or publicly, and of course the impossible questions of racial integration and racial equality. Beginning work on the problems and coordinating efforts that were beneficial to the city economically and racially was an extremely difficult task, and one that still begs the question of any city's mayor actually being able to alleviate economic and racial inequality.

Detroit has survived despite its massive poverty rate and its hard-hitting deindustrialization witnessed by the city over the past 50 years. As Thomas Sugrue, author of The Origins of the Urban Crisis agrees,

The bleak landscapes and unremitting poverty of Detroit in the 1970's and 1980's are the legacies of the transformation of the city's economy in the wake of World War II, and of the politics and culture of race that have their origins in the persistent housing and workplace discrimination of the postwar decades. What hope remains in the city comes from the continued efforts of city residents to resist the debilitating effects of poverty, racial tension, and industrial decline. But the rehabilitation of Detroit and other major American cities will require a more vigorous attempt to grapple with the enduring effects of the postwar transformation of the city, and creative responses, piece by piece, to the interconnected forces of race, residence, discrimination and industrial decline, the consequences of a troubled and still unresolved past.

Detroit has a long way to go in terms of construction, politics, economic leadership and public appearance. To solve Detroit's existing problems, it is crucial for meaningful and sympathetic politicians to work closely with grassroots organizing efforts for economic relief of city inhabitants. In order to conceive of possible solutions to this seemingly endless problem, one must examine the political dynamics of not only past and present mayors, but also the perspective of organizers and directors all the way down to the lowest economic rung of citizens in Detroit—the unemployed, the impoverished, and the homeless. This study will examine the lives and times of four different Detroiters; Coleman A. Young, Detroit's Mayor from 1974-1994, Dennis W. Archer, Detroit's Mayor from 1994-2001, Dr. Vernon Rayford, head of Just Love Ministries charitable organization and feeding program in Detroit, and Keith Livingston, a homeless man utilizing Just Love's services. Through discussing these different stories, the study will conclude with a proposal for the logical next step, a grassroots ideology reflected through an innovative shelter and rehabilitation facility.

Mayoral Politics

Many attempts to alleviate poverty in the city of Detroit have been made for several decades, but history has demonstrated that even hard-working mayors cannot be successful without an effective group of supporters. This chapter will explain the impenetrability of any politician, regardless of race and economics, to single handedly eradicate the urban plagues of unemployment, poverty, and homelessness within the city of Detroit. This section will also establish Detroit's two most pressing dilemmas, the dilemma of widespread racial integration within the city, and the dilemma of economic sustainability, and which of the two effects poverty and unemployment more thoroughly. Each mayor's attempts will be discussed, while demonstrating the fact that no Detroit politician who has surfaced in the modern urban environment has been able to solve both problems concurrently.

Race, capital, demographics and creativity were deterrents in achieving individual political success among the mayors. After the 1967 riots, the city of Detroit went from having a nearly 50-50 black-to-white ratio to a 75-25 black-to-white population by the year 1980. It was during this period that Detroit elected its first African American mayor into office in 1973. Coleman Alexander Young was Detroit's mayor for 20 years, serving five terms. During Young's tenure as mayor, he accomplished many, but not all of the goals that he set out for himself, including the integration of the police force, the creation of more affordable and suitable housing, and the dismantling of one of Detroit's most feared police regimes, the STRESS (Stop the Robberies, Enjoy Safe Streets) unit , responsible for many "accidental" police shootings, and a frequent subject in accusations of police brutality .

Coleman Young was not, however, faultless. In fact, much of today's urban plight in the city of Detroit has been blamed on its former mayor. Media outlets never looked kindly upon Young, and he remained in an adversarial position with reporters and journalists for nearly his entire political life. Young was stigmatized throughout his terms as a leader incredibly preoccupied with race. By alienating white suburbs and disenfranchising white business owners and executives, the city separated itself further and further between its black and white populations. The dividing line between the races became more and more tangible, and today, the infamous Eight Mile Road now cuts between the city and the suburbs marking black and white territories respectively. Young's campaign for Detroit's criminals and vandals to "Hit Eight Mile Road! " did not rub suburbanites the right way, to say the least. As the city and suburbs grew further and further apart in interests, politics, and skin color, it became clear that Young played a major role in perpetuating Detroit's division between races. As African American representatives moved to the forefront of Detroit politics, the few remaining whites slowly left the city.

The Life of Coleman A. Young

Coleman Alexander Young was born in 1918 in Tuscaloosa, Alabama. His mother and father relocated to Detroit's Black Bottom when Young was only five. He was the eldest of five children, all of whom attended the Detroit Public Schools. During the Young family's life in Detroit, the Black Bottom was stigmatized as a landmark for economic strife, joblessness, and a location that would benefit from low-cost affordable and/or public housing. At the turn of the century, Detroit was a popular spot for the relocation of those folks displaced by the migration that occurred after the emancipation of African American slaves in 1865. The Motor City attracted folks from Alabama, Missouri, and other southern states filled with unemployed free citizens looking for work. Detroit, renowned for being an area of great economic opportunity attracted many southerners to the unskilled labor opportunities within the city.

Young's family was no different in this trend. Young's father, also named Coleman, was a political amateur who tested the political waters in his community. Thus, Young was able to get a taste of politics through his father's activism. Throughout school, Young sensed the racial tensions that existed in the city. After his graduation from Eastern High School, Young received one of his most important lessons in racial acceptance and discrimination. Discouraged by his high school teachers and counselors, Young was blocked from applying to his first choice school, the University of Michigan . Young began to realize that the world, politically or socially, was in fact a white world. This mindset would shape his political career. Young's sense of division between black and white became a major theme in many of his policy changes, additions, and his attitude.

Young had a series of odd jobs until his responsibilities until 1942 when he was drafted to serve in World War II. Young became a Second Lieutenant for the Tuskeegee Airmen, an expendable black unit. As a pilot, Young was enthusiastic about being able to "fly a B-24 over Germany and [drop] bombs on those superior Aryan motherfuckers. " Young was discharged because of his infiltration of an all-white officers club at an Army camp, and his radical politics were a constant concern of his peers and commanding officers. Young returned to Detroit to then begin down his winding political path that would continue for more than 50 years. Upon his discharge from the Army, Young became director of organization for Wayne County's Congress of Industrial Organizations (now known as the AFL-CIO) in 1948. His extensive work as organizer would land him his unsuccessful bid for state senate from the Progressive Party, though, this loss would not be his last appearance in local politics. Young's progressivism was his largest influence in his politics. He was constantly reminded of the need for racial and economic justice, especially in the inner city, with which he was quite familiar. Because of his leftward lean, he was always at odds with his opponents over what resulted in Detroit's racial isolation. Coleman Young founded the Negro Labor Council in 1951, an organization known for their extreme left ideals . The Negro Labor Council was "responsible for gaining employment integration at Sears Roebuck and Co. nationwide, " while suspected to be a communist organization that was later disbanded in 1956. The allegations of Young's council being communist stigmatized his politics.

Political Background

Young unsuccessfully ran for city council and State Representative before he finally won a seat in Detroit's 4th congressional district as State Representative. Young became Michigan's Democratic Floor Leader in 1966, one year prior to the massive devastation of Detroit's 1967 riots. He quickly gained notoriety in local politics through his popularity in the African American community, which allowed him to climb the power ladder, the top rung of which would be his mayoral position. He remained State Representative for two terms, and in 1973 Young campaigned for mayor of Detroit. One of Detroit's better-known sheriffs, Sheriff John Nichols would be Young's opponent in Detroit's first black vs. white election of Mayor. From 1973 until the early 1990's, he stood as the symbol of Detroit for all of its residents.

Young entered office during the climax of white flight. He was confronted with several issues regarding race class, and the impossible task of balancing them together. One of Young's more difficult challenges was the integration of Detroit's police force which would make a statement for racial equality. But, Young also needed to economically revitalize the city somehow. When white folks abandoned the inner-city, so did the funding. With people, corporations, and businesses moving north, the capital followed the white flight. The city was left in economic ruin after the riots. Young's election in 1973 marked the beginning of a new era in Detroit, though Young was forced to inherit a Detroit confronting major race and economic issued that daunted the new mayor. With the promises of his 1973 campaign that had yet to be accomplished, his public appearances and community involvement made Detroiters curious to see what he could accomplish over time, if given another term.

In 1977, Detroit had its first black vs. black candidate election for Mayor. The year 1977 also marked the opening of one of Detroit's proudest accomplishments, the Renaissance Center, which at the time contained the five-star hotel The Westin as well as many ballrooms for elite receptions. The Renaissance Center is Detroit's largest and most impressive skyscraper and has only recently been replaced as one of the most technologically advanced centers in Detroit (now the Compuware Center holds the record for the most modern development in Detroit). The Renaissance Center, a 727-foot multi-cyclindrical, multistory mammoth is frequently shown in photographs and renderings of downtown Detroit's skyline. Needless to say, its construction most certainly spoke well for Young, and he trumpeted it in his re-election campaign in 1977. The Renaissance Center was imagined and designed by a nonprofit private development organization hoping to return some livelihood to Detroit by attracting commerce. The center cost $337 million to construct and currently boasts 5.5 million square feet of office space and 150,000 square feet of retail space . Today, the Renaissance Center is the proud home to one of Detroit's "Big Three" administrations, General Motors. The Renaissance Center remains one of the symbols of Detroit and is still the most recognized building downtown.

In 1977, Mayor Young began to sense the possibility of change in the economy with the election of Democratic President, Jimmy Carter, who was known for being progressive in his policies, and who was also known for looking kindly upon suffering urban metropolises. During his term, President Carter's recently constituted Urban Development Action Grant program approved over $107 million in grants for Detroit and instituted new federal policy that increased the city's block grant allocation from $30 million to $60 million . This allowed Detroit to build up some of their limited resources, demolish abandoned homes and buildings, and fix up public spaces. However, the help from the Carter administration would have been even more influential had his plan utilized some long-term action. While some urban enterprises were flourishing during this time period, the opportunity for change was slipping by, with the "merciless Regan years ", as Young referred to them, just around the corner. By the time Young's third re-election campaign was on the horizon in 1981, the city had been suffering from a massive deficit problem since just after the construction of the Renaissance Center.

Detroit's now infamous Joe Louis Arena was constructed in 1980. Named for the legendary heavyweight champion, Joe Louis, a popular and patriotic WWII era soldier and athlete, the arena is home to one of Detroit's favorite athletic enterprises, the Detroit Red Wings. The Detroit Red Wings are well-known for their back-to-back Stanley Cup victories in 1997 and 1998. The team was the inspiration of one of Detroit's most beloved nicknames, "Hockeytown". Paid for by a number of private beneficiaries, Detroit's contribution to Joe Louis was minimal. With the city running a $132 million deficit in 1981 after Joe Louis Arena's opening, residents remained impressed with Young's economic progress in the city, as new developments were showing up like clockwork prior to each re-election. The city re-elected Young by a 71% majority in November of 1981 despite Detroit's fiscal irreparability.

In the early 1980's Mayor Young found himself in the center of some major bribery-related lawsuits and accusations in the early 1980's, beginning a long trend of rumored corruption in

Detroit city politics. Both investigations have grown out of Mr. Young's efforts to direct more city business to black-owned companies. One centered on Magnum Oil, a company to which the city advanced $1 million at a low interest rate to buy bus fuel, which it then resold to the city. City officials said they had done so because the company could not obtain conventional financing...A second investigation also touched on Mr. Young. It involved whether Vista Disposal Inc. paid the former director of Detroit's Water and Sewerage Department, Charles Beckham, $16,000 in bribes to win a contract to haul sludge from the city's water treatment plant. Federal investigators installed a listening device in the Mayor's town house to record conversations by him, Mr. Beckham and Darralyn Bowers, the owner of Vista and a close friend.

The allegations against Mayor Young were dismissed in 1983, due to insufficient evidence, but the damage had been done. As the city of Detroit became synonymous with a negative political impression, the reflection of the constituent disappointment and disenfranchisement was obvious in Young's re-election campaign of 1985. Detroit had a meager 37.7% of its population get out to vote, thereby attaining Young's fourth success at his mayoral bid. The Mayor believed he needed to demonstrate some physical evidence that the city has worked on -- hence he proposed the idea of the "people mover" prior to his 1985 victory.

When one reflects on the idea of the people mover today over twenty years later, it is obvious that the project was an inherent failure for the entire city of Detroit and its suburbs. The people mover started out as an above-ground subway system that was mechanically operated from a different location. The automatic large-scale remote-control subway train has remained clean and roomy throughout its existence, while appearing quite technologically advanced. When the initial proposition was made for the people mover to be the bridge between the inner city and the suburbs, most urban and suburbanites were open and motivated about the idea of an efficient public transportation method for a high-traffic city. In a place where housing is segregated, where the automobile industry is constantly moving farther away from Detroit's metropolis, the people mover seemed like the perfect opportunity to close the gap between inner city and suburbs, the rich and the poor, the black and the white. Money was invested, and labor begun.

What had started out as the Motor City's answer to the high cost of vehicles eventually became a disappointment to the term "public transportation." Because of insufficient funds and a lack of support for the project from city dwellers and local politicians including the City Council, the people mover has little to show as its empty cars cycle around the downtown full of empty skyscrapers. Today the people mover simply serves as a way to get from one part of gentrified downtown to another part of gentrified downtown and serves no actual purpose for folks who would truly benefit from a functional public transportation method.

The failure of Detroit's people mover marked Mayor Young's last attempt at successful urban revitalization. Re-elected for his fifth term, Young took his seat as mayor for the last time in 1989. These late years for Young as mayor would set the tone for the election of Dennis W.

Archer, Detroit's next mayor from 1994-2001. Young had long tried to integrate the city hoping to bring whites back along with some substantial capital. However, since whites would only come to the city due to expensive economic development, it made it difficult for Young to pursue measures that would lead to black equality in addition to the satisfying the needs of white communities. Though, Young's attempts at reintegrating the police department were somewhat successful; in 1973 the Detroit Police Department was a meager 18% African American while in 1983, the police force was 32% African American .

Young had an extensive series of achievements under his belt as mayor for twenty years. Besides his integration of the Detroit Police Department and the erection of three major facilities in the downtown area, Young created one of many housing projects known as Victoria Park in 1974. By 1994, the project was responsible for nearly 15,000 new housing units. It was also on Young's watch that police brutality reports from Detroiters declined by 64% from 1975-1982. Young also successfully bid to have the Republican National Convention in the city of Detroit in 1980.

In 1992, Young considered his health and his increasing age deterrents for running again. Young wavered in his decision, but finally on the filing deadline of the Democratic mayoral primary, Mayor Young announced his decision to step down from his position. Stepping up were the fresh faces of Sharon McPhail, progressive city council member, and Dennis Archer, honored member of the American Bar Association and former Justice of the Michigan Supreme Court. Though McPhail's potential victory would have been the first victory by a woman—black or white—for the mayoral candidacy, Dennis Archer's mayoral campaign was a well-oiled program, one which achieved exactly what it set out to attain. Dennis Archer proved to be an unbeatable opponent, winning the Detroit vote in 1993 by a 53% majority. McPhail and a third candidate, Arthur B. Blackwell split the remaining 47%, with less than 30% having voted for McPhail in the democratic primary, which most often serves as an indication of the general election winner. January 1st, 1994 not only marked Dennis Archer's inauguration, but also the new mayor's 52nd birthday. While Archer admittedly said that Young was "a hard act to follow," he also admits that "[Young and I] have a lot more in common in terms of goals, such as our commitments to creating wealth and a level playing field for the Afro-Americans, [but] our styles of getting there are completely different. " Mayor Young, despite having employed Archer as his campaign manager in 1977 endorsed McPhail, due to her Young-esque politics and agenda. The New York Times describes Archer and Young to have been "at odds " with each other during the 1993 campaign.

Dennis Archer; Detroit's Second African American Mayor

Born in 1939 in Cassopolis, Michigan, just north of the Indiana border, Dennis Archer didn't always live in the city of Detroit. His father was a handyman with a third grade education, and it wasn't until after Archer graduated from Western Michigan University that he relocated to the city of Detroit 180 miles from his hometown to take part in local politics. After starting up his own law firm shortly after his graduation from college, Archer coincidentally became Mayor Young's campaign manager during his re-election efforts in 1977.

After his success in the managerial end of politics, Archer made the decision to run his own campaign for the Michigan Supreme Court. In 1986, he successfully became a Supreme Court Justice, elected for an eight-year term. However, it was no more than four years through his term when Archer realized there was a need for an inspiring leader for the City of Detroit, and he could be the one. In 1990, Archer's resigned from his position as Supreme Court Justice and he began to organize his election for the mayoral seat.

Not nearly as progressive as his predecessor, Mayor Archer had an agreeable public persona. He took his responsibilities as mayor to heart, and wasted no time coming up with solutions to the urban problems Detroit had yet to confront. The year that Archer was elected for his first of two terms, President Bill Clinton had already been in the White House for two years. Archer and Clinton had an unusually positive and close working relationship, which gave Archer a special advantage. Clinton devised a plan to rejuvenate and revitalize failing urban areas across the United States. His plan would recreate public spaces, offer new jobs and facilities, and demolish unsafe territories throughout the city, including Detroit's excess of abandoned homes. The plan would funnel subsistent capital into the city's governance and allow city leaders to make strides in future renovations. Clinton's plan was appropriately called the "Empowerment Zone" plan. Achieving an Empowerment Zone designation meant that over a period of ten years, the city of Detroit was going to receive federal funds to help uplift people to work to improve an 18-square-mile zone. In matching Clinton's plan for urban renewal, John Engler, the Governor of Michigan in the early 1990's, developed an initiative for "Renaissance Zones ", which also allowed Archer some additional financial resources to build upon. In combining the Empowerment and Renaissance Zone designations, Archer led the city in the creation thousands of new jobs not only through temporary construction and renovation positions but also through the opening of sustainable businesses, accomplishing at least half of Young's agenda for economic revitalization.

It did not take long to recognize the city's progress, largely due to Archer's influence. In 1995, the rate of unemployment in the city dropped from 1994's 13.4% to 1995's 8.2%. The Empowerment & Renaissance Zone designation initiatives proved a positive attribute. Archer promised voters that Detroit would become a city of world-class leadership status, and Archer also promised that by the year 2001, "...People will recognize Detroit as the best-run city in America ." Such claims made Archer appear unrealistic. However, his additions and contributions to the city would be invaluable in the long run. With Archer's first year in office under his belt, he began to propose new and innovative ways to develop Detroit's world-class status.

Between 1994 and 1996, Archer successfully attracted $2.2 billion in private investments for 82 commercial properties. Because Archer put so little weight on his race and the general race of the city, CEO's and business professionals came to know Detroit as a center for integrated commerce instead of its previous racially stigmatized economic disorder that Detroiters frequently associated with Young. Archer maintained this skill and desire as a key attribute of his administration. The influx of popularity forced property values in the city to rise by 25% in 1996. In the same year, Dennis Archer completed talks with General Motors to relocate their corporate offices downtown to the Renaissance Center, a shining reminder of why Detroit is stili called the Motor City.

Archer's talks with Mike Illitch of the Detroit Tigers and Bill Ford of the Detroit Lions also proved to be fruitful; a long-term plan was initiated to relocate the baseball and football teams into the downtown area from their current locations outside the city. The baseball field would be adopted by Comerica Bank, one of Michigan's larger banking corporations and would don the name "Comerica Park." The Lions' stadium, which would come just a couple years after the opening of Comerica Park, would be called "Ford Field" after Ford Motor Company, one of Detroit's greatest benefactors. The agreements were made and 1996 marked the beginning of the end for the outdated stadiums and with Detroit's lowest murder rate in 21 years.

Ending a banner year, the rise of new development was around the corner in 1997. Detroit has long since been known for its infamous night-before-Halloween mischief traditionally called Devil's Night, just short of an annual contained riot, where Detroit residents, typically disenfranchised youth, travel around the neighborhood committing arson and other crimes against property in their own areas. This was a long time practice in the city of Detroit and began during the Coleman Young's era. Homes were set afire throughout the city with very little relief on behalf of city officials, as the damage was widespread and dangerous. It was Mayor Archer who took the initiative to create a task force of sorts to enable Detroiters to act as volunteers reporting to a team if they witnessed Devil's Night crimes. Archer began this program during his first term, and the citizens of Detroit were pleased with the extra protection. Not only did the Devil's Night changed decrease the need for officers and municipal assistance, it also provided a sense of unity to the city and neighborhoods as a whole. It served as an indication that instead of uniting racially, Detroiters should unite as a community.

He changed the name — Devil's Night – to Angel's Night. In 1994, Mayor Archer's first year, there were 3,500 organized volunteers lining the residential streets in Detroit on Angel's Night. Three years later, Archer motivated the city to turn out 35,000 organized volunteers . It was the same year that the city of Detroit ranked #1 in Industry Week Magazine's listing of world-class communities based on their manufacturing statistics. Mayor Archer was sited by Newsweek Magazine as one of the 25 U.S. Mayors to watch in the upcoming years. Archer was aware of the fact that the momentum had to keep up on his watch, though Archer had already made some massive accomplishments that would have been unheard of in Mayor Young's era. Archer was re-elected to his second term in November of 1997.

Archer's concern with racial balance was not of imminent importance in his political agenda. His concern was the lack of funding in the city programs, largely due to Detroit's segregation. For years, both Young and Archer attempted to entice the city council into thinking that casino gambling would be the answer to many of the city's problems. The city council was notoriously opposed on the matter and it wasn't until Archer's proposal that the Council agreed to the idea. On April 9, 1998, Council approved the construction of three casinos inside city limits. Archer promised the city a massive revenue increase on behalf of the casinos, and construction began. Today, the three casinos, Motor City Casino, Greektown Casino, and the MGM Grand Casino are three of Detroit's most profitable facilities. Motor City Casino gutted the old Hostess factory, The Greektown Casino took over an indoor mini-mall called Trapper's Alley, and the MGM Grand was supposed to be a temporary casino, but has not yet moved from its massive newly constructed white cement facility.

The casinos amassed $100 million annually, and created jobs for nearly 8,000 people. As Archer has said, "...there's nothing like jobs to help people move up and out of poverty ". Unfortunately, many of the people filling positions in the casinos were mostly white transplants from the suburbs, and the opening of the casinos did not rehabilitate Detroit's impoverished population by a long shot. The casinos did generate enough capital to help Detroit with other publicly funded programs, and the initial proposition of the casinos promised much of their revenue to the failing Detroit Public Schools. In turn, eight percent of casino revenue was promised to the state Renaissance Fund for Economic Development, and two percent was promised to "local improvement" efforts, with the assumption that the Detroit Public Schools fall under the category of local improvement .

After the casinos had gained notoriety and become one of the city's biggest moneymakers, Archer began plans with corporate executives for the revamping of downtown Detroit's Washington Square. The proud bearer of Campus Martius which opened in 2004, Washington Square is Detroit's answer to Rockefeller Plaza ice skating and casual metropolitan dining. Directly across from the ice rink stands the exquisite Compuware building, Detroit's most recent architectural success. Campus Martius is also surrounded by Detroit's Hard Rock Café, in addition to a quaint Au Bon Pain cafe, across from a Borders bookstore. Detroit appeared to be on the rise with its new mayor, but the façade of success and prosperity was barely citywide.

THE REMAINING DILEMMA

One of Detroit's most significant problems remained unsolved. Nearly one-third of Detroit's population continued to be trapped in poverty, with attempts of migrating to the suburbs to be futile at best. The casinos did not provide substantial relief to the homeless, nor did the efforts of attracting white commerce to Detroit. Few, if any plans were made to revamp the truly devastated areas, and any invitation to embrace Detroit's developments were targeted toward the middle-to-upper classes. Statistical information gathered by the US Census Bureau illustrates that the poverty level did rise and fall a bit under different mayoral control, in addition to the steady rise and fall of the black and white populations.

Detroit Census Results From Three Generations[1]	1970 Mayor Young Elected: 1973	1990 Mayor Archer Elected: 1993	2000 Mayor Kilpatrick Elected: 2001
Total Population	348,413	1,027,974	951,270
African American Population	255,432 74%	777,916 76%	775,772 82%
White Population	86,576 25%	222,316 22%	116,599 12%
Number of Unemployed Individuals	27,730 14%	82,333 11%	53,259 8%
Number of Individuals Not In Labor Force	150,012 43%	341,985 33%	298,716 44%
Number of Families Living Below Poverty	28,903 24%	71,673 29%	47,920 22%
Number of Individuals Living Below Poverty	82,785 19%	328,467 32%	243,153 26%

Mayor Young's approval rating was surprisingly high during the city's economic recessions. Young was beloved by Detroiters, and seen as a prophet to the disenfranchised and seemingly forgotten African American population surrounded by a ghostly urban landscape. Young was a true working-class American, having pulled himself up by the bootstraps to a success in the political arena. Detroiters identified with Young, and saw him as a leader who could properly represent the working class city desperately trying to recover from economic and racial turmoil. His grip, however, on economic reality was rather unsteady, leaving Mayor Archer to deal with his debt of over $80 million within the city in 1994.

Throughout his tenure as Mayor, Young was known for alienating the suburban communities, those who had moved up and out of Detroit. The folks left in the city, Young's generation of Detroiters, were the true survivors, the lifetime Detroiters, and the Detroiters worthy of Young's political representation. Young's go-at-it-alone attitude along with his fierce public persona allowed Detroiters to admire Young, and allow suburbanites to dismiss him as a formidable politician. Young's frequent swearing in both conversation and addresses caused many to assume that the mayor couldn't be taken seriously. He also frequently represented himself and the city as the victims of the media. Young's attitude became Detroit's general impression among visitors and outsiders.

The standoffish Young who drew a sharp line between the suburbs and the city contributed greatly to Detroit's modern apartheid. With the election of Mayor Archer, city dwellers were guaranteed a better working relationship with their suburban neighbors. Archer attempted to re-enfranchise white business owners to relocate into the city and create a community where black and white work together to create a singular Detroit. Archer represented Detroit's trying to phasing out of its racial division and a Detroit on the upside of urban sustainability. The new mayor attracted a previously unheard of trend—whites slowly moving back to the city to live, and to work. Archer began the work on gentrification in the city by means of renovating old buildings and factories and turning them into upscale lofts and apartments.

The neighborhoods and communities that need the most help are often not prioritized. This is due to a lack of political representation, and a general impression among city-dwellers that such areas are lost causes. In a sense, the repair of suffering communities was the same conundrum that Young faced 30 years earlier. In the midst of the gentrification efforts, an observer might note that the additions and renovations done attract a different social class into the city.

While Archer and the new generation of corporate leadership took Detroit under their wings, the effort to improve the lives of native Detroiters lost its importance in the scheme of reindustrialization. While Archer's changes to the city have been welcome by businesspeople, they have also been problematic towards the impoverished population of Detroit. Archer's renovations and advancements became the symbols of modern Detroit, while very much representing the obsolescence of the Detroit utilized by the underclass.

The sense of unity that Young strove to attain while in office among African Americans was slowly being replaced by the desire to revamp such communities in order to make them more aesthetically pleasing to visitors and tourists. The plethora of new operations in the city has provided Detroiters with some hope that the local government will take a more meaningful approach at the city's redesign. Detroit's new renovations have only taken place in a very small portion of Detroit, the portion of Detroit that tourists, suburbanites, and corporate executives frequent. A widespread relief effort in Detroit is necessary for the city to demonstrate its self-sufficiency to its global counterparts, and the relief effort must exist within Detroit communities, not simply corporate properties .

Opposing Detroits

Mayor Young and Mayor Archer created different atmospheres within the city. Young set up the kind of Detroit that citizens can feel at home in, with neighbors and business owners relating to each other relating to the plight of the African American community. Young represented a poor community with poverty rates rising as his multiple terms progressed. His community of supporters was convinced that a properly-functioning Detroit must contain a plethora of African Americans fighting against economic odds to represent their city. Detroit Young's Detroit was poor, but united for the African American community. Archer's Detroit was one of more booming economic prosperity, and a Detroit containing a mixture of races and economic backgrounds. Archer's Detroit catered to the needs of the city's constant struggle for viable commerce and "world-class" economic status. Archer's steps towards integration were useful, as much of Detroit's business sector has been revamped. Suburbanites returned to the city in small numbers, and commerce began to serve a new class of Detroiters. Archer's Detroit was economically stable, but hardly targeted directly towards his African American constituency.

Detroiters had quite a choice in determining who the more prosperous mayor was. Young seemed to attract many voters, but Archer seemed to attract so much capital. The measure of success and progress in metropolises nationwide varies. In Detroit, however, the measure of success is quite different between Detroit and suburban Detroit. While Detroit identified with a mayor from the age of civil rights and the black struggle, suburban Detroit identified with the need for a stronger business atmosphere and the requirement that the city cleaned up its appearance. The problem, however, lies in the fact that suburban Detroiters don't vote for Detroit elections, which leads to the dilemma of which leader is the better representative all-inclusively for Detroit.

Mayor Archer was a proponent of physical improvement for the city of Detroit. The dereliction of Detroit only began to improve with the creation of new modern enterprises. However, joblessness, homelessness, and poverty still plague Detroit. An observer might pose the question: is Detroit utilizing its resources wisely? Should Detroit continue to try to attract a new generation of Detroiters from the suburbs, or attempt to re-spark the interests of native Detroiters?

It would require more government programs, more general assistance, and more public policy aimed at the unemployed. However, this conclusion also poses the question; can any city's mayor and/or local government fully solve the problem of poverty and joblessness? Mayor Young would say no.

"Education, drugs, homelessness, unwed mothers, crime, you name it—to varying degrees, every social issue is about jobs. If I could have brought enough jobs to Detroit, I would have gone down as the greatest mayor the world has ever seen. The same could be said for mayors of New York or Cleveland or Buffalo or Los Angeles or Philadelphia. The problem is, there's only so much a mayor can do about jobs...he can't keep a factory from folding and he can't change his climate and he can't control wages or utility bills, and as much as he might like and try to, he can't make another man's decisions. "

In the modern urban environment, there is a threshold as to what can be expected of local elected officials. The decentralization of Detroit's industrial facilities brought an added amount of stress to Young, as it would for any politician. As factory positions filled by workers in the northern suburbs, Detroiters became immune to the unemployment and underdevelopment surrounding them. Any politician can make a promise, however the support of the community and elected officials is required for effective change. As a representative of the city, a mayor should make every effort to reinvent a working landscape that the area can embrace. It is easy to see that both mayors did achieve some aspects of their imagined Detroit.

Having discussed the respective mayor's upbringings and political styles, the conclusion is simple—Young appealed to disenfranchised African American Detroiters, while Archer appealed to the upper-crust, not necessarily African American Detroiters. It would have been entirely possible for Young to have initiated many of the modern achievements that Archer proposed, but the differing personalities and priorities of the two politicians led to different views of development. Young's supporters formed from a common need to identify as an empowered group of African Americans. For Young to have begun talks with the executives with whom Archer had a working relationship, Young would have had to expand his horizons to admit that the city of Detroit could not function simply as a "chocolate city ", and that neighborhoods and industries must be integrated in order to support a united space. With the post-civil rights attitude still being fresh in the minds of many Detroiters, African American leadership motivated the population to take control of their political future. A small representation of this can be observed in the statistics of voter turnout in the city of Detroit through the Young era, Archer era, and Kilpatrick era. As time went on and each mayoral election took place, the number of voters in the city plummeted by year.

Young's limited progressive view required some expansion, and without a deeper sense of acceptance of his potential constituency, Young's peacemaking ability would continue at a very slow rate. A sense of open-mindedness would have allowed Young to achieve a positive working relationship with the suburban communities, and the same open-mindedness would have allowed Young to attract industries and corporations to serve as allies of the city. Much of Archer's ability to unite the city with the suburbs would have been impossible without Young's influence. For example, without having erected the famous Renaissance Center in 1977, Archer would have been unable to allow General Motors to relocate their offices to a nationally recognized location. Archer's peacemaking ability was necessary to build upon the advancements that Young had made over his 20-year term. Archer's generation marked Detroit's first opportunity at reindustrialization, a phrase no one expected to hear since the destruction of Detroit's livelihood between 1960 and 1970.

Archer also had an advantage over Young in terms of his credentials. While Young was a veteran and virtually a lifetime Detroiter, Archer's acute sense of law and knowledge of the legal system gave him an advantage in the field of professional relationships not only with his counterparts in the suburbs, but also in Archer's ability to attract commercial executives to Detroit. Archer's experience in the American Bar Association and also as a Supreme Court Justice granted him the tolerance necessary for a leader in a city like Detroit. Young's tough political persona, his reputation for frequent swearing, and his constant fight against the media did not auger well for him with respect to outsiders. Beginning with his bribery investigations, Young's paranoia about the media's negative portrayal was one of his attributes throughout his time as mayor.

"[When] asked if he felt he was the ultimate target of the investigations, Mayor Young said: "Of course, no doubt in my mind. From the time I took office, there has been an investigation of me... I'm not imagining these things. "

Young's achievements were strategically placed within election years, with each election cycle bringing some new industrial addition to the city. Archer's achievements were widespread and constant, never dependent on whether an election was pending. The two mayors opened the floodgates for a new generation of politicians to take hold of the city in 2001. With a new generation entering the political arena, the future of Detroit was up in the air. Campus Martius and Compuware were on their way into the city as Archer was on his way out. This was the same time that Detroit's population sunk to the under 1,000,000 status. The loss of Detroit's spot as one of the top ten largest US cities according to population would devastate Detroit's functionality because much of their federal funding would be revoked. Since cities with populations over 1,000,000 are granted over $50 million annually to operate, Detroit's fall out of this category would make the city no different from any other minimally funded cities in Michigan.

The city of Detroit cannot afford to lose its funding, as nearly a third of all Detroiters cannot even maintain a living wage. The social repercussions were evident in the election of Mayor Kwame Kilpatrick in 2001. On Kilpatrick's watch, many facilities providing for the homeless or disabled constituency were closed permanently, with Kilpatrick arguing that the lack of federal funding was responsible for such organizations falling to the very bottom in the list of Detroit's priorities.

The Mayoral Election: 2001

The candidates for the 2001 election for mayor were not only large in number, but with different ideas of how the city should function. Front runners surfaced after the September 11th primary. The Christian Science Monitor reported that "no fewer than 21 potential chief executives are traveling around town in search of votes. That's good news for the podium-rental business, but a bit confusing for voters ." The primary was able to whittle down the options for the next mayor. Detroit was faced with two strong candidates, city council president Gil Hill who is best known for his role on Beverly Hills Cop with Eddie Murphy, and Kwame Kilpatrick who was best known for being the son of a very influential congresswoman in Detroit, Carolyn Cheeks-Kilpatrick, having held the same office in the 13th US congressional district for 20 years. Hill had the municipal experience that voters would have looked for, from his experience in council and in the police force, and Kilpatrick had the political know-how having been the first African American State House Democratic leader as a state representative . Kilpatrick hoped to follow in his mother's footsteps as a well-respected local politician. After Kwame's victory, it was no surprise that in an Ebony article in 2002, he attributed his success to his family and particularly his mother, saying "I only hope to be half as good as she is ." With a name like Kilpatrick, Kwame managed to take Detroit by storm and make a name for himself as the "hip hop mayor" over time. However, the election between Kilpatrick and Hill marked a turning point in the city's history. The post-Young years brought prosperity through Mayor Archer, and now it was time for a bigger shift, that could potentially shift the city into high gear once again as a manufacturing capital of the world, the way Detroiters remember the city at its best. Gil Hill was a strong candidate. However being a 70-year old and having had a questionably nepotistic relationship with the police department worked against him. As an ex-police chief, some questions were raised about Hill's intentions regarding his campaign as to how Hill would be able to objectively make positive changes within the police force. As City Council President, Hill's tenure gave him the negative appeal of Detroit's stagnant and stubborn city council. As it turns out, Kwame arrived at exactly the right time back in 2001. The city and the local government was in the midst of trying to spark more interest in the downtown area by opening up professional parks and new technological advancements, such as the newest addition of wireless internet at Campus Martius Park . Detroiters were ready and willing to make a change in order to make the city more people friendly and functional. Detroiters recognized that major changes had to be made in order to get Detroit back on the map as a city working to rebuild its population to attain the over 1,000,000 status. James Ngare, Detroit resident, explained "I think it was just time to try something different " to justify Kilpatrick's 54% majority victory. Hill collected the remaining 46% of the vote according to the Detroit News, though the voter turnout was less than 25% of city residents.

Thirty-one year old Kwame Kilpatrick made a name for himself as the youngest mayor of Detroit in history. Because of his influence in the youth culture, Kilpatrick was able to touch base with young voters, often disenfranchised with local politics. Detroit residents were convinced that Kilpatrick might lift them out of the problems left existing in the city after Archer. Kilpatrick was seen as having fresh ideas and creative ways to implement them.

However, the youth of Detroit were only one demographic group that was impressed by Kilpatrick. He was a generally well-liked candidate by all age groups. Detroit Police Chief Jerry A. Oliver Sr. said "People can see themselves in the mayor's vision for the city. This is not some abstract vision that you can't really get a hold on, that you can't get your mind around. He can make a vision real in his comments to people. He can energize them to want to accomplish it. That's his strength. " Kilpatrick also instinctively reminded people of their former leader, Coleman Young, which encouraged many traditional voters. With the older generation, Kilpatrick seemed like someone who could make positive changes for the seniors, as 75-year-old Mattie Davis explains, "He reminds me a lot of Coleman Young. The way he carries himself, the way he talks to the people, whether you're poor, young, old, Black, White, he communicates with anyone. " Kwame had anticipated bringing more technological advancements into the city making, making better use of the underutilized riverfront area, and of course spouted the universal goals of all Detroit mayors—developing public transportation to a useful level, demolishing abandoned homes and facilities, and encouraging the increase of efficacy within municipal departments.

Kilpatrick won the hearts of mothers too, by showcasing his relationship with his mother. Mothers saw his positive influence being able to cross over age lines and be all-inclusive. At a health fair for senior citizens back in July of this year, Kilpatrick walked around the room wanting to touch him as if he was a patriarch. One older woman whispered to a girlfriend "He looks just like my boy. Just like him. "

Besides Kwame's youthfulness and his attention to the public, his goals of changing Detroit's national and international images were one of his attributes that opened the community's collective mind to the promise of a fresh thinker. With Kwame's attention to detail in the police department, including his proposal to conduct a national search for a new police chief, he soared above Hill as a legitimate lawmaker. A 24-year-old police officer, David Mahalab, voted for Kilpatrick because he was "talking about changing things, about conducting a national search for a new chief so we can get rid of the nepotism, favoritism, and cronyism. "

In addition, Kilpatrick was lucky enough to have Archer as his predecessor because Archer had gotten things moving in the economic and architectural realm of revitalization. The Compuware building, which would be responsible for the employment of 6,500 individuals was already under way, as was the new Campus Martius, a the center of town with an ice rink and little shops. The gentrification of Detroit was happening and Kilpatrick was lucky enough to walk right into it and let the advancements take place. This would allow Kilpatrick to make promises of economic success in the city. "Mr. Kilpatrick says he will seek to bring more high-tech companies into the city, and spread its centre's economic rebirth to its still struggling inner suburbs. "

A promise of making the city trendy came along with Kilpatrick. His diamond earring and designer suits gave people the impression of a well to do young, African American who would represent the city of Detroit definitively. This hope for a trendy revitalization in the city would not get him all that far, as little has been done since Kilpatrick's election in 2001 to bring a cultural rejuvenation to the city.

In 1995, Dennis Archer predicted that "by the year 2001, Detroit will be recognized as the city to look at for settling a national standard for delivering essential city service in a cost-effective, timely manner, and people will recognize Detroit as the best-run city in America. " Now in the year 2006, Detroiters are still waiting to see when the world-class status of Detroit will be realized. Kilpatrick has much work to do if he plans on leaving Detroit in better shape than it was when he entered office.

Detroit's identity rests in its mayor. Once Kilpatrick became the symbol of Detroit, he was happily labeled the "hip hop mayor" of the notorious Murder City. Kilpatrick, like other Detroit politicians, has not been able to successfully integrate Detroit's remaining dilemmas; improving the economy of the city, and desegregating the racially divided city and suburbs. The problems are greater than the potential of any local elected official, and it is for this reason that grassroots and community efforts are vital to the livelihood of Detroit.

FROM POLITICS TO PRACTICE

As former Mayor Coleman A. Young pointed out, there is only so much a mayor can do, regardless of geographical location and fiscal situations, about jobs, poverty, and the overall quality of life within a city. In an interview with Dennis Archer in January of 2006, Archer agreed with Young's opinion on the frustration of the mayoral position. As it has been demonstrated with current Mayor Kwame Kilpatrick, the mayor of Detroit has a responsibility to the city as a whole, and very little input on individual families living substandard lives. Because of his underlying responsibilities with city planning and municipal efforts, any Detroit mayor will be unable to fully solve the problem of poverty and widespread unemployment without an on-the-ground effort. Grassroots organizations and charitable institutions focused on helping the very bottom rung of Detroit's economic society have been the most successful in improving the quality of life. As grassroots organizers are not term limited or frequently voted out, such efforts make large strides in the social organization of the city. With mayors coming in and out of office, it is quite difficult to hang on to a sense of predictability with each leader's opposing agendas. The feeling of constant change has been well known in Detroit since Young left office in 1993. Each of the three most recent mayors of Detroit have had different goals for the city and different ways of executing their plans.

Granted, the respective mayors have had differing opportunities to align themselves and their agendas with national politicians. Mayor Young attributed a large portion of his urban failures and unresponsive proposals to the inadequate national leadership that was present during his tenure as mayor. Young operated with Republican presidents for the majority of his time in office. While Young did have President Carter on his side during the late 1970's, the period of subtle improvements in Detroit ended abruptly and was soon replaced by the Regan era. President Bush Sr. followed Regan, and the Republican legislature didn't look nearly as kindly upon Detroit as Carter and President Clinton did.

As Archer took office, Clinton was preparing for his second year as President. Clinton's apathy towards failing urban environments was well received in Detroit, with the implementation of the Empowerment Zones. Archer was fortunate enough to stand alongside Clinton throughout both of his terms as mayor. Kilpatrick had the task at hand of serving alongside George W. Bush, who was also not nearly as sympathetic towards the city as many of the more liberal presidents.

For this reason, it is necessary to utilize other methods of social organization outside of the political realm in order to make necessary changes within the city. The large group of folks who exist within the city labeled either as homeless, impoverished, or economically disenfranchised are needing avenues for assistance in getting back on their feet. These groups of people require immediate attention, and from an organization that is focused on the desire for an adequate quality of life.

Fortunately, many organizations of this caliber exist in the city of Detroit. Of course, it takes a much larger effort than anyone could imagine to fully alleviate poverty, and with more organizations located in the city limits than the city would ever be able to fund. However, the logical beginnings have already begun within the past several decades.

DETROIT RESCUE MISSION MINISTRIES

The Detroit Rescue Mission has been in existence for 98 years. Serving as Detroit's largest shelter for the homeless, the Detroit Rescue Mission is Detroit's best known institution in regards to aid for the impoverished. The DRMM is a Christian-based organization, providing shelter and rehabilitation services to over 1,000 people daily. The DRMM provides three different kinds of housing; emergency housing, transitional housing, and permanent housing. Emergency housing includes shelter for an evening plus hygienic care and optional services for vocational work or substance abuse resources. Transitional housing provides up to two years of temporary housing for folks in need, relocating families into homes or apartments allowing them to start back up on their feet. Permanent housing is used to help folks who are coming out of the impoverished community, unable to afford full rental costs in most homes. The DRMM requires 30% of the monthly rental fees to begin with economic rehabilitation for these permanent housing families

Wellness House

Wellness House serves the impoverished HIV/AIDS inflicted community of Detroit. Wellness House provides assisted living transitional housing as well as distribution of food, food vouchers and vitamins. Wellness House programs serve over 3,000 persons who live in 55 cities throughout five counties in southeastern Michigan. Since services are targeted to those with HIV/AIDS who are also living at or below poverty level, most Wellness House clients are in the City of Detroit; though their clients also are as far spread as Port Huron to Monroe. Wellness House's future, however, is not looking bright. Mayor Kilpatrick's 2004 budget reduced block grant funding to the agency by over 70% from the City's 2003 allocation and proposed 2004 City Council budget. At the end of 2004, the health department – also administrator of federal dollars for AIDS housing – cut a separate Wellness House housing budget by almost 30%. Wellness House began 2005 with almost half a million dollars in lost funding, with the mayor's office citing "inconsistencies in the awarding process ". The director of Wellness House, Rob Fetzer, and his community of supporters are currently scrambling to continue supplying provisions to these folks, but the local government has not been helpful in the matter.

Neighborhood Service Organization

NSO sits on Woodward Avenue in a small, divided building. NSO is a 24-hour walk-in center, which provides a safe haven for homeless persons or "those living a marginal existence." Food, clothing, resting spots, laundry facilities, showers, treatment and support services are available 24 hours a day, 7 days a week. NSO was established in 1955 as a private non-profit human service agency. The mission of NSO is "to compassionately reach out to people, empowering them to improve their lives ." Program focuses include: mental health, youth gun-violence prevention, persons with developmental disabilities, crisis intervention, suicide prevention, problem gambling, homelessness, substance abuse, grandparents raising grand children, home-based Headstart, home ownership counseling, and community development. However, NSO's clientele has been questionable, as violent crimes have frequently taken place inside their walls, along with some sexual violence reports prior to the center's separation of men's and women's quarters.

Other organizations serving the larger metro-Detroit area range from feeding programs to vocational rehabilitation. The charities are imperative to Detroit's economic rejuvenation, and more programs in the city deserve the attention of political figures. The aforementioned groups are some of the better known and more highly funded of the organizations within city limits. However the funds are still far too limited for the centers to operate at their full potential, and constant financial dilemmas have caused some of these shelters to close down, either temporarily or permanently. Granted, these organizations are not one of the top priorities of Michigan lawmakers, and their importance to the community has been completely understated. Empowering individuals to operate at their full potential requires a first step, which these shelters and many others within the city provide. This first step must be the transition from downfalls like drug addiction and unemployment into the utilization of an institution focused on self-help.

The grassroots organizations require some aid from the governmental side, and must beg the question of what, as a neighborhood, can a community do to change its course economically and socially. Detroiters and other city residents cannot rely on a political agenda to keep an area intact; it requires a widespread effort and a desire to improve the life of each individual. While the agendas of small neighborhoods and of political representatives differ greatly, it is difficult to extract common goals attained by common strategies from both sides. In combining opinions and tactics, it is important to break the cycle that Detroit has been stuck in—the racial tensions between individuals within city limits. The rejuvenation of Detroit, either physically or mentally, requires the participation of the entire community, or at least the participation of influential leaders like Rob Fetzer of Wellness House, Grace and James Boggs of Detroit Summer, employing creative youth within the area, and Dr. Rayford of the understated Just Love Ministry.

Dr. Rayford

"My dad came here in the early 1920's. He had come here, moved here from East St. Louis over to Detroit because he'd heard that there were jobs and so forth. So when he first got here, he didn't have any money and he was sitting in the park where Frank Murphy Hall of Justice sits now. He said he was sitting in that park and he was debating whether or not he was gonna leave, and he says a Baker car passed by and he saw a lady get out of a Baker car. He saw something drop from her purse and it rolled, and she went on so it rolled and with his eyes he followed it, it was a quarter. He said he took that quarter and he went to a bakery that was right around the corner, he got himself a cake and some milk and he went back to the park and he was sitting on the seat eating and a man came by and he said "Son do you want a job?" And he got a job! And that's what started him. Well the thing is, some fifty years afterward which is, sometime truth is stranger than fiction, I spent 29 years at the very spot that my dad first started up— that spot at Frank Murphy Hall of Justice, I was in that spot for 29 years. And I knew then that, hey, my destiny in terms of fact— I take things like they letting me know— I'm here by some greater power, in Detroit, I mean."

481 West Columbia is the home of Just Love Ministry, an assistance facility in the Cass Corridor of Detroit, one of the most poverty-stricken areas in the city. Just Love Ministry serves the homeless community of the inner-city with meals, prayer, support groups such as Alcoholics Anonymous and Narcotics Anonymous, in addition to serving as a small center to receive food and clothing. The building sits behind a large white church right off of one of Detroit's most traveled highways, I-75.

The one-story building itself is no more than 2,500 square feet. From the outside, two of its brick walls are painted a bright blue. There are grates on the doors and windows, and a small painted wooden sign reads "JUST LOVE" in red letters. Just Love's location is notable, as it is in very close proximity to the newly renovated sporting arenas downtown. The organization almost lost its space when the stadiums moved in. Government and city officials claimed that Just Love was in the middle of the "stadium path." Just Love expected an eviction notice, but one never came. The empty lots on either side of Just Love are now utilized, however, by employees of the arenas, or used as private parking lots.

An untrained eye might almost suspect that this isn't one of the truly bad parts of Detroit, as it is so close to the gentrified downtown area. It doesn't look like that many people are walking down the streets, and the traffic is not very heavy. Just Love is right off of Grand River Ave, one of the larger main roads in Detroit. The exit off of 1-75 onto Grand River has not been repaved in several years, potholes and major cracks in the road cause many of Detroit's automobile problems. Traffic lights in the downtrodden portions of Detroit such as the Cass Corridor serve only as a suggestion to yield.

As you travel west on Grand River you intersect West Columbia and make a right hand turn. From the corner, Just Love's big blue wall and wiry little door are visible. Once inside the building, there is a room just past the front door with a long table and a number of chairs. Around the walls of the room are benches attached to the walls, where people often sleep. There are about six doorways off of the main room each leading to smaller rooms. Four of the six rooms contain piles of clothing, toys, coats, books, and bags of food that need to be sorted. The other two rooms serve half as storage and half as offices for Dr. Rayford, executive director and Juanita Wood, assistant director.

The back of the shelter serves as a kitchen, a dining room, and a facility for prayers and meetings. One wall of the back room, which is much larger than the front room, has a mural spray painted with "PROJECT RESTORE" in large letters, with many pictures of symbols that are specific to Detroit surrounding the words. The mural is hopeful and bright, reading "Dedicated to those who decided to better themselves and their lives. Keep it up!"

I have been going to Just Love for various reasons since I was 11 years old. I have never walked into Just Love without seeing the faces of Dr. (Doc) Vernon Rayford, "Mother" Wood, and years ago, the late Gladys Rayford. Gladys, who passed away in June of 1997, a woman of grace and generosity, was a selfless individual constantly concerned about the greater good of the world, not herself. She was an attractive woman who came up with the notion of Just Love Ministry back in 1987. However, it was long before 1987 when she knew she had a calling and a mission.

The name Just Love Ministry doesn't seem very peculiar once you know the founder and her family. Gladys sat around her kitchen table eating dinner with her family for nearly four years before her ideas took shape. Her family knew of her passion for helping the less-fortunate, those who needed simple compassion to improve their lives. Gladys' children, and husband Vernon, would ask her simply "Well what is it that you want to do?" Gladys would reply, "I just want to *love* them. I just want to love them." Gladys, with the help of her husband, was able to occupy the first building, a building not nearly as large as their present location.

Gladys and Dr. Rayford have felt the need to instigate such an organization largely due to the fact that the government aid in the city of Detroit has not been sympathetic enough towards the downtrodden. Had general assistance and welfare programs benefited the homeless of Detroit, the Rayford's might not have been nearly as adamant about providing assistance. Had mayoral efforts been more aware of the problems in the impoverished community, there may have been a chance that Detroit's homeless would not see economic despair as a failure of the political system. Providing compassion, love, and support for the said community was absolutely necessary not only to Gladys, but to the organization of homeless that have slowly surfaced throughout the past thirty years.

Just Love Ministry started at the corner of Peterboro and Second, another intersection in Detroit marking an immensely troubled area. At the opening of Just Love on December 24, 1987 a worried Detroit police sergeant pulled Gladys aside. He asked her, "Do you know where you are? You're located at the corner of one of the highest drug trafficking corners in the city of Detroit." She happily replied "Oh is that right? Well then this is where I need to be."

Gladys' initial plan was to serve the poor folks of Detroit by providing some coffee, maybe some snacks and perhaps some games. Upon her entrance into the business of charity, Gladys found that there was a large need for a more organized meal program. With that in mind, Gladys and Dr. Rayford began a fundraising effort and attempted to publicize their organization locally. After meeting with a man who ran a local meat ministry and agreeing to serve Just Love with the necessary staples to feed a community, Gladys, Dr. Rayford, and a very limited volunteer staff began serving lunch on a daily basis. At that point in time, Just Love was serving meals to approximately 200 people a day. However, since the size of the facility was limited, the directors had to take folks in shifts of 50. As Dr. Rayford points out, "its needless to say that sometimes that took, feeding them in 50s, that meant that was about 4 shifts, and so that was almost…all day."

After two years, the facility's size became an issue and after about a year of uncertainty later, Just Love landed at their location in the Cass Corridor. While their rent was significantly higher at the Cass Corridor location, the Rayford' were seeing some limited funds come in from donations and benefactors. While it wasn't much, the money was just enough for the organization to function as it needed.

Today, Dr. Vernon Rayford is the head of Just Love, working hard to carry on Gladys' life mission, with nothing but optimism and a smile. A man in his early 70's, Dr. Rayford, or "Doc" as his clientele affectionately refer to him, spends every day at Just Love. Dr. Rayford has spent his entire life inside Detroit's city limits. While he is well traveled and well-read, Dr. Rayford concedes that he has no intention of leaving. He was "born here [in Detroit], I was raised here, I've lived my best years here and I'm gonna live and die here."

Dr. Rayford attended school in the days when Detroit was perhaps even more integrated than it is today. Dr. Rayford learned alongside many whites, specifically Jews. At the time when Dr. Rayford was a young student, the minority percentage of his classmates was somewhere between 5-10%. Today's schools are almost precisely the inverse, with an over 93% population of black students in Detroit, it is clear to see that Dr. Rayford's has witnessed in the city a massive change. This unequal percentage existed throughout his high school years, as he remained one of the minorities. The large racial discrepancies have always existed, and with a strong hold in the city of Detroit. While Dr. Rayford has openly admitted the only way for the city to rehabilitate is by transcending racial lines, he has also been pleased with the influx of African American political power within the city. It is imperative for the city's politicians to appropriately represent their constituencies.

Some time around 1945, Dr. Rayford's twin brother approached him with some exciting news. He said "Brother, you know what I found out? I discovered that I don't have to drink alcohol now to get high," he said, "you know I found out there's a clean high." The clean high he was referring to was none other than marijuana. The irony of the situation that Dr. Rayford found himself in was quite interesting. "…As I look back on it, [my brother] was pronouncing the very thing that was going to cause the greater problem of homelessness. Because the escalation of drugs, in the school and in the community, is one of the major factors in helping to disrupt and cause the greater problem of homelessness. Where men and women like my brother who had a great deal of potential fell victims to a problem which was bigger than they, and they were not able to overcome it and thereby with them falling victims, they didn't have the fight or the energy to keep fighting to try to overcome it, it therefore created homelessness."

Dr. Rayford explained his brother's self-destructive behavior as following down a very typical path. While he was a marijuana user, Dr. Rayford's brother found himself lost in habits as serious as a heroin addiction. Though Dr. Rayford's brother finally managed to kick the habit, Dr. Rayford is not a stranger to the destruction of individuals caused by drug addiction.

Dr. Rayford notes that many of his contemporaries found themselves in similar situations, where the salary from a day-to-day job would become not enough, and folks would begin breaking laws in order to keep up their habits, whether it be through car theft, a breaking and entering, or the robbing of a bank.

Dr. Rayford went on from high school to Wayne State University downtown and received his PhD in law. At college-age, Dr. Rayford became familiar with what would become the destruction of Detroit. Dr. Rayford explained that in a sociology class as an undergraduate, one professor's visitor made the observation that Detroit would not be able to recover from a growing drug problem on its own. As white flight took hold during Dr. Rayford's college years and after, this particular speaker told his class that "you think that you're leaving the problem. But by virtue of leaving the city, and not fighting this problem with drugs, etc., it's going to follow you." While most of Dr. Rayford's peers expressed disbelief at such a statement, the speaker turned out to be predicting the exact course of the city's future.

Dr. Rayford is extremely well-versed and experienced when it comes to dealing with the homeless community. Part of it may be his deep knowledge of the law, having served as a law librarian at Wayne for a number of years, but part of it also comes from his strong Christian faith. Dr. Rayford has two prefixes, the title of Doctor and the title of Reverend. Dr. Rayford is, among other things, a Christian preacher who proudly imbues his Christian faith into the practice of charity. As a reverend, he has taken on the responsibility of leading Just Love's weekly Sunday morning services and the weekly Thursday bible study, reinstating faith in the unfaithful and hope in the hopeless.

As defining a problem is always the first logical step in coming up with solutions, Dr. Rayford says he attributes homelessness not only to drugs but also to a lack of jobs. "I think we have to be about the business of creating opportunities," he explains. Without a booming auto industry like Detroit saw back in the 1950's and 60's, jobs have become a much rarer commodity. Besides the fact that the minimum wage has not been in line with a living wage, a job that even will provide minimum wage has become nearly impossible to get to. Without a properly functioning public transportation method, Detroiters are finding it harder and harder by the day to earn a living

"If you take all the spirit out of a person, and don't provide any opportunities, and they don't see any opportunities for growth, and they look into their future and all they see is nothing but hopelessness and that's all they see, then some of them tell me that I'm not gonna work for that, they'll say, "Doc, look what I got. I got this job for $5 an hour, I gotta go somewhere that takes me two and a half hours to get there, then if I don't have a car, I gotta walk 2 miles before I can get to the bus, and then after I catch the bus, if its at night, it takes another two and a half hours to get home." By that time, some hours have passed, just in traveling, trying to get to a job that's $5 an hour for eight hours. If I got a company that says ok I give $5 an hour and I'll provide your transportation [for a fee] and they turn right around and take almost all my money that I earn, when I really check it out I make about $3.50 an hour."

The educational system also has seemed to pose some problems in and around the homeless community. Dr. Rayford managed to transcend the usual experience and make the most of his schooling in the city of Detroit. Dr. Rayford mentioned a total lack of motivation on the part of today's students, which is not uncommon nationally. Since the 1970's after the major Detroit riots, Detroit has seen its young folks failing out of schools for a number of reasons. The cause and effects almost seem cyclical, as a lack of education leads to bad decisions, bad decisions lead to drugs, and drugs lead to desperation and poverty. Add into this equation that the impoverished community is conceiving and birthing kids into this troubled metropolis and sending them off to dysfunctional schools, and you are left with results that show little or no social progression.

Among his responsibilities as director of Just Love, Dr. Rayford's proudest accomplishment has been seeing his children grow and blossom into morally sound and socially aware adults. Dr. Rayford's son-in-law, Andrew, is in the midst of becoming a preacher, as Dr. Rayford has been. At a Sunday morning service on January 8th, 2006, Andrew was able to lead the weekly prayers. After having delivered an emotional sermon on how the new year should bring us all hope, and the understanding that it is by God's will that we are here today, celebrating a new year, Dr. Rayford had some inspirational words as well.

Those alert and spiritual audience members were fortunate enough to hear Dr. Rayford's explanation of why he calls Andrew his son, rather than referring to him still as a son-in-law. Dr. Rayford has mentally adopted Andrew as his son, and to him there is no line between in-laws and his immediate family. For many Detroiters, community and familial bonds are all they can rely on. Since the sense of community is quite strong in Detroit, most residents have found a common ground. Because of Detroit's overwhelming African American population, city dwellers have found hope in the idea of African American empowerment. Racial integrity is the one thing all Detroiters constantly work towards.

Most kids in Detroit are not as lucky as Dr. Rayford's. Dr. Rayford remains immensely concerned about the wellbeing of today's youth, because he knows that those will be the clientele that he is faced with in a decade or two. It worries him, because it seems like the transition from drugs to desperation to homelessness cannot be interfered with once it begins. With regards to students, Dr. Rayford explained

"...You may wonder why some of them don't see much hope, and the fact is we're not providing them with any. And if we don't provide them with much hope then they say, "well what's the sense of me going you say oh go to school and do what for our society? To help our society? When our society don't want any help? Won't even accept our help?" And there are kids who wanna do something, but then if you got people who say "I reject them" and don't say give them open arms and say "Lets go to work!" they want to work and do something, they don't want to see society as it is, and that's why we gotta start challenging them because you know some of them haven't been challenged."

To Dr. Rayford, negative local morale has also seemed to take on a significant role in unemployment and homelessness. While Dr. Rayford says that jobs are a large issue in the homeless community, he concedes "I think we need to also along with the jobs, we've got to deal with the persona of the person, we've got a job to do to assist people to feel better about themselves on the inside." To many homeless folks, it would appear that they have a relatively low sense of self-confidence. This, no doubt, is a side effect of self-destruction through bad choices and inadequate care. Dr. Rayford's sense of faith and charity is an advantage to anyone who walks through Just Love's doors. In many scenarios that Dr. Rayford has witnessed, the pronunciation of homelessness is only clearer when the individual feels inadequate about themselves. The significance of the name "Just Love" seems to make more and more sense, once a person is able to see just how supportive this organization is towards the individual and individual goals.

Because of his background in law, Dr. Rayford has had the ability to assist many of his clients in law-related issues. At the time when my interview took place with Dr. Rayford, he was in the midst of helping a gentleman write a letter to one of the district courts in Detroit explaining the client's innocence on a particular charge. While he is an exceptionally intelligent man, Dr. Rayford tends to stay out of the limelight of law. For all intents and purposes, Dr. Rayford is a retiree of the law industry and his focus now lies in social justice. He is experienced in the field of politics, as he understands the needs of a city like Detroit and what a local government should or should not be doing to aide in Detroit's fight against poverty. Unfortunately, as he agrees with much of Detroit's population, Dr. Rayford would admit that local government along with statewide and nationwide politicians have a responsibility to their public that has not been properly addressed. He argues that "for the most part we have leadership that is selfish." In addition to having a city council that gets little done, on top of having a mayor whose primary focus is far from the alleviation of poverty, one can easily see that Detroit is not headed down the proper path to re-enfranchise its population in terms of socioeconomics and labor. Dr. Rayford has become attached to the idea that he is required to assist others as he himself would want to be assisted. While local government has played the largest role in the integrity of the community, local government has also left to the public responsibility for its own rehabilitation. Dr. Rayford and Just Love have been the vehicles for the impoverished population to attain some sense of self-worth. Without Dr. Rayford's unfaltering generosity, many homeless Detroiters would have been unable to conclude that there is a life beyond poverty, and that organizations like Just Love must be utilized in order to reintegrate oneself back into respectable society.

The city's leadership, especially in the eyes of someone like Dr. Rayford, seems inadequate. One of Detroit's bigger problems is the fact many of the city's politicians are not in touch with the true problems in Detroit.

"I know, frankly, some of these people who think they know about Detroit, they're strangers to Detroit. They don't really know Detroit, even some of those politicians. They don't really know Detroit. They think they know, and man, we can tell, they don't know Detroit. Some of them came here in the 1960's when things started booming, but they weren't here when in the 1930's, 40's, and 50's, and even Archer, he don't really, I mean to think about it, he's a latecomer to Detroit. He was not from Detroit. He comes from Battle Creek. But I'm what I'm saying is most of them, even those on the council, most of those they're not native Detroiters, they came here during the time when things were good they got an education in the south, and then came to Detroit, but they're not Detroiters. They don't really know about Detroit. Most of them don't. Coleman Young was a Detroiter, he was rooted in Detroit, he was born in Detroit, but see what I'm saying is some of these others, their not Detroiters, really Detroiters…they don't really know the inner history…how the educational system was…that's why many of them don't really know the problem, but I was born in Detroit. And I know what the problems are."

Its no surprise that many Detroiters are not encouraged by the limited progress that Detroit has made. Many Detroiters also admit that they don't see a light at the end of this tunnel for the economic prosperity of their metropolis. However, Dr. Rayford has not given up on the city. "I learned a long time ago never to use the terms such as hopelessness, 'cause I was taught never to use that terms hopelessness or a term like never, I feel as though there is always hope." Dr. Rayford, a realistic optimist, has a great deal of understanding when it comes to Detroit. He understands the ins and outs like a true lifetime Detroiter. It isn't something you see every day and its people like Dr. Rayford who deserve the recognition that should come along with innately understanding a population as hard-to-read as the homeless. The city of Detroit should feel deeply indebted to Dr. Rayford and his family. Just Love Ministry has been a light in Detroit to many whose minds and spirits have been left in the dark. The importance of organizations like Just Love and true Samaritans like Dr. Rayford should never be underestimated, and it is only through the help of folks like the Rayford' that this city might have the capability to learn a lesson in self-preservation. While Just Love and other shelters are not the answer to poverty, they are a very beneficial first step to folks seeking help. Dr. Rayford maintains hope that the city can revive itself, albeit a slow and staggering process.

Keith Livingston

At Just Love Ministries, Dr. Rayford and Mother Wood see the same faces every day. The folks who frequent Just Love belong to a tight-knit community of the down-and-out individuals working to better themselves either physically, religiously, or emotionally. Looking around the main room, I can see many familiar faces that I've been seeing for years.

Danny, Dr. Rayford's nephew, often helps out around the shelter. A man of about 40 years, Danny has always represented the "quality control" aspect of the shelter; for over a decade, Danny could be found approving or denying requests of Just Love clients. Danny instinctively knew whether clients would use a winter coat for warmth, or for money. The only reason Danny has this instinct is because he, himself, was homeless for quite some time. After falling prey to drugs and other drawbacks, he gained inspiration from his uncle and the community members at Just Love, and now is a full-time employee at an automobile factory, living in a place of his own.

Another familiar face is that of Lenita. She has been coming to Just Love for years, and is always in the main room prior to prayer services, which she attends regularly, and meals. Lenita's face lights up the room when she sees me. "Hey, I know you!" she'll exclaim, remembering when she received hygienic items and winter clothes from my organization. Lenita has some mental deficiencies, and has been affectionately stigmatized within Just Love as "one of the crazy ones." With her extremely long braids and sporadic teeth, Lenita exemplifies the attitude at Just Love. Despite her homelessness, Lenita is always smiling and happy to see the people she recognizes.

Robert is another regular at Just Love, he happily greets and keeps track of many of Just Love's visitors. Dr. Rayford and Mother Wood have appointed him the general maintenance assistant within the building. In return for his services in handing out food, cleaning up the rooms, and serving meals, he (and two other men) occupies Just Love at night, sleeping in one of the back rooms, on top of a cot. Robert is always willing and able to help out wherever the directors need him, and always with a smile on his face.

If you spend any time at Just Love, you're bound to come across Keith Livingston. Keith is a large man in his mid 40's with a very deep, hoarse voice. He often wears his reading glasses, which have obviously made their way to him through charity, as the earpieces have been stretched to fit around his head. He always asks Dr. Rayford if any new eyeglasses have been donated to Just Love, in hopes of finding the correct prescription lens and/or properly fitting frame. Keith spends his days attending various Narcotics Anonymous meetings at different locations, studying for the work he's pursuing at Wayne State University, and networking in the hopes of finding a career or a viable home.

These folks all have a couple of things in common. Firstly, they are all homeless, aside from Danny, who has only recently worked his way into a home. Secondly, they are ex-drug users. Thirdly, these folks always have smiles on their faces. While the lack of a home and lack of positive political representation is at the forefront of their problems, they remain grateful for a safe haven that is free of drugs, violence, hate, and discrimination. Because Just Love exists, these folks have a purpose in life. They are members of a community that encourages them to thank God for each day they've lived on earth, always under the impression that things can only get better. Most of Just Love's clientele are also convinced that it is only by God's will that they in part have lived as long as they have, and the reason they've landed at Dr. Rayford's door. Because of Dr. Rayford's charismatic presence, Just Love's clients are thankful to have such a supportive community.

The community at Just Love is nearly all (98%) African American. They vote Democratic in major elections if they vote at all, and tend to be more progressive than suburban Democrats. People at Just Love seem to be nostalgic for the good old days of Coleman Young's African American motivated leadership, and the politics of African American empowerment that still play a significant role in their ideals. This misplaced nostalgia remains a powerful force in Detroit politics explaining, in part, why Detroit's leadership has followed the path it has.

Despite best efforts from concerned suburbanites, Detroit re-elected Mayor Kwame Kilpatrick in 2005. As stated in the previous chapters, suburbanites have no real voting power or political influence in the city of Detroit. In the 2005 election, Freman Hendrix stepped up as Kilpatrick's opponent. Hendrix was well known for working with Dennis Archer as his Chief of Staff, as well as being his Deputy Mayor throughout both of Archer's terms. Hendrix's stigma as being sympathetic to white businesses and not as focused on African American political power in the city hurt his campaign. Detroit was still seeing many developments taking place on Kilpatrick's watch, though in fact the changes originated with Archer. Kilpatrick in a sense walked into an administration after they cleaned up the city post-Young, and he was able to use Archer's good work in the city to his advantage as evidence justifying his re-election.

Suburbanites, particularly from white suburbs, traveled to Detroit to make a clamor about the state of the city, and how the only way Detroit would be able to make a comeback would be through a leader with business skills and experience working with Detroit benefactors. The suburban nonvoters aggressively campaigned for Hendrix, especially within the homeless community. They exemplified the importance of a new leader who wouldn't put economic identity and general assistance programs on the back burner, in addition to improving the overall state of what suburbanites view as a dying city. However, the campaigning backfired.

"Boy, when [suburbanites] started dumpin' on Detroit it was like them against us....tryin' to tell Detroiters how to vote... that made me vote for Kwame," Keith explained to me.

...yeah, they holler about the race issue because it was put in racial terms. A white guy from outside Detroit asked me, "well who did you vote for?" He came up to me and I was laughing,

I let him know I voted for Kwame 'cause I think he's a better guy. It was just the way, not only Kilpatrick, but Hendrix put it, like he was the candidate for the interests outside of Detroit. Detroit is very, very polarized, and it's a racial thing. Kwame pulled it off because homeless people voted [for the black candidate].

In spite of being homeless, Keith has taken on many projects that would deem him as something of a social activist, especially within the communities with which he is familiar, including the homeless, imprisoned, and ex-drug abusers. His work at Wayne State University was focused specifically on why the rate of African Americans in maximum security prisons is so high in today's society. However, Keith didn't always play such an active role in the community.

Keith Livingston was born in 1956, into a two-parent middle-class family. Keith had two older brothers, Michael and Andrew, both of whom avoided Keith's path of economic instability and rebellion. Keith's mother had a two-year college education and worked for the city. His father had graduated from high school and worked for the government. Keith and his family have lived in the city of Detroit for his whole life. Unlike his parents and brothers, Keith did not finish high school. Keith was a self-described "incorrigible" kid, and during his childhood he was sent to Sexton High School in Lansing, a school for troubled students. Keith admits to having been involved in some drugs, but none of the "hard stuff," having smoked marijuana by age 12, and having been a beer drinker.

In 1982, Keith was imprisoned in Jackson, Michigan's maximum security facility upon being convicted for first-degree manslaughter. Released in 1991, his prison term had been abbreviated due to his good behavior while incarcerated. And that's when he became involved in the crack-cocaine phenomenon.

I had got out of prison and I was going to school on a fellowship. I was in the doctorial program. I guess I felt that I was "less than" everyone else...it was purely psychological. I ended up using drugs, at that particular time I was messing with heroin, and I started dealing with the crack. I was teacher's assistant then too as a matter of fact, for criminal justice. They used to have a quiz section for Introductory Sociology and I taught the quiz section, and at that particular time, I started using drugs. Even though I thought I was less than, you know, I wasn't doing that bad in school, in fact I was doing real good, but things began to change. As a result of my drug use, I lost the fellowship the next year 'cause you know my grades went down. After school, I moved in with a friend, stayed upstairs, but eventually for me the drugs and not being able to find employment caused serious depression as a result and the drugs, my landlady didn't wanna be bothered so I became homeless.

In the three years between Keith's release from prison and his entrance into homelessness, his life fell apart largely due to crack. Keith received his fellowship upon his release from prison, having gotten set up with a professor from Bryn Mawr who was interested in the work that he did while studying in prison. Keith used the resources surrounding him during his incarceration and studied the only thing he was able to- his fellow inmates. Keith did some writing on self-esteem of prisoners, and the involvement in self-esteem in the African American movement. His work was titled "The Decriminalization of African American Males" and was well-received at Wayne State University, where he drew the attention of many faculty members, and in turn studied with several professors independently. Keith studied the social structure of prisoners, and attempted to make sense of the overpopulation of African Americans in jail. With obvious disappointment, Keith tells me that he "had an opportunity and I blew it."

Keith's inherent negative self-esteem issues are not uncommon among homeless men and women. Keith has been lucky enough to survive through the struggles of drug use and incarceration and make it to his 50th year. Also, because Keith has remained homeless, he has seen no physical proof that things may actually get better. All the while his attitude has stayed positive, and Keith works hard to achieve his goals. Since 1994, Keith has taken control of his future. Keith held some odd jobs, including a job in the Detroit airport, a truck driving position for Burlington Coat Factory.

Keith is a regular at Just Love Ministry. When asking both Dr. Rayford and Mother Wood who might be a good subject for this study, the two directors simultaneously recommended Keith. Prior to his days at Just Love, his friends and allies described him as a very angry man upon meeting Keith. He has openly admitted to having an overly aggressive attitude, and did not hesitate to explain how his anger affected his life, not only because of drugs, but because of his self-sustained negativity. Upon Keith's entrance into Just Love during Gladys' generation of running the shelter, he was diagnosed with bipolar disorder.

I look back on it, people were telling me the way I looked, I looked angry. I wasn't friendly and usually I think that was a defense mechanism in terms of being incarcerated, being in the streets down here, and I was angry, I was very violent towards individuals at that particular point in my life. I was mad at the world. So, I'd come into NSO... then I'd come here [to Just Love] to eat and get out of the cold in the wintertime, I'd lay down and sleep, and this is one of the places I would go, kind of like a soup kitchen shuffle that we'd make in the wintertime.

In the midst of our interviews, I was taught a new word, "bandos," a reference to the abandoned homes and buildings that he and several other shufflers would occupy at night. The occupation of bandos is common, especially in the city of Detroit, due to the city's overwhelming number of abandoned facilities. When Keith wasn't utilizing a bando, he turned to organizations like Just Love, The Neighborhood Service Organization (NSO), and the Detroit Rescue Mission (DRMM). Of the places he visited, he found that Just Love helped him the most, attributing his success of kicking his drug and alcohol habits to the guidance of the Rayfords' and the amenities offered by Just Love. Keith preferred Just Love over DRMM or NSO. Keith explained that the practices at DRMM were invasive, and in a way, dehumanizing to an ex-convict. "I would sleep in the Rescue Mission sometimes but I didn't like to go to there 'cause I had a thing about taking all my clothes off in a line to get in the shower. It reminded me of my incarceration." In Keith's days of unmanageable anger, he was in good company when utilizing services at NSO. For many homeless people, NSO has become a last resort. "That's where you go, you know, once you have no other place to go, I guess you gravitate around other people that don't have no other place to go and you learn how to survive." Keith was able to survive, and he thinks of his days at NSO having run concurrently with his self-medication on illegal drugs.

> I didn't think I had a problem when I was at Wayne, but then I'd come to the realization that every time I'd have some money, I'd end up broke. So I realized that it was definitely an addiction because I felt like I could not get out, drugs were a way out, cause I found many other ways out of homelessness on several occasions and the biggest dilemma I think, especially among men, is that they keep finding their way back here. I'd get homeless, I'd get a job, but usually when I got a job I was "in recovery" so to speak— I'd stopped using but a lot of times I went back to using drugs cause life still wasn't good to me— even clean I felt worse, so that's why I tend to think that I was self medicated. I guess [if] you go through it long enough you begin to realize {laugh} that you gotta make some changes without the drugs and you know, you still gonna be depressed, you'll still feel hopeless at times, but it's a change. I'd always go back to using because I felt miserable. But when I came to the realization that I had to actively work on changing my perception about things and in spite of me, and in spite of whatever happened, I guess I began to see that it's a lot of work to do, with me, just staying clean is not enough. You gotta work for it.

In other words, Keith is well aware of the fact that his homelessness is a consequence of his own actions. Many Detroiters are in the same boat as Keith, desperately trying to either kick a drug habit, find a steady job, or making ends meet within their families. However, Keith, in addition to many others, is convinced that there is definitely more that government associations could be doing to aide Detroit's homeless and assist them in their move up and out of poverty.

If an individual were to split up the Detroit population into two groups, the Coleman Young's Detroiters and Dennis Archer's Detroiters, Keith would fall into the former. While Young focused on the abolition of racism and the empowerment of African American elected officials, Archer focused on the economic sustainability of Detroit. Both mayors had very valid justifications for stressing their focuses. Since Keith's days as a young adult, he's been aware that race is no more than a socially constructed boundary which politicians and officers use as justification for unequal treatment of their constituencies. Keith has always referred to the media as the "social influence mechanism," a term he coined upon concluding the work he did at Wayne. From the media perspective, Keith has noticed that the world, whether or not it claims to be colorblind, is in black-and-white terms. As a result of the social influence mechanism, "emphasis that has been put on crime and usually the perception, or fear of crime exceeds the actual amount of crimes that actually happen," Keith explains. "Most people tend to see blacks as the ones that commit violent crimes, and those stereotypes are alive in a lot of people's minds." Keith knows that the severe racial polarization in Detroit has been the cause for concern among elected officials and Detroiters.

Keith focuses on crime and incarceration as symptoms of homelessness, as he has experienced them from an insider's perspective. Keith also knows that as a result of imprisonment, African American men in particular will come out of prison on the lowest rung of the social food chain. Keith was fortunate to have had something to show from his time in prison after he wrote "Decriminalization of African American Males." Most men are not so lucky. Keith is obviously smart, and is the type of person whose street smarts exceed his academic intelligence, and it is his ability to navigate around the questionable areas of Detroit that has allowed him to survive.

One of the biggest problems, Keith agrees, is the transition between homelessness and self-sustainability, and the lack of government aid that is included in the process. Keith thinks that there is a massive lack of programs designed for folks trying to rehabilitate economically or physically. Very few shelters in Detroit, if any, are all-inclusive centers that associate vocational counseling with drug rehabilitation while being able to provide a place to sleep at night. Because no centers of this nature really exist in Detroit on a large scale, impoverished Detroiters will find themselves hopping from place to place to attend Narcotics Anonymous meetings, after seeing a mental health counselor, followed by a career counseling session, not to mention the improbability of a drifter like Keith to provide himself with three square meals a day. Some folks, like Keith, are motivated to make the move from poverty to sustainability. Sadly, many Detroiters are simply disenfranchised by the whole process of trying to improve their lives; it ends up becoming a futile effort that leads to little or no avail. I asked Keith if he was in good company in terms of other homeless folks who are making an active effort to rehabilitate.

I think that there's some people wanting to better themselves, there's some, it's not all of them though. I think that it's just like you keep going to look for a job and you get turned down, eventually a lot of people give up. There's a lack of programs too so, people try, and they fail. You need a lot of support most people don't want to be involved in these support programs. Some people don't realize that basically when you come into programs like NA and AA, it's like a culture, its like a totally different design for living and patterns for interpreting reality, 'cause no matter what happens, if you get a job and you're successful, you become socially acceptable, whatever you go through.

I know guys who have been on this route, and some of them, even when they were dying of cancer, they would wait till the bitter end in terms of the pain before they would use any type of prescribed narcotics. I know some people that been through this thing— they starved, and I guess it all depends [on the person]. What shocked me is that you got people out there that's homeless, they're HIV+ who don't seek out help, they're women living like men because of the city. It's a psychological issue too. To me, it's a social psychological issue.

In defining the remaining problems that any local politicians might be able to address, Keith is convinced that the lack of public transportation has been extremely detrimental to Detroit's unemployed population. In Detroit, Keith remarks, there are virtually no jobs for unskilled employees. In the suburbs, jobs are frequently available, and many of Keith's peers have been employed north of Detroit, including Keith. However, the distance between what these men consider home and where jobs are available are nearly impossible to travel. "Places smaller than Detroit, like Salt Lake City, Utah they have more of a mass transit system than Detroit with the rails and the buses," Keith explains. The underdevelopment of Detroit's public transportation is the number one issue that Keith attributes unemployment to. Having a formidable public transportation method not only hurts Detroit, it also hurts the suburban communities in the sense that races are isolated in certain geographic areas, which can have no outcome other than the advancement of segregation within the surrounding cities.

Even with the addition of a quality system of public transportation, the issue of inadequate wages would not change. Minimum wage has taken on a personality completely independent of a living wage. The two are very different—as minimum wage is far less than what is considered a living wage in today's marketplace. Livable income is based upon reality, rather than the minimum wage assumption of the ability to survive in an imagined setting where, though most market prices rise throughout the years, the minimum wage has far from caught up to the regular rate of inflation in the United States. The wage dilemma, plus the need for decent public transportation have both been factors in the exacerbation of homelessness. I asked Keith what he would say if he were asked to sum up the causes of homelessness in a word—which of these urban plagues, out of race, economics, unemployment, transportation, drug usage, etc., would he attribute to homelessness the most.

I'd say economics. That's a factor because the stress from that causes a lot of problems. I'd say lack of jobs, like I say for males specifically, the "work" function is very much integral to the masculine role and that causes most people [to be] here, because they not getting any money, they feel social inequality. Especially in terms of one's self esteem in this country...and I wonder if that has some validity [in regards to] poor kids goin' to [underdeveloped/under funded] schools, that might be a factor on why most people from depressed areas do far worse than people that are not in pockets of poverty.

While remaining racially unified for the African American community, it would appear that Keith and his cohorts have a strong racial identity and cling to a sense of independence. The economic capabilities of racially isolated Detroit have been resoundingly insufficient. Keith notes that while race has been a major issue in the community, the problems in the racial schema are much more globally effective, while the economic disparities that the city has witnessed are much more exclusive to Detroit's specific geographic location. For Keith and the homeless community, programs of adequate assistance would help these folks invariably. Keith has the ability to take his life into his control and make what he wants from it, and he has already begun that process by doing the necessary research and making the necessary connections to faculty and administrators in the city to get back on his feet. Keith desires the life of a functioning member of society, not the life of an unmotivated panhandler like some of his contemporaries.

In order to make a reality out of the goals Keith has set up, he will be required to test his mental and physical motivation. However, there is little hope that Keith will be able to rehabilitate single handedly. He will require the aid of the community, the state, and the local government in order to reintegrate himself into his desired community as a respectable worker. To conceive of Keith's life several years from now would be virtually impossible without setting him up in the right place with the right resources. Resources must be made available to the disenfranchised politically undecided communities especially in Detroit. While Keith has employed the services of places like NSO, Keith has his complaints, and with all due respect.

I don't even go to NSO, because I remember going there fighting…A friend of mine that was working there got killed last year. Let me put it like this you got drug dealers and its like when you walk in there, there's a spirit in there …But anyway a woman killed a friend of mine named Garcia that was working there last year, stabbed him, and the girl I know that was working there I talked to her on the phone she's not there anymore but that kind of messed her up.

Keith has striven to distance himself from danger since his bouts with violence in the past. The kind of place that would benefit Keith and the homeless community working to improve the general quality of life would require feeling safe and confident about oneself and one's surroundings. Keith knows that in order for him to function as he wishes, a lot of psychological issues must be addressed to allow him to feel like a viable human being, an asset to the community, and most of all to raise his self-confidence. To live in an environment where you fear for your safety and health has proven to be a setback in the homeless community. Keith has always been of the opinion that in the homeless community where he lives and also in the community of prisoners he's been exposed to, there are many ways to add insult to injury and demean the sense of self either through drugs, violence, and other crime. The only way to tackle this problem of community-wide self-worth is not to try to eliminate poverty from the top political rung, but rather by starting with the alleviation of suffering from each individual. Housing, training, and life skills programs must be made available and open for such people. Starting with a rehabilitative program or facility, the community will regain its lost morale and hopefully rekindle the desire to improve the mind, body, and spirit of the downtrodden city.

"HELPING HOMES" REHABILITATION CENTER, DETROIT, MI

Necessity for Facility

With nearly 30% of families living in poverty in Detroit today, it has become obvious that the federal government has provided neither financial assistance nor working solutions to the failing city. Substandard housing has become the norm in Detroit, with many families lacking the simple ability to provide their households with proper plumbing or an operating phone line. The city has now turned to its public elected officials, who have had a difficult time for years attempting to tackle poverty. While it is nearly impossible for any city's mayor to eliminate homelessness, the focus of such politicians should rather be on the alleviation of suffering to individuals living in poverty. The lack of morale and the quality of life are two of the greatest deficiencies and setbacks for impoverished individuals.

Public housing is present in Detroit as it is in most large cities. The public housing sector is its own entity and should not be mistaken with the proposal of this unique shelter. Public housing suggests a form of payment in return for shelter. However, one can clearly see by looking at census statistics and by the financial state of the inner-city that public housing may simply be an unaffordable luxury for the downtrodden of the downtrodden, the poorest of the poor. A facility must exist that can allow those who want to help themselves-the homeless and impoverished who want nothing more than to get stable and back on their feet. As it stands, the city of Detroit not only forgets about and disregards its lowliest citizens, it discourages their existence by lacking the proper funds to repair shelters and improve the conditions of public facilities.

"Helping Homes," the next generation of innovative rehabilitation for the homeless and impoverished will attempt to serve a critical purpose in the city of Detroit. By opening the doors to this new facility, numerous homeless men, women and children will have the opportunity to lead normal lives, get back on their feet, and attain realistic career goals while learning how to value the self, mind, and body. In addition, Helping Homes will attempt to play an active role in serving the surrounding community by running a feeding program for other impoverished individuals.

This non-profit charitable shelter and organization can allow the hopes and dreams of citizens who are unemployed and disenfranchised to be realized.

Philosophy

What is the purpose of today's modern homeless shelter? It is not only to have a roof over the heads of the impoverished, but also to clothe, feed, and give hope to our nation's poor. Reverends, priests, and local activists are just a few of the people who have found it necessary to reverse the downward spiraling effect of Detroit. While many people are responsible for the limited rehabilitation of a select few of Detroit's underclass, there is no facility in existence that allows all rehabilitation services under one roof—the roof of their home in a Helping Home. Helping Homes will provide a clean, safe home that allows children to function and learn, and teaches adults valuable life lessons such as social and vocational skills, cooking, cleaning, and administrative skills.

The main theme of Helping Homes is the succinct message that you must be willing to help yourself. Admission and retention depend on this. There is no purpose in trying to impose oneself on a person in need who will not receive you. Helping Homes goes half the distance, and the tenant is required to go the other half. This half-and-half solution is the only way in which to ensure that anyone entering the shelter is a reliable and motivated individual.

Setup

To ensure the safety and success of the facility, twenty-four hour surveillance is necessary, along with attendance to the front desk at all times. In addition, the facility will be fully staffed by the tenants all taking responsibility for different tasks.

One Helping Home will house between 10-15 people, each with his or her own quarters. Bedrooms contain a matress, bed frame, bookshelf, a dresser, a desk with a lamp, a mirror, and a closet. These entities are required to attain the larger goal- self preservation and motivation. Bedrooms occupy the second and third floors of the home, ideally an abandoned or otherwise large empty home off of Woodward in Detroit. The house will be renovated, painted, and fixed up to proper living conditions. Each bedroom will have the ability to house a child, as well. Larger units will be made available for larger families.

The goal is not so much economic assimilation with the rest of the population, but to create an environment that allows our tenants not to be alienated from any community and to be treated with respect by their housemates and families. In a grassroots setting, these folks will be able to understand the importance of social organization from the bottom rung up. In addition, Helping Homes residents will learn a lesson in community organization and community bonding, as well as the tools to begin working up to a satisfactory standard of living by working together with their neighbors.

The first floor of the Helping Home is completely focused on respect for the community. There will be a living room with a television and couches, a nursery for children, offices of the necessary counselors, a library, a full kitchen, dining room, and another larger room for community meals.

Upon entrance to the house, there will be an individual to greet you and answer phone calls and requests, questions, and concerns of current and potential tenants. Two to three different residents will be required for two shifts in the day. These individuals will reside in the home, as well as all other attendants in the home. Their work, such as in a co-op, will be exchanged for their room and board.

Besides the receptionist, the home will have three to four cooks who prepare meals for the entire community. These tenants will be responsible for the upkeep of the kitchen, making sure that necessary food is available, and shopping for food for the community. If these people enter the home without any cooking experience and desire the position, training can be made available.

The feeding program sponsored by Helping Homes will require a room large enough to feed at least 50 people at one time, and the feeding program will serve not only as a benefit to the poor community, it will also allow an opportunity for those seeking aid from a Helping Home to enter the facility and see how it functions before deciding to apply for residency. The feeding program may also serve as a screening process for the shelter's directors to find worthy applicants for our program. The Helping Homes feeding program is always free for the public and is always respectful of confidentiality and privacy.

Helping Homes will employ another tenant as an attendant to any children. Of course, this service depends on the number and needs of kids. This person will be trained in CPR, first aid, and child care. They will be responsible for watching tenant's children while they are either at work or at a job interview. Child care is one of the most important aspects of life in the modern day community, and is by far one of the most expensive services and often difficult to come by for the impoverished community.

Another tenant will be responsible for keeping all communal spaces clean. This tenant will vacuum, straighten furniture, sweep and clean the bathrooms. During the summer, this tenant will be responsible for keeping the outside of the home clean and presentable. This will include any lawn mowing and landscaping or gardening to some extent.

A fourth tenant will be responsible for being the assistant administrator; this includes helping the administrator of the organization with making phone calls or executing any publicly related matters. This tenant will be responsible for reporting any complaints or issues that arise in the home.

There will be a fifth tenant to organize projects and outings for the community's weekly meeting or monthly outing. This tenant will dialogue with the administrative assistant to set up meetings if problems arise so that the entire community may work out issues together. This person will also be responsible for finding a nice occasional outing either to a restaurant, movie, play, museum, or concert. Money in a shelter of this nature is sparse at best, so this person will be responsible to talking to company representatives about getting group rates, and the eventual goal will be notable organizational and business skills.

Ideally there would be a library, and another occupation of a tenant would be responsible for the upkeep of the library and making sure that books are properly checked out. Another tenant will be responsible for the inventory of the home, making sure that any necessary supplies are available and making sure that the community members have all they need to live their healthy lifestyle, this includes doing inventory of the bathrooms, kitchens, etc. Tenants requiring goods or services should report to the inventory manager.

All of our funds to keep the home in working condition and to keep food on the table will have to come from donors. Ideally, we will collect enough money to pay all bills, cover supplies, and be able to have a nice evening out once a month. The fundraising aspect will be executed by professional agents. It would begin as most charitable organizations do, with a small base eventually reaching national status.

Services

There are a few positions, ideally volunteers, which will be absolutely necessary for the success of the home. Each home will have a part-time vocational counselor, responsible for helping each of our tenants find steady, full-time jobs. The vocational counselor will come in the evenings or some other flexible hours, and have time slots for each tenant to check on their progress. They will keep relevant job postings on their door for the community to see.

All tenants will be required to meet with a counselor at least bi-weekly. This counselor will not only be a great help to those who may need counseling, but also to all other tenants who may simply need an ear to listen. The counselor will be responsible for reporting progress back to the necessary authorities, making sure that the Helping Home is a proper fit for the specific individual. These counseling sessions will be required in order for placement to be secure in the home.

There will be a paid administrator who looks over the functionality of the home and any monetary or social matter that might arise either with public officials or neighbors. Our administrator will be the main public relations liaison for each individual home.

The shelter is partially responsible for the employment of our tenants through our vocational counselor and general counselor. The goal is not to give up on the folks that the rest of society has forgotten but to help them make themselves into the ideal people that they desire to be. Neighborhood drug counseling and/or NA/AA sessions will be required for those folks who require such rehabilitation.

Admission

As there are a limited number of spaces in the facility, screening and background checks will be required for each tenant. Ideally, this shelter will house folks who have the potential to succeed and help themselves along the way. Tenants will be required to either write or convey to the admissions director why they deserve the opportunity to be housed in such a facility. They will need to prove that they have the motivation to be rehabilitated. There will be no tolerance for violent ex-cons, serious drug abusers, or those folks requiring serious professional medical assistance will not be admitted. This is not to say that anyone with a criminal record or past drug problem will be rejected. Any dangerous folks simply cannot be allowed to enter our safe community.

The identities of all tenants, if desired, will be completely confidential. A monthly progress report is required for each tenant to ensure their progress. This report may either be filed by an administrator, counselor, or by the individual. Tenants occupy the facility at their own disposal. They may leave whenever they want, though a counselor will advise them as to whether it is in their best interest.

Since the facility houses a limited number of people, there will be a running waitlist to gain admission into the facility, and hopefully if the need was great enough, another Helping Home in the same area would be created.

Many shelters, especially in the metro-Detroit area are focused on the needs of battered women and children looking for a safe haven. While Helping Homes will accept such clients with open arms, the city of Detroit and many other places nationwide have put a lesser emphasis on men, single or otherwise. Helping Homes will have no sexual discrimination, and men will be welcomed and encouraged to join the community.

Transition Back to Independent Living

In order for the impoverished population to maintain a satisfactory standard of living, Helping Homes will be required to keep up with past tenants in order to check on their progress. To leave Helping Homes means one of two things, either the resident may have been discharged due to behavioral problems, or the resident may have finished running the course of rehabilitation in the home. Either way, the home is required to help folks transition out of communal living into Detroit's basic atmosphere. After having learned lessons in self-preservation and personal care, the hope is that these residents will be able to function as average members of society. Helping Homes is also required to help these folks phase out of the home by allowing their clients to return for any counseling, meals, or support that they might need. Helping Homes will also be responsible for placement of individuals into adequate housing situations. Without the constant support of an organization like Helping Homes, the work and success achieved in the program will be obsolete.

Policies/Rules, Terms of Eviction

In order to maintain the good name of the facility, it may be necessary to evict potential dangers in the community. Grounds of eviction include the following: any threats to other community members as evaluated by a counselor or by the administrative assistant, serious legal offenses, any theft or robberies within the community or ANY form of disrespect to neighbors, lewd behavior, mistreatment of other tenants or children, uncontrollable drug addiction, or medical problems that would necessitate moving from a Helping Home into a proper medical facility. Respecting one's neighbor is the most crucial aspect of the home, in learning how to build and maintain community and family. Therefore the privacy of each individual is key, and any threat to privacy will result in probation or eviction from the home. Each facility will be different, including varying quiet hours and hours of operation.

CONCLUSIONS

In examining the dichotomy of race and economics in the city of Detroit, one question remains; the "what now?" of the once booming metropolis. By looking at case studies of the respective mayors and the results of their administrations, Dr. Vernon Rayford and Keith Livingston exemplify the challenges facing the community. Keith's life has become the result of the ever-growing impossibility of integrating economic advancement with racial equality. Anger, depression, and hopelessness become the livelihood of the impoverished community. In order to begin tackling the question of future actions to take in Detroit, one must first understand the forefront issues in the city's suffering. What can be said for Detroit is that their representatives, both local elected officials on the state level in addition to the mayor, are representative of the community. Unfortunately, such adequate and unwavering representation will help Detroit build its reputation as a racially isolated city.

Mayor Coleman A. Young was one of the representatives that did an excellent job in the field of solidarity within the African American community. The resulting morale of the community proved Young's commitment to African American empowerment. Young's setback, however, was in the field of economic equality. Young did not force Detroit into poverty, though the actions taken between 1973 and 1993 did not help the monetary state of individuals throughout the city. Young's administration could have made a much bigger effort towards public assistance and a general assistance program that would have benefited folks seeing the backlash of deindustrialization through their unemployment.

Mayor Dennis Archer took an active role in trying to re-empower the city's unemployed through neighborhood programs and initiatives like the Empowerment Zone designation of 1994. Archer actively involved a new generation of professionals in Detroit's life cycle, a group of CEO's and business owners that were able to attract varying types of commerce into the city. Archer was the influential policy maker especially in terms of bringing a racial balance back to the city on the commercial end. However, Archer's setbacks were visible because the unification of the African American community was no longer the main focus of the local government as it had been in Young's administration. This was one factor that made Detroiters revoke their initial support of Archer, as he was seen as far too sympathetic to white business owners. Archer focused on bringing in new industries and new races, while forgetting to re-enfranchise the actual constituency.

The mixed agendas (whether stressing racial or economic justice) of both administrations have produced a community now disenfranchised by local politics. This community, whether educated or not, defaulted to voting in a leader (Kwame Kilpatrick) who could bring a sense of African American solidarity back to the inner city.

Political power has a negative stigma for the impoverished community. Seeing as this group has limited voting and financial power, this group is often the most distanced from the local political realm, and systematically prepared for economic failure due to a lack of programs and aid. Dr. Rayford's clients of Just Love Ministries would greatly benefit from a Helping Homes-style setup, or any kind of all-inclusive rehabilitative facility. The clients that enter Just Love Ministries have begun to take the future into their own hands. The ministry is a big step in the right direction, but again, a lack of funding from the local government has been a drawback in exactly how much aid Just Love can provide. Dr. Rayford isn't trying to eliminate poverty, and it was never his goal to save the entire city. However, what Dr. Rayford has done is quite unique impoverished community. Dr. Rayford has focused on improving the quality of life for the homeless and trying to alleviate some personal suffering on an individual basis. His mission for the city of Detroit is to unite across racial and economic lines, to work as a community, not as an African American vs. white world, or a rich vs. poor society.

It can be concluded that regardless of the politician, mayors cannot and will not solve poverty single handedly. While solidarity is present in the neighborhoods, the lack of resources has been very detrimental to the community. As a city of extremes, Detroiters have always been accustomed to the notion of civil disobedience through riots, racism through the civil rights era, and a drastically falling economy as the city depreciated in population. Political power is simply not the answer to poverty. While with politicians, a little lawmaking can go a long way in communities such as the impoverished, the alleviation of poverty cannot be expected for today's local government. While the government successfully dug a ditch of economic despair in Detroit, community members and local activists have done their best to stay afloat.

Dr. Rayford has said that Detroiters must separate themselves from the mindset that Detroit is the world around them. A global perspective, Dr. Rayford agrees, is the only way to go about improving the overall state of the city, by improving the state of the world. For someone like Keith Livingston, it is clear that with the proper tools and the correct administrators, a meaningful life is within the realm of possibility. Keith desires the ideal life—being able to function as an individual through avenues of career choices, housing assistance, and counseling. Keith is obviously intelligent, and understands the outcomes of his actions. He has begun taking control of his life by re-enrolling in school, and regularly attending NA/AA meetings, besides regularly checking in with his supporters at Just Love. Keith and his cohorts will require a well-rounded support system, but most importantly, his community will be required to understand that the impoverished population must be reintegrated into the functioning society. Acceptance from his community is integral, Keith and the rest of the community, in and around the city, will have to work as a team to pull Detroit out of its stagnant poverty.

5

POLITICAL CORRECTNESS

INTRODUCTION

As Russell Kirk wrote, one of conservatism's most important insights is that all ideologies are wrong. Ideology takes an intellectual system, a product of one or more philosophers, and says, "This system must be true." Inevitably, reality ends up contradicting the system, usually on a growing number of points. But the ideology, by its nature, cannot adjust to reality; to do so would be to abandon the system. Therefore, reality must be suppressed. If the ideology has power, it uses its power to undertake this suppression. It forbids writing or speaking certain facts. Its goal is to prevent not only expression of thoughts that contradict what "must be true," but thinking such thoughts. In the end, the result is inevitably the concentration camp, the gulag and the grave.

While some Americans have believed in ideologies, America itself never had an official, state ideology – up until now. But what happens today to Americans who suggest that there are differences among ethnic groups, or that the traditional social roles of men and women reflect their different natures, or that homosexuality is morally wrong? If they are public figures, they must grovel in the dirt in endless, canting apologies. If they are university students, they face star chamber courts and possible expulsion. If they are employees of private corporations, they may face loss of their jobs. What was their crime? Contradicting America's new state ideology of "Political Correctness." But what exactly is "Political Correctness?" Marxists have used the term for at least 80 years, as a broad synonym for "the General Line of the Party." It could be said that Political Correctness is the General Line of the Establishment in America today; certainly, no one who dares contradict it can be a member of that Establishment. But that still does not tell us what it really is. This short book, which Free Congress has decided to make available free over its website, seeks to answer that question. It does so in the only way any ideology can be understood, by looking at its historical origins, its method of analysis and several key components, including its place in higher education and its ties with the Feminist movement. Finally, it offers an annotated bibliography for those who wish to pursue the subject in greater depth.

Perhaps the most important question facing Americans today is, "Do we really want America to be an ideological state?" Because conservatives know where all ideologies lead, our answer, resoundingly, is "NO!" But if we expect to prevail and restore our country to full freedom of thought and expression, we need to know our enemy. We need to understand what Political Correctness really is. As you will soon see, if we can expose the true origins and nature of Political Correctness, we will have taken a giant step to its overthrow.

WHAT IS "POLITICAL CORRECTNESS"?

Most Americans look back on the 1950s as a good time. Our homes were safe, to the point where many people did not bother to lock their doors. Public schools were generally excellent, and their problems were things like talking in class and running in the halls. Most men treated women like ladies, and most ladies devoted their time and effort to making good homes, rearing their children well and helping their communities through volunteer work. Children grew up in two–parent households, and the mother was there to meet the child when he came home from school. Entertainment was something the whole family could enjoy.

What Happened?

If a man from America of the 1950s were suddenly introduced into America in the 2000s, he would hardly recognize it as the same country. He would be in immediate danger of getting mugged, carjacked or worse, because he would not have learned to live in constant fear. He would not know that he shouldn't go into certain parts of the city, that his car must not only be locked but equipped with an alarm, that he dare not go to sleep at night without locking the windows and bolting the doors – and setting the electronic security system.

If he brought his family with him, he and his wife would probably cheerfully pack their children off to the nearest public school. When the children came home in the afternoon and told them they had to go through a metal detector to get in the building, had been given some funny white powder by another kid and learned that homosexuality is normal and good, the parents would be uncomprehending. In the office, the man might light up a cigarette, drop a reference to the "little lady," and say he was happy to see the firm employing some Negroes in important positions. Any of those acts would earn a swift reprimand, and together they might get him fired.

When she went into the city to shop, the wife would put on a nice suit, hat, and possibly gloves. She would not understand why people stared, and mocked. And when the whole family sat down after dinner and turned on the television, they would not understand how pornography from some sleazy, blank-fronted "Adults Only" kiosk had gotten on their set. Were they able, our 1950s family would head back to the 1950s as fast as they could, with a gripping horror story to tell. Their story would be of a nation that had decayed and degenerated at a fantastic pace, moving in less than a half a century from the greatest country on earth to a Third World nation, overrun by crime, noise, drugs and dirt. The fall of Rome was graceful by comparison.

Why did it Happen?

Over the last forty years, America has been conquered by the same force that earlier took over Russia, China, Germany and Italy. That force is ideology. Here, as elsewhere, ideology has inflicted enormous damage on the traditional culture it came to dominate, fracturing it everywhere and sweeping much of it away. In its place came fear, and ruin. Russia will take a generation or more to recover from Communism, if it ever can.

The ideology that has taken over America goes most commonly by the name of "Political Correctness." Some people see it as a joke. It is not. It is deadly serious. It seeks to alter virtually all the rules, formal and informal, that govern relations among people and institutions. It wants to change behavior, thought, even the words we use. To a significant extent, it already has. Whoever or whatever controls language also controls thought. Who dares to speak of "ladies" now? Just what is "Political Correctness?" "Political Correctness" is in fact cultural Marxism – Marxism translated from economic into cultural terms. The effort to translate Marxism from economics into culture did not begin with the student rebellion of the 1960s. It goes back at least to the 1920s and the writings of the Italian Communist Antonio Gramsci. In 1923, in Germany, a group of Marxists founded an institute devoted to making the translation, the Institute of Social Research (later known as the Frankfurt School). One of its founders, George Lukacs, stated its purpose as answering the question, "Who shall save us from Western Civilization?" The Frankfurt School gained profound influence in American universities after many of its leading lights fled to the United States in the 1930s to escape National Socialism in Germany.

The Frankfurt School blended Marx with Freud, and later influences (some Fascist as well as Marxist) added linguistics to create "Critical Theory" and "deconstruction." These in turn greatly influenced education theory, and through institutions of higher education gave birth to what we now call "Political Correctness." The lineage is clear, and it is traceable right back to Karl Marx. The parallels between cultural Marxism and classical, economic Marxism are evident. Cultural Marxism, or Political Correctness, shares with classical Marxism the vision of a "classless society" i.e., a society not merely of equal opportunity, but equal condition. Since that vision contradicts human nature – because people are different, they end up unequal, regardless of the starting point – society will not accord with it unless forced. So, under both variants of Marxism, it is forced. This is the first major parallel between classical and cultural Marxism: *both are totalitarian ideologies*. The totalitarian nature of Political Correctness can be seen on campuses where "PC" has taken over the college: freedom of speech, of the press, and even of thought are all eliminated.

The second major parallel is that both cultural Marxism and classical, economic Marxism have *single-factor explanations of history.* Classical Marxism argues that all of history was determined by ownership of the means of production. Cultural Marxism says that history is wholly explained by which groups – defined by sex, race and sexual normality or abnormality – have power over which other groups. The third parallel is that both varieties of Marxism *declare certain groups virtuous and others evil a priori*, that is, without regard for the actual behavior of individuals. Classical Marxism defines workers and peasants as virtuous and the bourgeoisie (the middle class) and other owners of capital as evil. Political Correctness defines blacks, Hispanics, Feminist women, homosexuals and some additional minority groups as virtuous and white men as evil. (Political Correctness does not recognize the existence of non-Feminist women and defines blacks who reject Political Correctness as whites).

The fourth parallel is in means: *expropriation.* Economic Marxists, where they obtained power, expropriated the property of the bourgeoisie and handed it to the state, as the "representative" of the workers and the peasants. Cultural Marxists, when they gain power (including through our own government), lay penalties on white men and others who disagree with them and give privileges to the groups they favor. Affirmative action is an example. Finally, both varieties of Marxists employ a method of analysis *designed to show the correctness of their ideology in every situation.* For classical Marxists, the analysis is economic. For cultural Marxists, the analysis is linguistic: deconstruction. Deconstruction "proves" that any "text," past or present, illustrates the oppression of blacks, women, homosexuals, etc. by reading that meaning into words of the text (regardless of their actual meaning). Both methods are, of course, phony analyses that twist the evidence to fit preordained conclusions, but they lend a "scientific" air to the ideology. These parallels are neither remarkable nor coincidental. They exist because Political Correctness is directly derived from classical Marxism, and is in fact merely a variant of Marxism. Through most of the history of Marxism, cultural Marxists were "read out" of the movement by classical, economic Marxists. Today, with economic Marxism dead, cultural Marxism has filled its shoes. The medium has changed, but the message is the same: a society of radical egalitarianism enforced by the power of the state.

Political Correctness now looms over American society like a colossus. It has taken over both political parties – recent Republican conventions were choreographed according to its dictates, while cultural conservatives were shown the door – and is enforced by many laws and government regulations. It almost totally controls the most powerful element in our culture, the entertainment industry. It dominates both public and higher education: many a college campus is a small, ivy-covered North Korea. It has even captured the clergy in many Christian churches. Anyone in the Establishment who departs from its dictates swiftly ceases to be a member of the Establishment. The remainder of this short book will explore the subject of Political Correctness further: its history, its method of analysis (deconstruction), and the means by which it has attained its influence, especially through education. But one more question must be addressed at the outset, the most vital question: how can Americans combat Political Correctness and retake their society from the cultural Marxists?

To that end, it is not sufficient to criticize Political Correctness. It tolerates a certain amount of criticism, even gentle mocking. It does so through no genuine tolerance for other points of view, but in order to disarm its opponents, to let itself seem less menacing than it is. The cultural Marxists do not yet have total power, and they are too wise to appear totalitarian until their victory is assured. Rather, those who would defeat cultural Marxism must defy it. They must use words it forbids, and refuse to use the words it mandates; remember, sex is better than gender. They must shout from the housetops the realities it seeks to suppress, such as the facts that violent crime is disproportionately committed by blacks and that most cases of AIDS are voluntary, i.e., acquired from immoral sexual acts. They must refuse to turn their children over to public schools.

Above all, those who would defy Political Correctness must behave according to the old rules of our culture, not the new rules the cultural Marxists lay down. Ladies should be wives and homemakers, not cops or soldiers, and men should still hold doors open for ladies. Children should not be born out of wedlock. Open homosexuals should be shunned. Jurors should not accept race as an excuse for murder. Defiance spreads. When other Americans see one person defy Political Correctness and survive – and you still can, for now – they are emboldened. They are tempted to defy it, too, and some will. The ripples from a single act of defiance, of one instance of walking up to the clay idol and breaking off its nose, can range far. There is nothing the Politically Correct fear more than open defiance, and for good reason; it is their chief vulnerability. That should lead cultural conservatives to defy cultural Marxism at every turn.

While the hour is late, the battle is not decided. Very few Americans realize that Political Correctness is in fact Marxism in a different set of clothes. As that realization spreads, defiance will spread with it. At present, Political Correctness prospers by disguising itself. Through defiance, and through education on our own part (which should be part of every act of defiance), we can strip away its camouflage and reveal the Marxism beneath the window-dressing of "sensitivity," "tolerance" and "multiculturalism." Who dares, wins.

THE HISTORICAL ROOTS OF "POLITICAL CORRECTNESS"

America is today dominated by an alien system of beliefs, attitudes and values that we have come to know as "Political Correctness." Political Correctness seeks to impose a uniformity of thought and behavior on all Americans and is therefore totalitarian in nature. Its roots lie in a version of Marxism which seeks a radical inversion of the traditional culture in order to create a social revolution. Social revolution has a long history, conceivably going as far back as Plato's *Republic*. But it was the French Revolution of 1789 that inspired Karl Marx to develop his theories in the nineteenth century. In the twentieth century, the success of the Bolshevik Revolution of 1917 in Russia set off a wave of optimistic expectation among the Marxist forces in Europe and America that the new proletarian world of equality was finally coming into being. Russia, as the first communist nation in the world, would lead the revolutionary forces to victory.

The Marxist revolutionary forces in Europe leaped at this opportunity. Following the end of World War I, there was a Communist "Spartacist uprising in Berlin, Germany lead by Rosa Luxemburg; the creation of a "Soviet" in Bavaria led by Kurt Eisner; and a Hungarian communist republic established by Bela Kun in 1919. At the time, there was great concern that all of Europe might fall under the banner of Bolshevism. This sense of impeding doom was given vivid life by Trotsky's Red Army invasion of Poland in 1919. However, the Red Army was defeated by Polish forces at the battle of the Vistula in 1920. The Spartacist, Bavarian Soviet and Bela Kun governments all failed to gain widespread support from the workers and after a brief time they were all overthrown. These events created a quandary for the Marxist revolutionaries in Europe. Under Marxist economic theory, the oppressed workers were supposed to be the beneficiaries of a social revolution that would place them on top of the power structure. When these revolutionary opportunities presented themselves, however, the workers did not respond. The Marxist revolutionaries did not blame their theory for these failures. They blamed the workers.

One group of Marxist intellectuals resolved their quandary by an analysis that focused on society's cultural "superstructure" rather than on the economic substructures as Marx did. The Italian Marxist Antonio Gramsci and Hungarian Marxist Georg Lukacs contributed the most to this new cultural Marxism. Antonio Gramsci worked for the Communist International during 1923-24 in Moscow and Vienna. He was later imprisoned in one of Mussolini's jails where he wrote his famous "Prison Notebooks." Among Marxists, Gramsci is noted for his theory of cultural hegemony as the means to class dominance. In his view, a new "Communist man" had to be created before any political revolution was possible. This led to a focus on the efforts of intellectuals in the fields of education and culture. Gramsci envisioned a long march through the society's institutions, including the government, the judiciary, the military, the schools and the media. He also concluded that so long as the workers had a Christian soul, they would not respond to revolutionary appeals.

Georg Lukacs was the son a wealthy Hungarian banker. Lukacs began his political life as an agent of the Communist International. His book *History and Class Consciousness* gained him recognition as the leading Marxist theorist since Karl Marx. Lukacs believed that for a new Marxist culture to emerge, the existing culture must be destroyed. He said, "I saw the revolutionary destruction of society as the one and only solution to the cultural contradictions of the epoch," and, "Such a worldwide overturning of values cannot take place without the annihilation of the old values and the creation of new ones by the revolutionaries." When he became Deputy Commissar for Culture in the Bolshevik Bela Kun regime in Hungary in 1919, Lukacs launched what became known as "Cultural Terrorism." As part of this terrorism he instituted a radical sex education program in Hungarian schools. Hungarian children were instructed in free love, sexual intercourse, the archaic nature of middle-class family codes, the out-datedness of monogamy, and the irrelevance of religion, which deprives man of all pleasures. Women, too, were called to rebel against the sexual mores of the time. Lukacs's campaign of "Cultural Terrorism" was a precursor to what Political Correctness would later bring to American schools. In 1923, Lukacs and other Marxist intellectuals associated with the Communist Party of Germany founded the Institute of Social Research at Frankfurt University in Frankfurt, Germany. The Institute, which became known as the Frankfurt School, was modeled after the Marx-Engels Institute in Moscow. In 1933, when Nazis came to power in Germany, the members of the Frankfurt School fled. Most came to the United States. The members of the Frankfurt School conducted numerous studies on the beliefs, attitudes and values they believed lay behind the rise of National Socialism in Germany.

The Frankfurt School's studies combined Marxist analysis with Freudian psychoanalysis to form the basis of what became known as "Critical Theory." Critical Theory was essentially destructive criticism of the main elements of Western culture, including Christianity, capitalism, authority, the family, patriarchy, hierarchy, morality, tradition, sexual restraint, loyalty, patriotism, nationalism, heredity, ethnocentrism, convention and conservatism. These criticisms were reflected in such works of the Frankfurt School as Erich Fromm's *Escape from Freedom* and *The Dogma of Christ*, Wilhelm's Reich's *The Mass Psychology of Fascism* and Theodor Adorno's *The Authoritarian Personality*. *The Authoritarian Personality*, published in 1950, substantially influenced American psychologists and social scientists. The book was premised on one basic idea, that the presence in a society of Christianity, capitalism and the patriarchal-authoritarian family created a character prone to racial prejudice and German fascism. *The Authoritarian Personality* became a handbook for a national campaign against any kind of prejudice or discrimination on the theory that if these evils were not eradicated, another Holocaust might occur on the American continent. This campaign, in turn, provided a basis for Political Correctness. Critical Theory incorporated sub-theories which themselves were intended to chip away at specific elements of the existing culture, including "matriarchal theory," "androgyny theory," "personality theory," "authority theory," "family theory," "sexuality theory," "racial theory," "legal theory" and "literary theory." Put into practice, these theories were to be used to overthrow the prevailing social order and usher in social revolution based on cultural Marxism.

To achieve this, the Critical Theorists of the Frankfurt School recognized that traditional beliefs and the existing social structure would have to be destroyed and then replaced. The patriarchal social structure would be replaced with matriarchy; the belief that men and women are different and properly have different roles would be replaced with androgyny; and the belief that heterosexuality is normal would be replaced with the belief that homosexuality is "normal."

As a grand scheme intended to deny the intrinsic worth of white, heterosexual males, the Critical Theorists of the Frankfurt School opened the door to the racial and sexual antagonisms of the Trotskyites. Leon Trotsky believed that oppressed blacks could be the vanguard of a communist revolution in North America. He denounced white workers who were prejudiced against blacks and instructed them to unite with the blacks in revolution. Trotsky's ideas were adopted by many of the student leaders of the 1960s counterculture movement, who attempted to elevate the black revolutionaries to positions of leadership in their movement. The student revolutionaries were also strongly influenced by the ideas of Herbert Marcuse, another member of the Frankfurt School. Marcuse preached the "Great Refusal," a rejection of all basic Western concepts, sexual liberation and the merits of feminist and black revolutions. His primary thesis was that university students, ghetto blacks, the alienated, the asocial, and the Third World could take the place of the proletariat in the Communist revolution. In his book, *An Essay on Liberation*, Marcuse proclaimed his goals of a radical transvaluation of values; the relaxation of taboos, cultural subversion; Critical Theory; and a linguistic rebellion that would amount to a methodical reversal of meaning. As for racial conflict, Marcuse wrote that white men are guilty and that blacks are the most natural force of rebellion.

Marcuse may be the most important member of the Frankfurt School in terms of the origins of Political Correctness, because he was the critical link to the counterculture of the 1960s. His objective was clear: "One can rightfully speak of a cultural revolution, since the protest is directed toward the whole cultural establishment, including morality of existing society..." His means was liberating the powerful, primeval force of sex from its civilized restraints, a message preached in his book, *Eros and Civilization*, published in 1955. Marcuse became one of the main gurus of the 1960s adolescent sexual rebellion; he himself coined the expression, "make love, not war." With that role, the chain of Marxist influence via the Frankfurt School was completed: from Lukacs's service as Deputy Commissar for Culture in the Bolshevik Hungarian government in 1919 to American students burning the flag and taking over college administration buildings in the 1960s. Today, many of these same colleges are bastions of Political Correctness, and the former student radicals have become the faculties.

One of the most important contributors to Political Correctness was Betty Friedan. Through her book *The Feminine Mystique,* Friedan became the mother of the modern feminist movement in America. Friedan was not a member of the Frankfurt School, but she was strongly influenced by it. Her work offers a useful case study of the Marxist roots of Political Correctness. Friedan devoted almost a full chapter of *The Feminine Mystique* to Abraham Maslow's theory of self-actualization. Maslow was a social psychologist who in his early years did research on female dominance and sexuality. Maslow was a friend of Herbert Marcuse at Bandeis University and had met Erich Fromm in 1936. He was strongly impressed by Fromm's Frankfurt School ideology. He wrote an article, "The Authoritarian Character Structure," published in 1944, that reflected the personality theory of Critical Theory. Maslow was also impressed with the work of Wilhelm Reich, who was another Frankfurt School originator of personality theory.

The significance of the historical roots of Political Correctness cannot be fully appreciated unless Betty Friedan's revolution in sex roles is viewed for what it really was – a manifestation of the social revolutionary process begun by Karl Marx. Friedan's reliance on Abraham Maslow's reflection of Frankfurt School ideology is simply one indicator. Other indicators include the correspondence of Friedan's revolution in sex roles with Georg Lukacs' annihilation of old values and the creation of new ones, and with Herbert Marcuse's transvaluation of values. But the idea of transforming a patriarchy into a matriarchy – which is what a sex-role inversion is designed to do – can be connected directed to Friedrich Engels book *The Origin of the Family, Private Property, and the Sate.* First published in 1884, this book popularized the now-accepted feminist belief that deep-rooted discrimination against the oppressed female sex was a function of patriarchy. The belief that matriarchy was the solution to patriarchy flows from Marx's comments in *The German Ideology*, published in 1845. In this work Marx advanced the idea that wives and children were the first property of the patriarchal male.

The Frankfurt School's matriarchal theory (and its near-relation, androgyny theory) both originated from these sources. When addressing the general public, advocates of Political Correctness – or cultural Marxism, to give it its true name – present their beliefs attractively. It's all just a matter of being "sensitive" to other people, they say. They use words such as "tolerance" and "diversity," asking, "Why can't we all just get along?" The reality is different. Political Correctness is not at all about "being nice," unless one thinks gulags are nice places. Political Correctness is Marxism, with all that implies: loss of freedom of expression, thought control, inversion of the traditional social order and, ultimately, a totalitarian state. If anything, the cultural Marxism created by the Frankfurt School is more horrifying than the old, economic Marxism that ruined Russia. At least the economic Marxists did not exalt sexual perversion and attempt to create a matriarchy, as the Frankfurt School and its descendants have done.

This short essay has sought to show one critical linkage, that between classical Marxism and the ingredients of the "cultural revolution" that broke out in America in the 1960s. The appendices to this paper offer a "wiring diagram" which may make the trail easier to follow, along with a more detailed look at some of the main actors. Of course, the action does not stop in the '60s; the workings of Frankfurt School are yet very much with us, especially in the field of education. That topic, and other present-day effects of Frankfurt School thinking, will be the subjects of future chapters in this book.

THE ORIGINS OF POLITICAL CORRECTNESS IN HIGHER EDUCATION

While the ideology of Political Correctness is hardly restricted to our campuses, there is no doubt it originated there. The intellectual roots of this phenomenon stretch back over centuries. Ultimately, the origins of PC can be traced to the rise of modern ideology and its quest for power. In contrast to the classical and Judeo-Christian traditions, which stressed man's need to understand the moral order and conform himself to it, modern ideologies have sought to dominate and control the world. In the twentieth century these ideologies finally gained political power in Communist states. But in the West, ideology has not been able to make such a direct assault on our traditions of ordered liberty. Rather, radical intellectuals have sought to undermine the foundations of knowledge itself, concentrating their efforts on the transformation of the university.

The turning point in the academy came in the 1960s, when militant students launched a guerilla attack on the traditions of Western culture and the liberal arts. Seeing that they could not gain lasting power through demonstrations alone, many of these militants opted to remain "in the system," going on to become professors themselves. This generation of "tenured radicals" (to use Roger Kimball's phrase) has now become the establishment in the vast majority of our institutions of higher learning. As university presidents, deans, and department chairmen, they have set about hiring other ideologues in their own image and have instigated the repressive policies we know as Political Correctness. These politicized academics will be extremely difficult to dislodge from their current positions of power.

Ideology vs. Liberal Education

The stakes in this war of ideas are high, for they include the very concept of freedom itself. Americans have always understood the intimate and vital connection between liberal education and political liberty. That is why Political Correctness is nothing less than a death blow aimed at the heart of our republic. In his seminal book, *The Idea of a University*, Cardinal John Henry Newman defined the "liberal arts" as a pursuit of knowledge for its own sake. By way of contrast, he defined the "servile arts" as those modes of study that serve only specific, immediate ends. The liberal arts are liberating, Newman argued, because they enable men to discover the underlying principles that guide us toward wisdom and virtue. Were he alive today, Newman would view Political Correctness as "servile" because its purpose is to advance a political agenda to a position of national power. Militant professors in increasing numbers are shamelessly turning their podiums into pulpits, abandoning the search for objective truth and setting about the task of indoctrinating their students.

The Devastated Curriculum

The proponents of Political Correctness have concentrated their efforts on the core of a liberal education, the curriculum. Their efforts will radically alter what new generations of Americans will learn. In this battle the handmaiden of Political Correctness has been the "multicultural" movement. A number of critics have rightly pointed out that multiculturalism is more than an argument for courses that concentrate on groups that at one time were disadvantaged or oppressed. Rather, multiculturalism involves the systematic restructuring of the curriculum so as to hinder students from learning about the Western tradition. Since the ulterior motive behind Political Correctness is an attempt to restructure American society along egalitarian lines, it is imperative for its proponents to instill in the minds of students a thoroughgoing cultural relativism. Perhaps the most disturbing aspect of the Politically Correct assault on the curriculum is that it has occurred at many of America's elite universities. Take, for example, the case of Stanford University, an institution that has long played a leadership role in American higher education. Stanford eliminated its long-standing Western civilization requirement in 1988 and replaced it with a multicultural program known as "Cultures, Ideas, and Values." Under this new program freshmen at Stanford can just as easily study Marxist revolutionaries in Central America as they can Plato, Shakespeare or Newton.

Stanford has also led the movement away from serious study of history. Students at Stanford, like students at all but one of the other top 50 universities in the United States, are not required to take a single course in history. Instead, they are offered a choice of courses under the heading of "American Cultures." According to one recent graduate of Stanford, it is impossible to fulfill the "American Cultures" requirement by studying Protestantism, Irish Americans, or the American West, while courses that do fulfill the requirement include "Film and Literature: US-Mexico Border Representations" and "Contemporary Ethnic Drama." Stanford students must also take courses in "World Cultures" and "Gender Studies" that include "Chicana Expressive Culture" and "Misogyny and Feminism in the Renaissance."

Because elite institutions such as Stanford set an example for the rest of American higher education, other universities eagerly adopt these devastating assaults on the curriculum. This "trickle-down" effect will have a long-lasting impact on the way future generations of Americans will be educated.

Intolerance and the Assault on Freedom

The two pillars that have traditionally sustained the liberal arts are academic freedom and freedom of speech. Without the freedom to pursue the truth and to write and speak freely, authentic scholarship is impossible. But both of these fundamental freedoms have been routinely abrogated by the establishment of speech codes, "sensitivity" classes, and a general atmosphere of fear and intimidation on campus. For example, younger professors who have not received tenure must not only be careful of what they say, but of what they publish. Ideological university administrators in the 1990s have created an environment dominated by suspicion that is far more intense than anything spawned by anti-Communist Senator Joseph McCarthy in the 1950s. The most tragic victims of this age of Political Correctness are the students. The traditional goal of a liberal arts education – acculturation, whereby students absorb the inherited wisdom of the past – has been set aside. Increasingly, a university education today seems to involve rote learning of political opinions. When all is said and done, Political Correctness substitutes smug feelings of righteousness for the traditional habits of critical thinking. One distinguished scholar recently lamented that "higher education is increasingly about acquiring attitudes and opinions that one puts on like a uniform." Because the academy is a relatively isolated world, it can allow politicized administrators to turn the campus into a laboratory for experiments in social transformation.

When critics of Political Correctness have compared the atmosphere on campus to that of a totalitarian state, liberal pundits have been quick to denounce them as hysterical. Few of these pundits have any first-hand experience of daily life on campus.

The Movement for Academic Reform

Despite the institutional power of the campus radicals, forces are at work seeking to spur authentic academic reform. The academic reform movement relies on the principles of accountability, communication and a commitment to authentic scholarship. One force of academic reform is a growing demand among parents for greater accountability from colleges and universities. At a time when studies show that students are paying more and learning less than ever before, parents in increasing numbers are becoming discriminating consumers.

Another force is independent student newspapers whose journalists publicize the antics of Political Correctness on campus. In the past, campus radicals thrived in the enclosed world of the university, but their actions are no longer going undetected. The advent of conservative student newspapers on dozens of campuses has forced campus militants into the open where they are most vulnerable to the scrutiny of an exasperated public. Two years ago, those who fund the Collegiate Network asked the Intercollegiate Studies Institute to take over the administration of their program to support and enhance responsible student journalism. The Collegiate Network contributes seed money, practical help and intellectual guidance to the 60 conservative student newspapers which provide alternative forums of discussion at many of the nations most elite (and closedminded) universities.

These alternatives papers have identified abuses at all levels of academic life and engaged in investigative journalism that has been remarkably fair and accurate. Perhaps the most well-known "scoop" came from Yale University's alternative paper, *Light & Truth*, a publication supported by the Collegiate Network. The editors of *Light & Truth* discovered that the $20 million gift of alumnus Lee Bass was not being used for its intended purpose of supporting an integrated course in Western civilization. Their report broke open the scandal, which ended when Yale returned Mr. Bass's money. The subsequent furor cost Yale a great deal more than Mr. Bass's $20 million – both in monetary terms and in the loss of confidence of many Yale donors that the current administration can be trusted.

Not all the scandals uncovered by alternative campus papers are of this magnitude, but there are innumerable abuses that can be exposed by investigative student journalism. The law school at the University of North Carolina, Chapel Hill, banned representatives of the U.S. military from setting up recruiting tables there, despite receiving federal tax dollars from the Defense Department. An article about this outrageous assault on freedom that ran in both the student-run *Carolina Review* and in the national student newspaper published by ISI, *CAMPUS*, raised a hue and cry on and off campus. North Carolina legislators took immediate action and passed a bill prohibiting taxpayer-supported schools from discriminating against the military when prospective employers come to the university.

At the University of Wisconsin, Madison, the *UWM Times*, a conservative student newspaper, revealed that a university administrator had been soliciting signatures for local Democrat candidates for public office, in direct violation of a state law forbidding university employees from engaging in political campaigning. The university chancellor, despite having issued a directive against such campaigning, refused to reprimand the administrator in question – perhaps because the chancellor himself violated both the state law and his own directive by signing one of the petitions while at work. The story was picked up by the *Milwaukee Journal-Sentinel* and the abuse was brought to an end. Now that alternative newspapers and organizations dedicated to academic reform are spreading the word, the larger communities that surround our institutions of higher education are getting more involved in serious academic reform. For example, the National Association of Scholars is encouraging university trustees to take a more active and vocal role in opposing the excesses of Political Correctness. Efforts of this type must be expanded and intensified.

In the long run, the most direct method of defeating the inquisitors of Political Correctness is simply to stand up to them. Individual acts of defiance often entail serious risks: students can face star-chamber proceedings that are humiliating and demoralizing while faculty can lose their bids to receive tenure. But every act of resistance causes a ripple, encouraging others to stand up to ideological intimidation. With the support of a significant number of parents, donors and alumni, these Davids may yet slay the Goliaths who tower over them.

The Fire of True-Learning

Perhaps the strongest force for true academic reform is that which seeks to defeat the ideological depredations of Political Correctness by winning the war of ideas. The best students have a questioning intelligence that cannot be satisfied with political slogans. When such students have access to serious scholarship they respond with enthusiasm. Even today acculturation still takes place under the mentorship of outstanding scholars at various institutions around the country. Moreover, some colleges and universities continue to swim against the ideological tides of our time. The Intercollegiate Studies Institute (ISI), in conjunction with the Templeton Foundation, has identified the best professors, departments, colleges and textbooks in American higher education today. This program, the Templeton Honor Rolls for Education in a Free Society, celebrates excellence and serves as a guide for parents and students contemplating the daunting choice of which college or university to attend.

By singling out the best in higher education, the Templeton Honor Rolls also encourage donors to reward universities that preserve the traditions of the free society. Prospective college students, their parents and donors can also benefit from a comprehensive guide to 100 of the top institutions of higher learning in America published by the ISI. The guide contains substantial, essay-length treatments of all 100 institutions, including 80 elite schools that were selected on the basis of competitive admissions standards and 20 schools that ISI particularly recommends for their commitment to a liberal arts education. The ISI college guide warns students about the ideological dangers on the campuses and steers them in the direction of the best professors and departments. As best-selling author William J. Bennett wrote of this project, "All too often, Americans treat colleges and universities with a deference that prevents them from asking hard questions and demanding real results. But if there is ever to be genuine, long-lasting education reform, parents and students will have to become shrewder and better-informed consumers of education. The ISI guide is a powerful tool in this effort."

One of Edmund Burke's most famous sayings is that "the only thing necessary for the triumph of evil is for good men to do nothing." For generations, Americans have treated higher education with respect and awe – a token of their faith in the liberating power of the liberal arts. But in the face of Political Correctness, it is time for the American public to temper its respect with a critical sensibility and to undertake a more direct effort to call academia to account. It is time for good men and women to demand that American higher education live up to its best traditions and eschew the tyranny of Political Correctness.

POLITICAL CORRECTNESS: DECONSTRUCTION AND LITERATURE

Literature is, if not the most important cultural indicator, at least a significant benchmark of a society's level of civilization. Our nature and environment combine to form each individual mind, which in turn expresses itself in words. Literature, as the words society collectively holds up as exemplary, is then a starting point of sorts – a window into the culture.

Today's literary field is therefore worth examining for the insights it provides into our current cultural milieu. The contemporary American literary field is awash in "isms:" Marxism, Freudianism, feminism, and so on. Most of these are the academic cousins of what is called in the common culture "Political Correctness." Literary theorists take their particular brand of criticism and apply it to literature in an effort to find self-affirmation in a "discovered" meaning of the text. For a feminist critic, for example, no longer does Andrew Marvel's "Upon Appleton House" have the beauty of the grounds as its theme; it speaks instead of the evils of a patriarchal line of inheritance. These "cultural critics," so named because they critique literature based on the point of view of a particular culture, arose in the 1960s, but their schools of criticism only truly began to pick up steam with the arrival of the school of deconstruction in the 1970s. The works of the father of deconstruction, Jacques Derrida, began to be translated from the French by American professor Gayatri Spivak in the mid-1970s, a time when the U.S. literary scene was ripe for its influence. The economic Marxists were alive and well on American campuses, and the cultural critics were still being fed by the radicalism of the times. Feminists, "queer theorists" and "literature-by-people of color" critics had gained a foothold in the earlier decade, but they had in their meager arsenals only a vague feeling of repression. What they lacked was philosophical backing – the courage prompted by having their own *logos*. The arrival of deconstruction from France provided that philosophy.

At that time, that generation of academics was doing what all academics do, telling the previous generation that it had it all wrong. In this case the rebellion was against the New Critics – so-called even now, decades after their prime. The New Critics specialized in finding the meaning of texts without regard to background information such as authorial intent, a process that had "the text is everything" as its guiding principle. The new generation of critics set out to turn that principle on its head. Instead of "the text is everything," the new generation claimed that "everything is text" and turned to analyzing anything and everything in relation to the literary work. If a poet wrote a poem that included a female character, the critics would look into the poet's relationship with his mother, his wife, his sister and so on in an effort to offer up an interpretation of the work.

This could have (and often did have) the positive effect of using biographic information to gain new understanding of the work; however, these new interpretations were not attempts to discern the true meaning of the work (as the New Critics had done) or even to discover the author's intended meaning (as traditional readings attempted). This new generation of critics instead became prime practitioners of what is known in literary circles as "cultural criticism." They strained to view literature from the "woman's point of view" or the "gay point of view" or the "radical minority point of view." Their attempts were not to find meaning – they were influenced too greatly by relativists for that – but to find sexism, racism or "homophobia" in the works of male, European or heterosexual authors.

Derridean deconstruction became a tool for these cultural critics. Simply stated, deconstruction is a school of thought that posits that words have no meaning. Instead, words have "traces" of meaning. The meaning of a word is continually disappearing, leaving us with only the memory, or trace, of what that meaning once was. (Similar to Heidegger's term being, Derrida often uses the crossed-out word trace in an effort to indicate a meaning that is simultaneously present and disappearing.) A metaphor may be helpful to understand the underlying philosophy of deconstructionism. If I say the word "pen," then you think of the object there in the desk drawer. But if I throw the pen at someone, then the word "pen" begins to lose the benign meaning of a writing apparatus with ink; to use deconstructionist terms, the original understanding of the word "pen" undergoes erasure to leave only a trace. Instead the word "pen" becomes associated with a weapon, a projectile, a means of expressing (perhaps) anger. If the pen strikes someone, then the word "pen" to that person means something painful, a personal injury, impetus for striking back and so on.

These meanings constantly grow and change because the human mind is always interpreting and reinterpreting. Because of this, deconstruction argues, it never fully settles on *the* stable meaning for the word "pen." Based on this linguistic argument, deconstructionists conclude that since any meanings in words are so quickly diffused, we can never really communicate at all. Words no longer have meaning.1 The postmodern catch word "differance," along with terms like "erasure" and "trace," entered American scholarship through Derrida's writings. By combining the concepts of (and the French words for) "deferment" and "difference," Derrida came up with this name for the endless deferment of meaning that takes place. Derrida claims that differance is the reason that words cannot have meanings; the mind continually understands things in different ways so that the original meaning loses its importance as the *proper* meaning - it becomes a mere trace. Ultimately this is insufficient for today's cultural critics – they need words to mean things so that they can point to artistic works and bemoan how they illustrate or exemplify the repression of minority cultures. But other than its general philosophy, deconstruction offered something more important. It offered the techniques to "show" how all language deconstructs itself.

The deconstructionists specialized in "deconstructing" literary works – although they steadfastly insist that the works deconstruct themselves and the critic only illustrates how this happens. These techniques of deconstruction usually involve isolating the surface meaning of the literary work – the "traditionalist" meaning – and attempting to show how the work itself violates that traditional meaning. For example, they will take a love poem and pick apart the language until they find something that they can interpret as unloving. Elizabeth Barrett Browning's sonnet "How Do I Love Thee? Let Me Count The Ways," ends with the words "I shall but love thee better in death." The clever deconstructionists might combine these with Browning's earlier words, "when feeling out of bounds for the edge of beauty and ideal grace," to conclude that Mrs. Browning is actually reaching for her husband's death. "Why is she looking for the *edge* of beauty?" the deconstructionist asks. "She clearly does not want to remain in or before beauty; instead, she is seeking some way around it." The deconstructionist attributes this apparent disparity to the problem with language, "differance," and quickly concludes that the poem – like all other language – has no meaning.

Once they realized the power of this school of thought, the cultural critics embraced it readily, for here they discovered a method of attack on the traditional interpretations of literary works. They used deconstruction to remove traditional meaning and replaced it with *new* meaning. That meaning was the Political Correctness that infests our society today. For example, after the traditional meaning of "How Do I Love Thee?" has been destabilized in the process described above, a feminist critic might come along and - in the absence of a stable traditional interpretation – declare that the poem is "really" concerned with how women in nineteenth-century England were conditioned to see themselves as secondary to men.

Since "everything is text" in the postmodern mantra, the cultural critics did not hesitate to apply their methods to music, movies, television and anything they encountered. They found that they could remove the meaning from all cultural phenomena and substitute the values of whichever group they preferred. For example, homosexual analysts could remove the truth from the Bible and instead interpret it as full of homophobic hate – God's truth was torn down, and a human political agenda was inserted.

This example is not particularly outrageous, as Derrida's stated goal in deconstructionism was to remove the idea of what he called the "transcendental signified." Standard models of linguistics operate with respect to a signifier-signified pair. The signifier is the word, and the signified is that which the word represents. When differance enters the picture, the thing signified is deferred continually until it can be deferred no longer – that is, until it reaches into the realm of metaphysics. The final meaning reached by any word is God, as He is the ultimate meaning of traditional Western thought.2 The "transcendental signified" of which Derrida is trying to rid himself and the Western world is in fact God. Derrida labels belief in God a product of deficient Western thinking, and in true Nietzchean fashion he claims that God is a construct of language rather than the other way around. Naturally, Derrida quickly became the darling of the American university establishment. He lectured at universities along the Eastern seaboard, and grew to love that area of America. Soon America returned that affection by granting him a position in the English department of Yale University. Yale then began to draw to other deconstructionists and postmodernists; J. Hillis Miller, Geoffrey Hartman and others. Another European, Paul DeMan, also came to America and began teaching deconstruction. DeMan's history provides yet another reason why deconstructionists sought so avidly to remove meaning from language. In pre-World War II Belgium, DeMan had worked for an explicitly pro-Nazi newspaper. DeMan's detractors note that removing the meaning from language was an excellent way to dismiss his pro-Nazi writings.

Through deconstruction the cultural critics adopted a tool that turned literature, philosophy and culture into nonsense. For instance, in his own writing, in order to remain true to his own philosophy, Derrida eschews all forms of the verb "to be." In deconstructionist terms the verb "to be" implies meaning; thus, it cannot exist. Derrida therefore goes back and crosses out all "to be" verbs, making his writing all but incomprehensible. In beginning to attack the signifier-signified construction, Derrida writes "the sign is that ill-named thing, the only one, that escapes the instituting question of philosophy: 'What is…?'" At the same time Derrida is attempting to communicate his ideas about traditional linguistic models, he is forced by his own philosophy to scratch out the very words that allow him to communicate.

If Derrida were to follow the logic of his own theories he would find that the very concept of communicating his ideas by written or spoken word should be impossible. If deconstructionist theories were even remotely accurate, all verbal communication – and by extension all other forms of communication – would be impossible. As New Critic Dr. M. H. Abrams of Cornell University states, "I hope that Derrida remembers that words do mean things next time someone warns him of an oncoming bus." Not only does the embrace of deconstruction harm logical philosophy, it also renders the creation of literature virtually impossible. If words mean nothing, then they are nothing more than sounds. True, Lewis Carroll did create a well-known poem using nonsensical but pleasant-sounding words, but how many poems like "jabberwocky" can be created before we reach the saturation point? (Some would argue that we have already reached that point.)

As university literature departments "progress," the divide widens between those who produce literature and those who analyze and teach it. While Samuel Taylor Coleridge, T.S. Eliot and an entire cadre of great authors were well-educated men, it seems that a literary education in an American university actually *hinders* one's ability to write well. As professors of literature embrace the philosophy of deconstruction they lose the ability to write beautifully because meaning is necessary for beautiful writing. As a result, a distinction has emerged within English departments between M.F.A. (Master of Fine Arts) and Ph.D. programs – to the extent that they now have distinct faculties. America's greatest hope for good literature today lies not in the universities, but in the "amateurs" writing after their nine to five work days or while the kids are at school. The intelligentsia has forgotten its literature in its haste to promote its politics. Already there is a backlash against deconstructionism.

Just as the current thriving generation of critics looked upon New Criticism as passé, so the students of today are beginning to look upon deconstruction as obsolete. Derrida still lectured up to his recent death (he spoke in Washington, D.C. as recently as 1995), but, like their forebears, today's literature students are beginning to rise up and tell their predecessors that they had it all wrong. A primary factor in this backlash is the difficulty that lies in communicating deconstructionist ideas (note that what is offered here is merely an outline, not the actual methods of deconstructing a literary work). As a result of this difficulty, today's MTV generation has stumbled upon a positive side effect of their fifteen-second attention spans: They lack the patience to wade through Derrida's nearly unintelligible syntax and decipher his terminology.

Unfortunately, that has not stopped the cultural critics from indoctrinating this new generation in feminist interpretation, Marxist philosophy and so-called "queer theory." Requirements for reading Shakespeare, Milton, Chaucer, and other dead white males are disappearing to be replaced by options to take studies in "the Roles of Women in the Renaissance" (an excuse to lament the sexism of the past) or "The Bible as Literature" (a course designed to denigrate the Bible as cleverly crafted fiction instead of God's truth).

Deconstruction has succeeded in destabilizing the traditional meanings of texts. What happens next remains to be seen, but there are indications that its influence is waning. Already we see Shakespearean plays revived in the cinema; "Much Ado About Nothing," "Hamlet," and "Romeo and Juliet" – all recently adapted for the screen – have long since been abandoned by the American academy in favor of lesser works. Jane Austen's novels, once highly touted by the intelligentsia as undiscovered works of a female author, are now derided in our universities as being too conservative because of their themes of love and marriage. The popular culture has, in a moment of taste, seen the worth of these and revived them as cinema adaptations. But the real death knell for deconstruction will sound when the next generation of literary critics realizes that the very nature of what it does – read, think, analyze – is antithetical to deconstruction's philosophical goals.

The reliable savior of the intelligentsia is the common man and his common sense. Common sense dictates that words do mean things, and as deconstruction posits otherwise it will be relegated to the margins of society. Sadly, its effects will linger on – it has given a sense of validity to cultural criticism and established a marketplace for its ideas. The deconstructionists are already abandoning their enclave at Yale as their school of thought is eclipsed by trendier, simpler and narrower ideologues. These are the feminists, Marxists and queer theorists – none of whom are leaving their tenured offices peacefully. Instead, they have begun to recruit and train new graduate students to take their places. Applications for graduate and teaching degrees are at an all time high as these campus establishment "radicals" encourage the next generation to help them enshrine their ideology permanently in the American university system.

RADICAL FEMINISM AND POLITICAL CORRECTNESS

Perhaps no aspect of Political Correctness is more prominent in American life today than feminist ideology. Is feminism, like the rest of Political Correctness, based on the cultural Marxism imported from Germany in the 1930s? While feminism's history in America certainly extends longer than sixty years, its flowering in recent decades has been interwoven with the unfolding social revolution carried forward by cultural Marxists.

Where do we see radical feminism ascendant? It is on television, where nearly every major offering has a female "power figure" and the plots and characters emphasize inferiority of the male and superiority of the female. It is in the military, where expanding opportunity for women, even in combat positions, has been accompanied by double standards and then lowered standards, as well as by a decline in enlistment of young men, while "warriors" in the services are leaving in droves. It is in government-mandated employment preferences and practices that benefit women and use "sexual harassment" charges to keep men in line. It is in colleges where women's gender studies proliferate and "affirmative action" is applied in admissions and employment. It is in other employment, public and private, where in addition to affirmative action, "sensitivity training" is given unprecedented time and attention. It is in public schools, where "self awareness" and "self-esteem" are increasingly promoted while academic learning declines. And sadly, we see that "a woman's right to choose" leads many fellow Americans, including many with stewardship of public law and culture, to believe it is "the right thing to do" to allow the most helpless to be put to death. While it is the theme of this essay that the radical feminist movement is embraced by present day Political Correctness ideology, derived from cultural Marxism, feminism as such does have earlier roots. Feminism was conceived and birthed in America in the 1830s, in the generation experiencing the first stage of the industrial revolution. Women, who for centuries had shared the challenges of surviving in an agrarian life, were becoming part of a middle-class gentry with more time and energy to spend writing newspaper articles and novels for their "sisters." The initial stages of the feminization of American culture had started.

These feminists, radical in their time, became a staple of the idealistic Transcendentalists, who included Ralph Waldo Emerson, Henry David Thoreau and many radical Unitarian ministers of the day. They were also abolitionists, bent on destroying slavery and Southern culture as well. Spurred by the rhetoric of Harriet Beecher Stowe (author of *Uncle Tom's Cabin*), Julia Ward Howe (author of the words to "The Battle Hymn of the Republic"), and Margaret Fuller (the first radical feminist newspaper columnist), the men and women of this idealist Transcendentalist generation propelled our nation toward Civil War. Who were these Transcendentalist idealists, and why should we be reminded of them today? They were the precursors of today's idealistic Boomer generation. While we cannot draw a continuous link between the Transcendentalists and today's Boomers, their characteristics are very similar. We may glimpse where the elite Boomers are leading us by reviewing the history of the Transcendentalists and their causes. The Transcendentalists supported abolition of slavery, women's rights, temperance, pacifism (but not in the anti-slavery cause), and other causes which we now observe in New Age popular culture. They developed into spiritualism (talking with the dead), Eastern mysticism and phrenology (discerning personality by the shape of one's skull). They would be right at home in today's New Age milieu. Luther George Williams points out, referring to women's groups and civil rights groups that:

Freed slaves secured the vote only after the 13th, 14th and 15th Amendments (ratified in 1870), but women fared worse. They did not receive the vote until the passage of the 19th Amendment in 1920. However, the substantial political victories that these groups achieved (during the Civil War period) guaranteed that they would remain allies. Today, their political organizations dominate every aspect of society, politics and education in America – including the military. Indeed, the present-day radical feminist assault on VMI and the Citadel has a political parallel to the Transcendentalist activism of the Civil War period. This current assault is in part a continuation of a century-old effort to destroy Southern culture. In contrast to today's radical feminists, social feminists of the 1890s and early 20th century were of a less totalitarian character. They stood for women's suffrage but also advocated the strengthening of the family.

Today, the feminization of American culture, moving rapidly since the 1960s continues to intensify. Radical Feminists demand that women be allowed to "choose" entry to the infantry, artillery, special forces and combat engineering positions in the Army and Marine Corps. These demands follow the Feminization of combat aviation in the U.S. Navy, Air Force and Army since 1993. The feminization of American politics was advanced in the 1996 presidential election, when parties produced "feminized" conventions featuring soft, emotional, Oprah Winfrey-type orations and sentimental film clips of the presidential candidates. Both candidates were portrayed as soft, gentle, emotion-driven creatures sufficiently in touch with their feelings that all women across America would feel "comfortable" in their care. With 60 million female votes at stake, both parties pandered to America's "feminine" side.

There is no doubt in the media that the "man of today" is expected to be a touchyfeely subspecies who bows to the radical feminist agenda. He is a staple of Hollywood, the television network sitcoms and movies, and the political pundits of talk shows. The feminization is becoming so noticeable that newspapers and magazines are picking up on it. For example, the *Washington Times* and *National Review* magazines combined to tell us that "behind the breezy celebration of 'guy stuff' in today's men's magazine lurks a crisis of confidence. What does it mean to be masculine in the 90s?" It is revealed that today's men's magazines (*Esquire, GQ, Men's Health, Men's Fitness, Men's Journal, Details, Maxim, Men's Perspective)*"are all geared to a new feminized man...." Some examples? The old masculine attitude toward personal appearance is disappearing. If memory serves, our fathers' acts of personal upkeep were mostly limited to shaving and putting on a tie. According to Lowry:

[I]t's hard to imagine [them] interested in articles on 'A Flat Belly for the Beach' (Verge), or the three new men's fragrances for the fall season (GQ), or even 'The New Fall Suit' (Esquire). But somewhere along the line men became less concerned with being strong and silent, and more worried about making themselves pretty. Indeed the feminization of American culture is nearly completed. And the last bastion of male domination, the U.S. military, is under assault. If this "feminization" trend were driven only by radical feminists seeking to pull down a perceived male-dominated hierarchy, there would be more hope that the cycles of history would move America toward a stable accommodation between men and women. But the drive is deeper, and it will not be satisfied by any accommodation. The radical feminists have embraced and been embraced by the wider and deeper movement of cultural Marxism. For dedicated Marxists, the strategy is to attack at every point where an apparent disparity leaves a potential constituency of "oppressed" persons – in this case women, who are the largest of all constituencies. Cultural Marxists, men and women, are making the most of it, and the theory developed by the Frankfurt School provides the ideology.

The Frankfurt School theorized that the authoritarian personality is a product of the patriarchal family. This idea is in turn directly connected to Engels's *The Origins of the Family, Private Property and the State,* which promotes matriarchy. Furthermore, it was Karl Marx who wrote in *The Communist Manifesto* about the radical notion of a "community of women." He also, in 1845, wrote disparagingly in his *The German Ideology* of the idea that the family was the basic unit of society.

The concept of the "authoritarian personality" is not just to be interpreted primarily as a model for the conduct of warfare against prejudice as such. It is a handbook for psychological warfare against the American male, to render him unwilling to defend traditional beliefs and values.

In other words, the aim was to emasculate him. Undoubtedly the Institute for Social Research at Frankfurt University meant this, as it used the term "psychological techniques for changing personality." The "authoritarian personality," studied in the 1940s and 1950s by American followers of the Frankfurt School, prepared the way for such psychological warfare against the male gender role. The aim was promoted by Herbert Marcuse and others under the guise of "women's liberation" and under the New Left movement in the 1960s. Evidence that psychological techniques for changing personality are intended to focus in particular on the emasculation of the American male has also been provided by Abraham Maslow, founder of "third force humanist psychology" and promoter of psychotherapeutic techniques in public school classrooms. He wrote that "the next step in personal evolution is a transcendence of both masculinity and femininity to general humanness." Cultural Marxist stalwarts apparently know exactly what they want to do and how they plan to do it. They have actually already succeeded in accomplishing much of their agenda.

How did this situation come about in American universities? Gertrude Himmelfarb has observed that it slipped past traditional academics almost unobserved until it was too late. It occurred so "quietly" that when they "looked up", postmodernism was upon them with a vengeance. "They were surrounded by such a tidal wave of faddish multicultural subjects such as radical feminism, deconstructed relativism as history and other courses" which undermine the perpetuation of Western civilization.10 Indeed, this tidal wave slipped by just as Antonio Gramsci and the Frankfurt School had envisioned – a quiet revolution that could not be resisted by force. The Frankfurt School had devised the concept of designating the opponents of the Marxist cultural revolution as "authoritarian characters." According to available accounts: There was a meeting of American scholars at a conference on religious and racial prejudice in 1944. Over the next five years, a Frankfurt School team under the direction of Max Horkheimer conducted in-depth social and psychological profiles of Americans under a project entitled "Studies of Prejudice."

One of the results was a book entitled "The Authoritarian Personality" by Theodor Adorno, et al, that summarized one of the largest public opinion surveys ever undertaken in the United States. It was published in 1950, and conformed to the original Critical Theory in every respect. As a document which testified to the belief system of the Frankfurt School revolutionaries it was essentially anti-God, anti- Christian, anti-family, anti-nationalist, anti-patriot, anti-conservative, antihereditarian, anti-ethnocentric, anti-masculine, anti-tradition, and anti-morality.

All of these are elements in critical theory. "Cultural Marxism," as preached by the Frankfurt School alumni in the U.S., is being implemented by the elite Boomers. This has laid the foundation for and spurred the widely popular and destructive concepts of "affirmative action," "multiculturalism" and "diversity." One can't escape these terms today. They have grown from the study of anti-Semitism and discrimination by the Institute for Social Research during the 1940s and the systematic infusion of the language of "discrimination," "civil rights," 'women's rights," and other "minority rights" into American culture.

According to Raehn: Critical Theory as applied mass psychology has led to the deconstruction of gender in the American culture. Following Critical Theory, the distinction between masculinity and femininity will disappear. The traditional roles of the mothers and fathers are to be dissolved so that patriarchy will be ended. Children are not to be raised according to their biological genders and gender roles according to their biological differences. This reflects the Frankfurt School rationale for the disintegration of the traditional family. Thus, one of the basic tenets of Critical Theory was the necessity to break down the traditional family. The Frankfurt School scholars preached: Even a partial breakdown of parental authority in the family might tend to increase the readiness of a coming generation to accept social change. The transformation of American culture envisioned by the cultural Marxists goes further than pursuing gender equality. Embodied in their agenda is "matriarchal theory," under which they purpose to transform American culture to be female-dominated. This is a direct throwback to Wilhelm Reich, a Frankfurt School member who considered matriarchal theory in psychoanalytic terms. In 1993, he wrote in "The Mass Psychology of Fascism" that matriarchy was the only genuine family type of "natural society."

Erich Fromm, another charter member of the Institute, was one of the most active advocates of matriarchal theory. Fromm was especially taken with the idea that all love and altruistic feelings were ultimately derived from the maternal love necessitated by the extended period of human pregnancy and postnatal care: Love thus was not dependent on sexuality, as Freud had supposed. In fact, sex was more often tied to hatred and destruction. Masculinity and femininity were not reflections of "essential" sexual differences, as the romantics had thought. They were derived instead from differences in life functions, which were in part socially determined.

This dogma was a precedent for today's radical feminist pronouncements appearing in newspapers and in TV programs, including TV newscasts. For its promoters, male and female roles result from cultural indoctrination – an indoctrination carried out by the male patriarchy to the detriment of women. Indeed, cultural Marxism has, in the 1990s, melded with radical feminism in the elite Boomer generation, that throwback to the dangerous Transcendentalists of the early 19th century. A cauldron of discontent is forming in our nation, a discontent which has the potential to dismantle American civilization. Destructive criticism of primary elements of American culture inspired the 1960s counter-culture revolution. Idealistic Boomers coming of age strove to transform the prevailing culture into its opposites, in the spirit of social revolution. Now the elite Boomers are in positions of power, and they are working to destroy the nation's historic institutions. They aim to destroy as well the heritage we call "Western Civilization."

Richard Bernstein has written in his book on multiculturalism, "the Marxist revolutionary process for the past several decades in America has centered on race and sex warfare rather than class warfare" as in earlier times. This reflects a scheme more total than economics to restructure American society. As the social revolutionaries readily proclaim, their purpose is to destroy the hegemony of white males. To accomplish this, all barriers to the introduction of more women and minorities throughout the "power structure" are to be brought down by all means available. Laws and lawsuits, intimidation, and demonizing of white males as racists and sexists are pursued through the mass media and the universities. The psycho–dynamic of the revolutionary process aim for psychic disempowerment – decapitation – of those who oppose. Steve Forbes has emphasized:

This country's founders recognized three primal values in the Declaration of Independence, and they ranked them properly: Life, liberty, and the pursuit of happiness. Forbes observes that if the order of these fundamental human rights is switched – with happiness before liberty or liberty before life – we come to moral chaos and social anarchy. This very condition is what Judge Robert Bork describes as "modern liberalism." He defines its characteristics as "'radical egalitarianism' (equality of outcomes rather than of opportunities) and 'radical individualism' (the drastic reduction of limit to personal gratification)."

Judge Bork also identifies radical feminism as "the most destructive and fanatical" element of this modern liberalism. He further describes radical feminism as "totalitarian in spirit." Most Americans do not realize that they, through their institutions, are being led by social revolutionaries who think in terms of the continuing destruction of the existing social order in order to create a new one. The revolutionaries are New Age Elite Boomers. They now control the public institutions in the United States. Their "quiet" revolution, beginning with the counter-culture revolution of their youth, is nearing completion. A key, or even a dominant element because purportedly it represents that largest political and social constituency among their potential followers, is feminism. The Marxist movement in its "quiet" cultural latter-day phase is seemingly sweeping all before it. With its sway over the media, fully in the grip of feminism, it is hard to discern the stirrings of a counter-culture. Are the elite Boomers, the New Totalitarians, the most dangerous generation in America's history? William Strauss and Neil Howe suggest so, in their book *Generations: The History of America's Future – 1584 – 2069*. 19 James Kurth writes:

The United States itself has become a great power that opposes much of what was once thought of as Western Civilization, especially its cultural achievements and its social arrangements. The major American elites – those in power in politics, business, the media, and academia – now use American power, especially the "soft power" of information, communications, and popular entertainment, to displace Western Civilization not only in America but also in Europe.

Will American men, of every race, and more traditionalist women of every age and circumstances – who may well be a silent majority of their sex – rise to challenge Political Correctness? Or will American men continue in voluntary submission toward a future of peonage under a new American matriarchy? Would that be a precursor to a condition of anarchy, and an end to America's experiment with democracy? It may well be that the fate of American civilization depends on American men steadfastly resisting Politically Correct feminism. Even more, they must resourcefully oppose the wider grip of Political Correctness, the cultural Marxism for which radical feminism is only one avenue of attack.

Further Readings on the Frankfurt School

Another fact from that long-ago year, 1923, is equally significant: the intended name for the Frankfurt School was the Institute for Marxism. The Institute's father and funder, Felix Weil, wrote in 1971 that he "wanted the Institute to become known, and perhaps famous, due to its contributions to Marxism as a scientific discipline…" Beginning a tradition Political Correctness still carries on, Weil and others decided that they could operate more effectively if they concealed their Marxism; hence, on reflection, they chose the neutral-sounding name, the Institute for Social Research (Insitut für Sozialforschung). But "Weil's heartfelt wish was still to create a foundation similar to the Marx-Engels Institute in Moscow – equipped with a staff of professors and students, with libraries and archives – and one day to present it to a German Soviet Republic." In 1933, this disguised "Institute for Marxism" left Germany and reestablished itself in New York City, where in time it shifted its focus to injecting its ideology into American society. The most readable English-language history of the Frankfurt School is Martin Jay's book, The Dialectical Imagination: A History of the Frankfurt School and the Institute for Social Research, 1932 - 1950 (University of California Press, Berkeley, CA, 1973 – new edition in 1996). This book is in print in paperback and can be ordered through any bookstore. The reader should be aware that Jay's book is, in the words of another work on the Frankfurt School, a "semiofficial' history, which is to say that it is largely uncritical. Like virtually all other English-language authors on the Institute, Jay is on the political left. Nonetheless, the book provides a solid factual introduction to the Frankfurt School, and the reader should have little trouble discerning in it the roots and origins of today's Political Correctness.

In his first chapter, "The Creation of the Institut für Sozialforschung and Its First Frankfurt Years," Jay lays bare the Institute's Marxist origins and nature, and equally its efforts to conceal both: "The original idea of calling it the Institut für Marxismus (Institute for Marxism) was abandoned as too provocative, and a more Aesopian alternative was sought (not for the last time in the Frankfurt School's history)." Of the Institute's first director, Carl Grünberg, Jay writes, "Grünberg concluded his opening address by clearly stating his personal allegiance to Marxism as a scientific methodology. Just as liberalism, state socialism, and the historical school had institutional homes elsewhere, so Marxism would be the ruling principle at the Institut." Jay's first chapter also introduces the Institute's critical shift that laid the basis for today's Political Correctness, a.k.a. cultural Marxism: "if it can be said that in early years of its history the Institut concerned itself primarily with an analysis of bourgeois society's socio-economic substructure, in the years after 1930 its prime interest lay in its cultural superstructure."

The second chapter, "The Genius of Critical Theory," gets at the heart of the "Critical Studies" departments that now serve as the fonts of Political Correctness on American college campuses. All of these are branches and descendants of the Critical Theory first developed in the 1930s by the Frankfurt School. The term "Critical Theory" is itself something of a play on words. One is tempted to ask, "OK, what is the theory?" The answer is, "The theory is to criticize." Jay writes, "Critical Theory, as its name implies, was expressed through a series of critiques of other thinkers and philosophical traditions...Only by confronting it in its own terms, as a gadly of other systems, can it be fully understood." The goal of Critical Theory was not truth, but praxis, or revolutionary action: bringing the current society and culture down through unremitting, destructive criticism. According to Jay, "The true object of Marxism, Horkheimer argued (Max Horkheimer succeeded Carl Grünberg as director of the Institute in July, 1930), was not the uncovering of immutable truths, but the fostering of social change." The central question facing the Institute in the early 1930s was how to apply Marxism to the culture. The title of Jay's third chapter gives the answer: "The Integration of Psychoanalysis." Here, Jay's book falls down to some extent, in that it does not offer a clear understanding of how the Institute integrated Marx and Freud. The answer appears to be that Freud's later critiques were made conditional on a capitalist, bourgeois order: a revolutionary, post-capitalist society could "liberate" man from his Freudian repression.

Here again one sees key aspects of Political Correctness emerging, including a demand for sexual "liberation" and the attack on "patriarchal" Western culture. If the precise nature of the blending of Marx and Freud is left open by Jay, his next chapter makes the blend's application clear: "The Institute's First Studies of Authority." The Institute left Germany for New York in 1933 because the Nazis came to power in Germany. Not surprisingly, one of the Institute's first tasks in New York was to oppose Nazism. It did so largely by concocting a psychological "test" for an "authoritarian personality." Supposedly, people with this authoritarian personality were likely to support Nazism. Both the concept and the methodology were doubtful at best. But the Institute's work laid down an important tool for the left, namely a notion that anyone on the right was psychologically unbalanced. And it marked a key turning for the Institute in the birth of Political Correctness in America, in that the empirical research the studies demanded was done on Americans. Ultimately, the result was Institute member Theodor Adorno's vastly influential book, The Authoritarian Personality, published in 1950.

Jay's fifth chapter, "The Institute's Analysis of Nazism," continues the theme of the "authoritarian personality." But his sixth, "Aesthetic Theory and the Critique of Mass Culture," provides an answer to the question of why most "serious" modern art and music is so awful. It is intended to be. Theodor Adorno was the Institute's lead figure on high culture – he began life as a music critic and promoter of Schönberg – and his view was that in the face of the "repressiveness" of bourgeois society, art could only be "true" if it were alienating, reflecting the alienated society around it. Jay quotes Adorno: "A successful work...is not one which resolves objective contradictions in a spurious harmony, but one which expresses the idea of harmony negatively by embodying the contradictions, pure and uncompromised, in its innermost structure."

Adorno despised the new mass culture – film, radio, and jazz – in what seems to be a case of missed opportunity: today, the entertainment industry is the single most powerful promoter of Political Correctness. Another key Frankfurt School figure, Walter Benjamin, did see the potential: "he paradoxically held out hope for the progressive potential of politicized, collectivized art."10 At some point, someone – the question of who lies beyond the boundaries of Jay's book – put Benjamin's perception together with the Frankfurt School's general view, which Jay summarizes as "the Institut came to feel that the culture industry enslaved men in far more subtle and effective ways than the crude methods of domination practiced in earlier eras."

In the remainder of the book, Jay traces the (sort of) empirical work of the Institute in the 1940s, which was beset by the same problems as their earlier survey "research," and follows the Institute in its return to Frankfurt, Germany after World War II. But by this point, the reader will already have the picture. He will have seen how Marxism was translated from economic into cultural terms; discerned the themes of sexual liberation, feminism, "victims" and so on that make up today's Political Correctness; and found in Critical Theory the origins of the endless wailing about "racism, sexism and homophobia" that "PC" pours forth. One key piece of history is missing: "an analysis of Marcuse's influential transmission of the Frankfurt School's work to a new American audience in the 1960s," as Jay puts it in his epilogue. Also, Jay curiously passes over with only the most minimal discussion the effective move of the Institute, in the persons of Horkheimer and Adorno, to Los Angeles during the war. Did the connections they built there play any role in injecting the Frankfurt School's philosophy into American film and, after the war, television? Jay does not touch upon the subject. But for the reader new to the Frankfurt School as the source of today's Political Correctness, Jay's The Dialectical Imagination offers a solid base. The book concludes with an extensive (though not annotated) bibliography of works by and about the Frankfurt School.

As to other accessible works about the Frankfurt School, the definitive modern work in German has recently been translated into English: The Frankfurt School: Its History, Theories and Political Significance by Rolf Wiggershaus, (translated by Michael Robertson, The MIT Press, Cambridge, MA, first paperback edition 1995). This covers much of the same ground as Martin Jay's book, although it also follows the Institute from its post-war return to Germany up to Adorno's death in 1969. Wiggershaus is more detailed than Jay, and, although he too is on the left politically, he is more critical than Jay. In the book's Afterword, Wiggershaus offers a brief look (and a hostile one) at some German conservative critiques of the Frankfurt School. A picture emerges that will seem familiar to Americans entrapped in the coils of Political Correctness:

Since the publication in 1970 of his book The Poverty of Critical Theory, Rohrmoser has promulgated, in constantly varying forms, the view that Marcuse, Adorno, and Horkheimer were the terrorists' intellectual foster-parents, who were using cultural revolution to destroy the traditions of the Christian West. Academics such as Ernst Topitsch and Kurt Sontheimer, who saw themselves as educators and liberal democrats, followed in Rohrmoser's footsteps. In 1972 Topitsch, a critical rationalist who was Professor of Philosophy in Graz, had stated that behind the slogans of "rational discussion" and "dialogue free of domination" there was being established at the universities "a distinct terrorism of political convictions such as never existed before, even under Nazi tyranny." Additional works on the Frankfurt School include:

- The Frankfurt School by T.B. Bottomore (Tavistock, London, 1984). Another history written by a sympathizer; you are better off with Jay or Wiggershaus.
- "The New Dark Age: The Frankfurt School and 'Political Correctness'" by Michael Minnicino, in Fidelio, Vol. 1, No. 1, Winter 1992 (KMW Publishing, Washington, DC) One of the few looks at the Frankfurt School by someone not a sympathizer, this long journal article explains the role of the Institute for Social Research in creating the ideology we now know as "Political Correctness." Unfortunately, its value is reduced by some digressions that lack credibility.
- Angela Davis: An Autobiography by Angela Davis (Random House, New York 1974) Angela Davis, a leading American black radical and Communist Party member, was described by Frankfurt School member Herbert Marcuse as "my best student." She also studied in Frankfurt under Adorno. This book shows the link between the Institute for Social Research and the New Left of the 1960s through the eyes of a key participant.
- The Young Lukacs and the Origins of Western Marxism by Andrew Arato (Seabury Press, New York, 1979). The author is, as usual, a sympathizer, but this work shows the key role Lukacs played in the thinking of the Frankfurt School and, later, the New Left.
- The Origin of Negative Dialectics: Theodor W. Adorno, Walter Benjamin and the Frankfurt Institute by Susan Buck-Morss (Free Press, New York, 1977). An important book on the relationship of the Frankfurt School and Critical Theory to the New Left.
- Introduction to Critical Theory: Horkheimer to Habermas by David Held (University of California Press, Berkeley, 1980). Yet another history by a fan of the Frankfurt School, but valuable for its discussion of the impact of Nietzsche on key Frankfurt School figures. Beyond these secondary works lies the vast literature produced by members of the Frankfurt School itself. Some key works were written in English, and many of those written in German are available in translation. As is usually the case with Marxist works, the prose style and vocabulary are often so convoluted as to make them almost unreadable. Further, the refusal of the Frankfurt School to make its own future vision plain led many of its members to write in aphorisms, which adds yet another layer of impenetrableness.

One work, however, is of such importance that it must be recommended despite its difficulty: Eros and Civilization by Herbert Marcuse (Beacon Press, Boston, first paperback edition in 1974 and still in print). Subtitled A Philosophical Inquiry into Freud, this book holds center stage for two reasons. First, it completes the task of integrating Marx and Freud. While the Marxism is *sotto voce*, the whole framework of the book is in fact Marxist, and it is through the framework that Freud is considered. Second, Eros and Civilization and its author were the key means of transmission by which the intellectual work of the Frankfurt School was injected into the student rebellion of the 1960s. This book became the bible of the young radicals who took over America's college campuses from 1965 onward, and who are still there as faculty members. In brief, Eros and Civilization urges total rebellion against traditional Western culture – the "Great Refusal" – and promises a Candyland utopia of free sex and no work to those who join the revolution. About two-thirds of the way through the book, Marcuse offers this summary of its arguments:

Our definition of the specific historical character of the established reality principle led to a reexamination of what Freud considered to be universal validity. We questioned this validity in view of the historical possibility of the abolition of the repressive controls imposed by civilization. The very achievements of this civilization seemed to make the performance principle obsolete, to make the repressive utilization of the instincts archaic. But the idea of a non-repressive civilization on the basis of the achievements of the performance principle encountered the argument that instinctual liberation (and consequently total liberation) would explode civilization itself, since the latter is sustained only through renunciation and work (labor) – in other words, through the repressive utilization of instinctual energy. Freed from these constraints, man would exist without work and without order; he would fall back into nature, which would destroy culture. To meet this argument, we recalled certain archetypes of imagination which, in contrast to the culture-heroes of repressive productivity, symbolized creative receptivity. These archetypes envisioned the fulfillment of man and nature, not through domination and exploitation, but through release of inherent libidinal forces. We then set ourselves the task of "verifying" these symbols – that is to say, demonstrating their truth value as symbols of a reality beyond the performance principle. We thought that the representative content of the Orphic and Narcissistic images was the erotic reconciliation (union) of man and nature in the aesthetic attitude, where order is beauty and work is play.

Marcuse continues after this summary to lay out the erotic content of the "reality beyond the performance principle," i.e., a new civilization where work and productivity were unimportant. "The basic experience in this (aesthetic) dimension is sensuous rather than conceptual," that is, feelings are more important than logic: "The discipline of aesthetics installs the *order of sensuousness* as against the *order of reason*."

"In German, *sensuousness* and *sensuality* are still rendered by one and the same term: *Sinnlichkeit*. It connotes instinctual (especially sexual) gratification... No longer used as a full-time instrument of labor, the body would be resexualized... (which) would first manifest itself in a reactivation of all erotogenic zones and, consequently, in a resurgence of pre-genital polymorphous sexuality and in a decline of genital supremacy. The body in its entirety would become an object of cathexis, a thing to be enjoyed – an instrument of pleasure. This change in the value and scope of libidinal relations would lead to a disintegration of the institutions in which the private interpersonal relations have been organized, particularly the monogamic and patriarchal family."

This in a book which Marcuse dedicated to Sophie Marcuse, his wife of fifty years! It is easy to see how this message – "If it feels good, do it" – published in 1955 resonated with the student rebels of the 1960s.

Marcuse understood what most of the rest of his Frankfurt School colleagues did not: the way to destroy Western civilization – the objective set forth by George Lukacs in 1919 – was not through abstruse theory, but through sex, drugs, and rock 'n' roll. Marcuse wrote other works for the new generation that spawned the New Left – One Dimensional Man (1964), Critique of Pure Tolerance (1965), An Essay on Liberation (1969), Counterrevolution and Revolt (1972). But Eros and Civilization was and remains the key work, the one that put the match to the tinder. Other central works by members of the Frankfurt School include:

- The Authoritarian Personality by Theodor Adorno (Harper, New York, 1950). This book is the basis for everything that followed that portrayed conservatism as a psychological defect. It had enormous impact, not least on education theory.
- Dialectic of Enlightenment by Theodor Adorno and Max Horkheimer (trans. by John Cumming, Verso, London, 1979). A complex philosophical work written during World War II largely in response to Nazism (and extensively devoted to discussions of anti-Semitism), this work seeks to find a kernel of "liberating" reason in the ruins of the Enlightenment.
- Minima Moralia: Reflections from a Damaged Life by Theodor Adorno (trans. E.F.N. Jophcott, New Left Books, London, 1974). A book of aphorisms, almost entirely incomprehensible, but the effective conclusion of Adorno's work.
- Escape from Freedom by Erich Fromm (Farrar & Rinehart, New York, 1941, still in print in paperback) Fromm was the Institute's "happy face," and this book was often required reading at colleges in the 1960s. The thesis is that man's nature causes him to throw his freedom away and embrace fascism unless he "masters society and subordinates the economic machine to the purposes of human happiness," i.e., adopts socialism. At this point Fromm was in the process of breaking away from the Institute and his subsequent works cannot be considered as part of the Frankfurt School corpus.
- Eclipse of Reason (Oxford University Press, New York, 1947). Essentially a sequel to Dialectic of Enlightenment, the book is heavily the work of Adorno and other Frankfurt School personages, although only Horkheimer name appeared on it. Its contents are based on a series of lectures Horkheimer gave at Columbia University in 1944. The prose style is surprisingly readable, but the contents are odd; there is throughout a strong nostalgia, which was normally anathema to the Frankfurt School. The key chapter, "The Revolt of Nature," reflects a strange Retro anarchism: "The victory of civilization is too complete

to be true. Therefore, adjustment in our times involves an element of resentment and suppressed fury."

- Critical Theory: Selected Essays by Max Horkheimer (trans. Matthew O'Connell, Seabury Press, New York, 1972). The essay, "Traditional and Critical Theory" is especially important.
- The Essential Frankfurt School Reader, ed. By Andrew Arato and Eike Gebhardt (Continuum, New York, 1982, in print in paperback) Not an introduction to the Frankfurt School, but rather a reprinting of Frankfurt School essays not available elsewhere, this book is more useful to the specialist than the novice. Nonetheless, both the editors' lengthy introductions and some of the essays are useful (once again, the editors are solidly on the Left politically, and their style is as heavy as that of the Frankfurt School's members).

This small bibliography will be enough to get an interested reader started; the full literature on and by the Frankfurt School is immense, as the bibliographies in Jay's and Wiggershaus's books attest. What has been missing from it, at least in English, is a readable book, written for the layman, that explains the Frankfurt School and its works in terms of the creation of Political Correctness. This short volume is at least a start in filling that gap.

6

WHY WOMEN SHOULD RULE THE WORLD

WHY MEN ARE NOT FEMINISTS

It's a strange fact that when Feminists used to take to the streets agitating for sexual equality, you rarely see men marching along with them. You can find both sexes protesting about worker's rights, race equality, and the rights of homosexuals, but Feminism? If you find men involved they always seem to want to keep quiet about it. The only man I heard openly advocating Feminism was the English poet Robert Graves. Yet he was criticised by many Feminists because they claimed his brand of Feminism was not about equality, but that women should rule the world.

Feminism is about the equality of the sexes and this makes perfect sense to most women. From the time of Mary Wollstonecraft's *A Vindication Of The Rights Of women* in 1792, until now, women have written countless book on sex equality. Yet we don't find many male authors writing about Feminism, unless it is about why it can't work. (like *The Inevitability of Patriarchy*). Nor do we find many men protesting on the street about this either. Men either make jokes about Feminism and political correctness or claim that Feminism has gone too far and men now are being discriminated against! Or they just keep quiet about the whole subject.

In my personal experience I have found that Feminists themselves regard many men who voice any sympathy about Feminism with deep suspicion. Most Feminists groups have a very strict rule about not allowing men into their groups. Which is a strange rule for a group that advocates, equality, political correctness and anti-discrimination.. Though I can understand why they don't want men in their groups. There is admittedly the problem of some, big I am, turning up and lecturing them on why Feminism won't work, or attempt to take over. This was the experience of Feminists during the 1970s. They then allowed men into their groups, but even very sympathetic and well-intended men still tended to dominate the conversation and compete with women within the group. For this reason most Feminist groups ended up banning men.

The most famous case of this was the Greenham Common Peace Camp. In 1981 a group of 36 women started a protest against the deployment of cruise missiles at an American Air Base, at Greenham Common. This began a mass protest of both men and women but soon the women started to ban men from their camps around the site. Some camps placed a complete ban on men while others only allowed men to join them to protest during the daytime. This was given as one of the reasons why the Greenham Common protest was so successful, because men didn't interfere with the unity of the women.

Yet the very fact of banning men undermines the Feminist ideal of sexual equality. Because it is a admission by Feminists that they cannot make equality with men work, even in just Feminist meetings and protest movements. So if they are willing to acknowledge that they cannot create equality with men in groups that actually advocate sexual equality. Now do they expect to do the same in all other aspects of life?

So why is sexual equality strongly advocated by women but men show little interest? The obvious reason would be that women have something to gain through sexual equality. Whist men have something to lose. That is to say, men would lose dominance over women. While women have progressed from a position of servitude to that of equal opportunities in the West at least. This is true in all aspects of life. If you are a serf, slave or live in poverty, then equality sounds like a really great idea. If on the other hand, you are a wealthy member of the ruling elite, then of course, equality is a very dangerous, stupid and totally impracticable idea.

Perhaps this argument might be a bit too hard on men. After all it was 100% male governments in the early 20th century who voted to give women equal voting rights. It was also male dominated legislative chambers who voted to pass equal opportunity laws for women in the 1960s and 70s. So it does seem that the majority of men in the Western world are not actually opposed to Feminism, and secretly many men seem to support it. Yet even men who will support Feminist women, do not seem that enthusiastic about sexual equality. The problem might be that equality is a totally alien concept to the masculine mind.

For many men the whole of life is a big competitive game. In fact some men do talk about, "the game of life". The only trouble with treating life as one big game is that there will always be winners and losers. Which doesn't seem to be a problem if you are a winner, but a real problem if you happen to be a loser. If you happen to come from a wealthy family and have gone to university and have a well paid job, like a lawyer. Then you are not going to see a problem with treating life as just one big game, because you are on the winning team. It is of interest that many people who do live in poverty are contemptuously referred to as losers by some of the well off. They will even go as far as to claim that it is people's own fault if they live in poverty. Forgetting that in a world of winners and losers, you cannot have winners without losers.

In fact in any competitive game the losers always far outnumber winners. We can see this in any sporting competition you might have hundreds of individuals or teams enter it, but in the end you can only have one winner. So in a competition like the football World Cup it was started with hundreds of teams seeking qualification, but all finally got defeated and knocked out, except for the single winner. The same is true of the game of life, the poor and powerless far outnumber the rich and powerful.

Men have dominated our world for the last five thousand years. Yet if we go through every society ruled by men, what we don't find is any form of equality. Even political movements that have set out with the firm intention to create equality have totally failed in this. If we go back to the English Civil War of 1642-8 between the King Charles 1 and Parliament, it was started because of the dictatorial behaviour of Charles 1 who wanted to dissolve Parliament and rule alone. This created a bitterly fought war, (the worst internal war in English history) and guess what happened? Cromwell, the commander-in-chief of the Parliament forces became dictator and it was HE who ended up dissolving Parliament! Which was supposed to be what the Civil war was all about. The idealists of the time agitated to create an equal society, but they soon ended up in jail or on the scaffold. (Even equal rights between men and women were briefly discussed before Cromwell took control). The dictatorship of Cromwell was so bad that within a few years after his death, Charles 2 the son of the hated Charles 1, was invited back to rule England.

Egalitarianism was also the aim of the French Revolution in the 18th century, yet again all they created was a dictatorship and a reign of terror ruled by people like Robespierre and later Napoleon. Who was so competitive that he tried to conquer the world. The same was to happen in the communist revolutions of the 20th century where brutal dictators like Stalin and Mao Tse-tung took power. All these revolutions ended up creating tyrants, far worse than the ones they replaced. So the lesson here was that violent revolution is probably the worse possible way to try and create equality. Because all you do is to replace one group of very competitive men with another group of competitive men. What is more, the new rulers are likely to be also very violent men, because this was the way they obtained power.

The exception to this rule is the American Revolution. Where although the commander-in-chief of the revolutionary army George Washington did also became the President. Fortunately unlike Cromwell he didn't lose sight of why the revolution was fought. In his term of office he showed he believed in Democracy and wasn't interested in becoming a dictator. Another exception was Marshell Tito who although he was an extremely ruthless and violent partisan leader during World War Two. When he became dictator of Yugoslavia he turned out to be a reasonably enlightened leader. He was able to keep the Balkans in peace while he was in power, but unfortunately when he died the whole country split apart into violence. So it is possible for men of violence to become reasonable enlighten rulers but unfortunately they are a small minority.

Men themselves have seen that our very unequal world is a problem, and have attempted to do something about it through political movements like Communism, Socialism and Democracy. Unfortunately in all these systems only Democracy has worked. Though even with Democracy it took a long time to find a way to make it possible. The ancient Greeks and Romans tried it out, but it created so many disputes, it was finally given up as impossibility. So people switched back to dictatorship and kingship. Men have for a long time been searching for better ways to rule their societies. It is a sign of progress that Democracy was finally made to work in modern times after it was abandoned two thousand years ago in ancient Greece and Rome.

The problem with the failure of Communism and Socialism as well as the failure of Democracy in ancient times is that it takes away all hope of creating a just and equal society. Capitalists claim that competition is essential to motivate men. Some even go, as far to claim, "greed is good". This is perfectly true from the viewpoint of a wealthy businessman. From the viewpoint of those living in poverty, greed is a source of frustration, envy and even hatred. So it means that in positive way greed can motivate men to work hard to achieve their desires. Or in a negative way it can motivate men towards hatred, envy, crime and violent revolution. Also greed is not the best motivation for political leaders, as it is more likely to make them corrupt, or to become conquers of other nations. While competitive desires seem to motive politicians to want power for its own sake. That is to say they have become a winner, (the champion politician of their country) and the exercise of power is all they are interested in.

Yet we cannot just blame dictators and world leaders for all the ills of the world. They are ordinary competitive men who just happen to get to the top of the heap. All men, it seems, like nothing better to do than to be involved in competitive games with each other. If they are not playing competitive games with other men, then they like to watch them, as we can see with the great popularity of sport on TV. Because of this, it is men's competitive instinct that has made capitalism such a success in our world. One of the reasons why Communism and Socialism failed was that it didn't allow competitiveness in industry. Resulting in communist industry stagnating and becoming very inefficient, while in the Western world industry was made very efficient and progressive by the competition between industrial companies. Democracy is also only possible because of competition between political parties for power. That is the upside of competition but it also has a terrible downside.

Rulers of countries have for centuries competed with each other so vigorously that they have gone to war with each other. Conquers like Alexander the Great, Julius Caesar, Genghis Khan, Napoleon and Hitler have conquered and destroyed many countries and caused the deaths of millions of people. Just so they can proudly say, "wow, look how many countries I've conquered". In fact their attitude doesn't seem to be much different to say a famous tennis player who has won the grand slam, and wants to be remembered as the greatest tennis player of all time. The difference is that the only harm a great sporting hero causes is the bruised egos of some of his opponents. With a great conqueror we are talking about widespread death, destruction and suffering of millions of people. So for five thousand years of human history, competition between countries and rulers has led to countless wars and acts of genocide. This became so bad in the 20th century that whole cities were destroyed in the Second World War through aerial bombing. As well as the many instances of genocide practised in Nazi Germany, Cambodia, The Balkans and Rwanda. Also in the Cold War between NATO counties and the Soviet Union both sides armed themselves with enough nuclear weapons to destroy the planet many times over.

The competition between the USSR and the USA became really crazy during the Cold War. In the 1950s and early 60s, there was competition about who could produce the biggest nuclear explosion. The Soviet Union won this one. A hydrogen bomb test conducted by the Soviet Union in 1961 detonated with an explosive force of 50 megatons, or 3300 times the power of the Hiroshima and Nagasaki bombs, which were "only" 1-1.5 kilotons. The winning Soviet explosion was so large that it punched through atmosphere above it, right into outer space. It frightened both sides so much they decided to give up on this, one-up man ship game, as scientists on both sides informed their leaders that a bigger explosion might do permanent damage to the biosphere. There was also a concern that nuclear testing in the atmosphere was producing radiation fall out. Even though the politicians of the time claimed, "that there was no scientific proof that fall out from nuclear bombs was harmful to humans." How many times since have we the public receive reassurances like this? Anyway you can't let little problems like the radiation poisoning of whole countries, get in the way of being able to proudly say, "we built the biggest bomb in the world". Can you?

Then there was the space race where both sides spent billions of dollars just to get the first man on the moon. As well as a competition about who had the most nuclear missiles. At the end of the Cold War the USSR had 39,000 nuclear warheads while USA had "only" 24,000. Why both sides needed so many nuclear weapons was never made clear. It was just another case of the competitive spirit among men getting completely out of hand. Yet because of it, for four decades from the 1950s to the 1980s people all over the world lived in fear of a Third World War that would wipe out the whole human race.

There was even one case where a defect in the defence computer of the Soviet Union, told its operators that they were under missile attack from the USA. Fortunately the man in charge knew that the computer wasn't reliable and waited for confirmation from other sources, before he would give the order to launch a counter strike. He was then thrown out of the military for disobeying orders! Still it was better than being court marshalled and then shot, as would normally happen in the USSR. I suppose the only consolation he had, was that he is the only man ever; who can claim he single-handedly saved the world. It is total insanity that because of fierce competition between the super powers, we came that close to committing global suicide. The Americans indirectly admitted to this insanity by naming their nuclear strategy M.A.D (Mutually

Assured Destruction). This then means that men's competitive instinct rules out completely any chance of men creating an equal society or overcoming the suffering of poverty. Because it is natural for men to compete with each other about, "who is boss around here"? We live in a "winner takes it all" world where the rich and powerful want more and more power and wealth and the poor get nothing.

USA is the most competitive capitalist country in the world; this undoubtedly makes it the most dynamic and go-ahead state in the world. The downside of this ferocious competition is that 0.5% of the population of the USA own as much as the bottom 90%. It is no wonder the rich and wealthy like capitalism so much. It is these individuals that own all TV stations, film companies and newspapers, so it is natural for them to use the media to sing the praises of capitalism as much as they can. USA is the richest country in the world yet 45 million of its people live below the poverty line and over 40% have no medical cover.

To add insult to injury the rich don't even pay taxes. In most Western countries an entire industry has been created to help the rich to minimise their payment of taxation. So successful has this industry become that accountants make a mockery of taxation laws and use myriad of personal allowances, pension rights, deductible expenses and reinvestment allowances to allow their rich clients not to pay taxation. As one American millionairess once remarked, "Only poor people pay taxes".

The rich also put their money in overseas accounts, well away from the reach of the taxman. The point is that this means that it is only the poor and middle class have to pay the taxes, to keep the infrastructure of individual countries going, as well as to pay for the trillion dollar arms industry. The reason why this happens it that this wealthy rule the world, and so can make up their own rules and laws to suit themselves. It is also the big advantage of globalisation, as it makes it so much easier for the super rich to dodge taxation.

We live in a world where, it seems "nice guys come last". The fact is that you are unlikely to be the leader of a country, a religion or international business by being a compassionate, caring and loving person. The only exception to this I know is Nelson Mandela, he became president of South Africa because the previous white minority government was under pressure to give in to majority rule. Fortunately because Nelson Mandela the leader of the biggest party was a genuine forgiving and caring man, it was easy for the white politicians to hand power over to him. So we had a non-violent hand over of power to majority rule. Had Nelson Mandela been a different sort of person, the white minority in power may of wanted to fight it out, like they did in Zimbabwe. This was because they had to deal with a very different sort of leader in Robert Mugabe, who has since become another brutal dictator.

So it is possible for a caring and compassionate politician to make a positive difference to our world. Unfortunately Nelson Mandela is more the exception that proves the rule. Most politicians get to these positions of power through being ruthless, aggressive and devious. Political leaders even make claims that they are very tough and ruthless to get votes. Then we wonder why we live in an unjust and uncaring world. The point is that because we live in a world where only the most competitive, ruthless and Machiavellian people get to the top, it is no wonder that equality seems totally impossible in our world.

So where does this leave Feminism? Nowhere unfortunately. Today in the Western world we have laws to enforce equal opportunity. Now note the phrasing here, it says equal OPPORTUNITY not sex EQUALITY. Yes, by law women can in theory be equal to men, the catch is, women have to play the man's game and behave like competitive men.

This is the problem identified by Feminists themselves. Over more than a generation after the first equal opportunity laws were passed in the Western world, women on average are still paid far less then men, while the vast majority of the top jobs are still in the hands of men. If we look at this problem worldwide we find that women only own 1% of the world's wealth. This means that 99% of world's wealth is still owned by men. It makes you realise that the great progress that women seem to have made over the 20th century for equality, is still very much an illusion. Perhaps the only thing you can say about it that it is better than perhaps the 0001% that existed in the 19th century. Where women by law had few rights to own any property and didn't even have the right to vote. The problem for Feminists is that if women want to get top jobs they have to act like a Margaret Thatcher and become totally ruthless and uncaring. It seems only a small minority of women want to do this.

The solution given by Feminists is that we have to change the whole structure of society, because every social system in the world was created by men, for men. So they reflect men's competitive instincts and strengths. This then means if we have Democracy we have to have ferocious competition between political parties for power. If we don't have this, Democracy is eroded to the degree that it doesn't matter which party you vote for, the policies are the same. (Which is true in both the UK and the USA today). The same is true for the capitalist system. Capitalism only works while there is again ruthless competition between companies. If one company becomes too successful it will take over its competitors or put them out of business. Then it becomes a monopoly with no competition. Or if you are only left with a few large companies they will start to wonder why they need to compete with each other, when it is so much easier to co-operate. So they form a secret cartel and we soon have price fixing and complacency. This has happen in all the older industries. In the first half of the 20th century there were hundreds of car and aircraft companies competing with each other for customers. At the end of the 20th century there are only two large companies in the world that make commercial airlines and only a handful of car manufacturers, who are all in each other's pockets.

This then means that if the Feminists have their way and ruthless competition is eliminated, then men would be at a serious disadvantage, because without competition men do seem to lose interest in what they are doing. This is clearly demonstrated in communist countries where industries stagnated because of the lack of competition. Communists only did well in competing or fighting against the USA, as we can see in Vietnam, where a third world country defeated a super power. (Though admittedly they were well armed by the Soviet Union). This was also true in the space race. In fact during most of the 1950s and 60s the USSR was far ahead of USA in putting the first satellite, the first man, the first woman and the first space station in space. They only missed out on the main prize of putting the first man on the moon, and since then have lagged far behind. Now, without the competition between the Soviet Union and America, space exploration has stagnated.

So it seems competition is essential for men to be efficient. The problem is that competition can lead to possible global suicide, as we saw in the Cold War. It also creates a world of winners and losers, where the majority of the people of the world are losers in that they live in poverty. While the small minority of winners keep all the wealth of the world in their greedy hands. Another problem is that in a competitive world everyone is so busy looking after number one and no one is looking where they are going. This can create unbelievable cock-ups.

In 1960 the oil producing countries of Iran, Iraq, Kuwait, Saudi Arabia and Venezuela got together to form a cartel called OPEC because they wanted to prevent the trend of falling oil prices. Later on other oil producing counties also joined. Then in 1973 Egypt and Syria attacked Israel to try and regain all the territory they had lost in the previous Six-Day War of 1967. At first the war went well for the Arab states and Israel appealed to USA for more weapons. President Nixon acceded to this request and publicly proposed a $2.2 billion military aid package for Israel. This greatly angered the Arab countries that decided to use the power of OPEC as an oil weapon.

OPEC imposed an oil embargo on USA and Europe and agreed a $3.00 a barrel price rise. In the end this didn't make any difference and Israel won the war. Yet as a result of the greatly increased oil price OPEC countries found themselves awash with so much money, they didn't know what to do with it. Some of them bought brand new toys like the latest weapons that arms dealers could supply them, and what was left over they invested in international banks. Now this was to cause a big problem because the banks didn't know what to do with the surplus money either, until someone had the bright idea of loaning the money to poor third world countries. The theory being that developing countries would be able to invest in projects to industrialise their countries. That was the theory; the reality was a total disaster.

Most third world countries are ruled by corrupt dictatorships, so the money that was lent, went into buying arms, and starting a third world arms race. Which suited countries like Britain, as arms are its biggest export earner. As well as the USA because it is, the biggest arms exporter in the world. Money was also squandered on large inappropriate projects. Which again suited many Western governments, as it was Western engineering companies that built dams and other grandiose schemes the politicians thought up. Also unfortunately much of the money simply ended up in the pockets of corrupt officials. The only exception to this for a while was India, which was ruled at the time by Indira Gandhi. Although she took the opportunity to borrow from the World Bank she was prudent enough to make sure she was able to pay back later everything she borrowed. Unfortunately she was assassinated in 1984 and her son Rajiv Gandhi became leader. He didn't have any of his mother's prudence and borrowed heavily and soon found he was unable to pay the money back, plunging India into debt.

The result was that all these third world countries were unable not only to pay back the original debt but unable to pay back the INTEREST on the debt. The IMF and World Bank stepped in and demanded that these countries started to go over to planting cash crops like cotton for export money and not crops to feed their own people. They also demanded cut backs on government spending. The result was these governments cut back on health care and education for the people. (You couldn't seriously expect them to cut back on far more important things like arms, bribes and high salaries for important government officials, could you?) Which was a disaster because without proper education for the people, there is no way a developing country can catch up with the developed world. Also without proper health care, and using land to grow cash crops for export, there has been an increase in the mortality rate of people in the third world through disease and starvation.

The scale of this tragedy can been seen by the following statistics. Internationally, 815 million people worldwide go hungry. We live on a planet where 55% of the 12 million child deaths each year are caused by malnutrition. And it's getting worse. According to the United Nations, the poorest countries are worse off now, than they were 30 years ago.

The irony of this is that if any third world country wants to have a fight with its neighbour or have a civil war, guns and a limitless supply of ammunition are readily available. Yet money for education, heath care is in short supply for these countries, but then you got to get your priorities right haven't you? You cannot deny men the fun of playing with exciting toys like machine guns; tanks and flamethrowers can you?

Yet we have to be fair about this, men in the last few hundred years have made progress. Back in the 18th century it was commonplace for criminals to be flogged, tortured and executed for minor offences. People would die of starvation in the streets of major European cities and slavery was still practised. All this extreme brutality has slowly been banned in the West by exclusively male governments. This means that men in power are capable of compassion for their fellow human beings.

It means that men do have a choice. They are more than capable of being extremely brutal, as we have seen in so many cases of torture, violence and genocide even in our world of today. Yet this is not true of all men and we can find many examples of men who are capable of caring for others. Philanthropists like William Wilberforce (1759-1833) and Granville Sharp (1735-1813) who devoted their lives to abolishing slavery or John Barnardo (1845-1905) who set up homes for destitute children. Are examples of this. Yet a man doesn't have to be a wealthy philanthropist to be caring of others. Many ordinary men are caring of others. Unfortunately not enough of the loving and compassionate people get into positions of power to create a peaceful and caring world.

So what causes men to become extremely brutal while others devote their lives to caring for others? The simplistic answer is that some men are good while others are evil. Which explains nothing and this explanation does more harm than good. A better explanation comes from evolutionary theory, the study of early humans and primate studies. This science tells us where we come from and why we are like we are. Unfortunately these studies have also been distorted through sexual bias by male academics, who are blinded to the role of women and the feminine in the evolution of the human species. A more balanced approach would give us a far deeper insight to the human condition.

This is something I will explore in the following chapters. Showing that if we are aware of the masculine bias in evolutionary theory, history and early human studies. We can discover why men have created a world of conflict, violence and suffering and what can be done to change this.

7

THE SELFISH GENE, (AND OTHER FEEBLE EXCUSES MADE UP BY MEN)

Back in the 1960s at when the women's Liberation Movement was going strong, women libbers were claiming that men and women were exactly the same. They claimed this for two reasons-

1. Men previously were claiming that women were not as intelligent as men. In fact in the 19th century male scientists "proved" that women had smaller brains then men. The idea that perhaps these male scientists might be a little biased never crossed anyone's mind. After all scientists are above human failings like emotions, bias and prejudice. These super humans can see the facts logically and clearly without human emotions. So of course they cannot possibly make a mistake, can they? They were also claiming that women were too emotional to make sensible decisions. After all women would get too emotional to make rational decisions like ordering hundreds of thousands of men to die in the face of machine gun fire. Or use gas warfare, as a more efficient way to kill and blind people. Like they did in the First World War.
2. In the 1960s the fashionable scientific theory then was that it was our upbringing that made us what we are. So Feminists seized on this and claimed it was only cultural bias in the way we brought up children that made the sexes different. Great theory, but somehow in practice it didn't work out like this. Feminist mothers and schoolteachers worked hard at treating little boys and girls exactly the same. So little Johnny was given a doll to play with, which he immediately took apart, or used as a football. While little Mary was given a train set, which she didn't know what to do with. No matter what

Feminist mothers did, they found that the majority of little girls still liked playing with dolls and the majority of little boys still liked playing with toy guns.

Since then it has become clear that the sexes are very different. Scientists have discovered that the brains of men and women are not the same and are wired up very differently. Also the latest fashionable scientific theory is that, "it's all in the jeans". Genetics has taken over as the "theory of everything" to do with human and animal life. This then means a man cannot behave like a woman or a woman behave like a man, unless they have the genes within them to make them that way.

So is that it? Is it impossible for men and women to be different because it is programmed in our genes? Will this mean that men always want to compete and fight each other and try to blow up the world with nuclear bombs? And will women always be nice and kind and end up at the bottom of the heap in our competitive world? Well not quite. In the "nature verse nurture" debate there is surprisingly a third possibility. That both our genes AND the way we were brought up could influence our behaviour. We could even be influenced by the way we choose to think. (Which is a very revolutionary idea that politicians and marketing people don't want to hear). After all we are supposed to be the most intelligent creatures on this earth, aren't we? Well you would think so, but from the crazy way we run our world, a case could be made that we are the most stupidest animal on this earth. After all although we are very clever monkeys, we seem to use to use our brains to mostly find better ways to inflict, pain, hate, violence and suffering on each other. We are so intelligent that we can produce a space ship that can fly to the moon. Yet we are unable to find a solution to far more important problems like world poverty. To quote UN statistics.

1 billion people live in 'extreme poverty' and 2 billion people live in 'poverty'. 17 million people die every year from easily preventable causes, of which 11 million are children- that is 30,000 children dying each day from hunger and preventable diseases. 800 million people are hungry. 1 billion people do not have access to clean water and 2 billion do not have proper sanitation. The world's richest 1% of people earn as much combined annual income as the bottom 57%.

Why are we so stupid that we have all our priorities so completely wrong? In that we put our best brains and trillions of dollars into finding better ways to kill each other. Yet in comparison we put hardly any intellectual or material capital into making this world a better place for ALL people to live in. We are also supposed to have free will. (Though not if the politicians can help it). Yet few of us seem to use it and we follow the herd like sheep. In fact throughout history people who are slightly different from the norm are persecuted and have even been murdered for this, "crime".

The biggest problem with the nature v nurture debate is that it is also very political. In no way should political leanings get in the way of scientific inquiry, but then, science is practised by human beings. So it means that the belief that it is, "all in the jeans" is a powerful argument for conservatism. Which means that human nature is the way it is because it has been programmed in our genes. Which in turn justifies the status quo, which is war, capitalism and poverty. Those who advocate nurture are looking for social change and are mostly feminists, pacifists or left wing activists. So in means in recent years the scientific beliefs that it is only genes that determine our behaviour has been used as a very powerful argument for the forces of conservatism. Though as I will explain later in this book this argument is a two edged sword.

The Selfish Gene theory by Richard Dawkins is presented as a very powerful argument for conservatism and capitalism to the degree it has become a standard textbook in American universities. As it claims that the only purpose in life is for gene to reproduce themselves, and we all compete with each other to ensure it is our genes that produce the next generation.

Reproduction is the most important instinct all animals have. To the degree it will take precedence over personal survival. As in the case of the octopus. When the mother lays her eggs she will slowly starve to death looking after her eggs until they hatch. Some female insects die when they lay their eggs and the first meal the larvae has, when they hatch, is the body of their own mother. In the case of some species of spiders, the female eats the male after they have mated, (apparently sex gives her a appetite). The praying mantis also has similar habits. While the male is mating, the female have been observed to eat his head, yet the headless body will continue to mate. Which is a confirmation of what many women say about men.

"Their brains are in the end of their penis' ".

Although these instincts seem to be brutal, it still makes sense because if any species of animal is to endure, then it has to ensure its offspring will survive to adulthood.

This then is why in most species of animals the mother has very powerful maternal instincts. In the evolutionary theories invented by neo-Dawinists they always focus on the power and strength of the males. Yet the most important factor in the survival of any species is the behaviour of females. To be fair the Selfish Gene theory does acknowledge the role of the mother.

He is willing to accept that except for some species of birds, it is females who have most to do with ensuring the next generation will survive and go on to reproduce again. Whist for many species the male has very little to do with helping their offspring and in some cases will hinder and sabotage the efforts of the mother to protect and care for her young. Yet Dawkins seem to see this as a clever strategy by males in putting all his efforts into passing on his genes to as many females as possible.

So what is the role of the male in survival of the species? In most species of birds the male bird behaves like "a new man" in that they help to make nests, and sit on eggs and feed the chicks. This is not the case in most mammals, which is what we are. Male lions have been witnessed killing cubs whom he hasn't fathered. Lionesses do most of the hunting in prides but the male lion will use his larger size to bully the lionesses away to feed first, or even steal the food completely from the lionesses. In spite of the fact, it is far more important for the survival of the pride, and his own off spring, that lionesses take priory in feeding, if she has to suckle young or is pregnant. In many mammals the only job the male does is to impregnate the females.

Of course we human males are not like this, are we? If we get a girl pregnant we always stick by her and help look after the kid, don't we? Well, some of us do. A very large number of young men leave girls who get pregnant and refuse to pay maintenance. After all, the child might not be his! And anyway it wasn't his idea to have children! She should have taken the pill or something. Why can't she just get an abortion? I mean he had nothing to do with it, did he? All he wanted was a bit of fun and certainly not being saddled with a screaming brat, the rest of his life.

In most species of mammals the females are more than capable of feeding and protecting her young herself. Even in herd animals except in the case of buffaloes and cattle the males don't get involved in protecting the young, and will run off like everyone else if approached by a predator. So if males don't do much in caring and protecting of the young, what do they do? It seems what they do best, is fight each other.

Fighting seems to be the common pastime among most types of male animals. We have animals like stags, bulls and rams that every spring goes in for bashing their heads together. Or giraffes who also use their head as a weapon as they swing it on their long neck. Which makes boxing, and the damage that can be done to the brain by being punched in the head, seem quite sane and sensible. So why do male animals go in for head banging and inflicting damage to each other? According to evolutionists it has something to do with the male sex drive.

In the "survival of the fittest" theory, it is important that only the strongest male animals mates with the females. So the instinct for males to fight each other is a test of strength to ensure that only the strongest will pass on their genes to the next generation. Though this theory doesn't always work out in practice. Studies done on the coyote show that although male coyotes will fight each other for the privilege of mating, the females will not always pick the winner. Some females have been observed driving off the winner and mating with the loser. Clearly this is a case where coyotes need someone to teach them how the theory of evolution works.

If we take all the knowledge we have on the observation of animals in the wild and apply it to human behaviour we can see a similarity. It was once normal for non-Christian kings and tribal chiefs to have more than a hundred wives and hundreds of children. Which makes sense, in evolutionary theory, because he would be the alpha male in the community. So would have a desire to pass on his genes to as many offspring as possible. In this way, he is not behaving much differently from a stag or lion who have a harem of females and tries to mate with all of them. Many alpha males in the animal world have territories, which they fight for against other males. Again we see similar behaviour among humans. Kings, and tribal chiefs, would also have territories that he would claim as his, and fight other kings or chiefs who trespass on his borders. It is even possible to make out a case for genocide using this argument. Lions will kill cubs that are not his when he takes over a pride. So it would also be "normal" for conquerors to kill and wipe out those who are not the same race as themselves. Which is what happened when Europeans invaded the Americas and Australia, where the native people were slaughtered and very nearly wiped out.

So that's all right then. It is "normal" for men to fight each other, have wars between countries and even practice genocide. Which is great if you are a psychopath and enjoy killing other people. You can kill as many other people as you like, and it's all right, because it is all about the survival of the fittest! If you are the sort of person who is a bit of a wimp, because you actually care about others, then there is a real problem with these theories.

In recent years neo-Darwinism has used genetics to back up theories of the selfish gene. According to his theory the whole of life is basically selfish. Now this as a purely erudite theory confined to ivory towers of the academic world. Unfortunately such theories tend to leak out into real life. Where it tells people it is perfectly all right to be selfish. Then we have social Darwinism, which can be used to justify all sorts of selfish and brutal behaviour. It was taken to the extreme by the Nazis who used the concept of the "survival of the fittest" as one of their justifications for practising genocide on Jews, Slavs and Gypsies.

The problem is that men who do take a very masculine point of view invent these theories. We hear about, "man the mighty hunter" theories where at one time scientists claimed that it was Stone-Age hunters that caused the extinction of Mammoths and other giant animals of the Ice-Age. Now this theory has changed and it is accepted that it was rapid climate change that caused this mass extinction. At one time when male palaeontologists found the sites of human settlements in the Stone Age they would concentrate on flints used in hunting. It was only when female palaeontologists also began to excavate these sites that they began to notice other stones that would have been used to grind up seeds. (Stones that male scientists had previously discarded as being of no importance). So we can see that the masculine attitudes of male scientists and academics can greatly influence their theories and what they discover.

As men are naturally competitive and think that the whole of life is a game of winners and losers. It would make sense that men see evolutionary theory the same way. They would concentrate on any competition they see like a predator going after a grazing animal, and totally ignore any example of co-operation. Like the way bees and plants work together, in that the plant gives the bees pollen, while the bee fertilised other flowers by transporting the pollen from flower to flower. Or plants producing fruit for animals to eat, then the fruit has seeds inside them that are planted in the ground when the animal defecates. Or birds that feed off the hides of large grazing animals, who allow them to do this, as the bird get rid of troublesome insects. There are as many observations in the wild of life co-operating with each other, as there are of life competing against each other. Also in any competition, no forms of life can afford to become winners. Predators that become too successful can end up making extinct the animals they feed on, and in turn will become extinct through starvation.

Neo-Darwinian theories tell us that male animals have an instinct to impregnate and pass on his genes to as many females as possible. This then makes sense of young men's desires to "sow their wild oats". It also makes sense of why many young men have a very cavalier attitude towards birth control. Where many men claim that, "having sex with a condom is like having a shower in a raincoat." I know when I was a young man in the 1960s I was told of a trick to fool young women. Apparently these young men would cut the bottom off condoms. Then in the half-light of having sex in the back of a car the girl would see him put on the condom ring, not realising that the bottom half was missing. The problem with this was that illegitimate children were still a very big issue in the 1960s and abortion was still illegal. I do wonder about the tragedies caused by tricks like this with young pregnant girls being thrown out of their homes to fend for themselves, for "disgracing" their parents. But then as explained to me, "any girl who has sex before marriage is only a whore or slut". So that's all right.

Its strange how people never worked out the inconstancy of this? It was a taboo then that young women didn't have sex before marriage, but the attitude also was there was something seriously wrong with a young man who was still a virgin by the time he was 18. With whom were young men supposed to have sex with? Prostitutes, "sluts" and "whores" of course. These women made young men feel like "real men" and were rewarded by being treated with contempt and derision.

These sorts of attitudes are even more tragic in Africa. Many young men in Africa refuse to use condoms, which allows Aids to flourish in that continent. Causing deaths to millions of people. But not to worry, these young men have found the prefect solution to the Aids problem. Apparently if you have sex with a virgin, it cures Aids. Yea really! What is more, the younger the girl the better it works. You don't say! So of course it means men with Aids are perfectly justified in raping pre-adolescent girls. I mean you wouldn't want to stop men from being cured of Aids would you? All right it didn't work the first few times they tried it, but perhaps they haven't done it enough times. Or the girls weren't young enough, but keep at it and it will eventually work. Won't it?

In the meantime, what about the young girls being given Aids by these men before they are even teenagers? There is a deafening silence about this, but then as evolutionists will explain, men have a powerful instinct to pass on his genes to as many women as possible. So the poor boys can't help it. There, there. (Though it has to be admitted that condoms as not as easy to obtain in the African bush as they are in any Western town or city. Also recent research shows that Aids also may be carried by contaminated needles when vaccinating the population for other diseases).

The irresponsible attitude of many men is also fuelling the Aids epidemic in the West. It seem there is a type of man who has the mentality of a psychopath and will use their penis as a genuine killing weapon. In that, they are aware they have Aids or HIV and yet will knowingly infect other men and women and will get very offended if it is suggested they use a condom.

The very irresponsible attitude of many men .towards women, children and other men puts doubt on another theory invented by academic men about the Stone Age. The theory was that, not only was man, "the great white hunter", (even in pictures of Stone-Age men in Africa he was painted as white up until very recently), he was a good husband as well. The man went out killing Mammoths and presumably carried it to the cave on his back to feed his family. He also protected his wife and children by fighting off Sabre Tooth Tigers and Giant Wolves. (What a man). The reasoning why Stone Age man would do this is because he had this instinct to pass on his genes so he needed to protect his women and children to do so. This attitude doesn't seem to have been passed down to many modern men, who do their best to get out of paying child support. Also this theory assumes that men in the Stone Age were married or pair bonded. Marriage, and pair bonding, is an idea invented by religions like the Christian Church, (The Muslims allow men to have many wives as did the Chinese up until the communist take-over). The Church also need laws, taboos and social censor to enforce marriage. If marriage or pair bonding was natural for us, the Church wouldn't needs to force us to marry and stay faithful. (Which large numbers of people don't do). The reason religions enforce customs that women remain faithful to one man, is that it is the only way a man can be sure that the children of women he lives with are his. With the break down of marriage in recent years we find men who are happy to live with and support women with children who are not his. Clearly this in another case where these men need to be re-educated about their desire to pass on their genes. Perhaps if they are taught neo-Darwinian they will, "naturally" kill the children their partners previously had with another man and then force her to become pregnant with this sperm.

Now anyone reading this book might get the impression I disagree with Darwin's theory of evolution. I am not against the theory that says that one species of animal evolved from another. That has been proven in the fossil record. The problem is the means by which this happened. Theories like, "the survival of the fittest", "nature red in tooth and claw", or "the selfish gene" are just reflections of a very competitive, masculine point of view. If a man is competitive, aggressive and selfish in his attitude then he will naturally want to claim that the whole of life is like this, as it justifies his belligerent behaviour. In much the same way as a bigoted and intolerant priest will want to claim that god is very judgmental and punitive, for the same reason.

"The survival of the fittest" and "selfish gene" theories are not the only shows in town. There is another theory around that doesn't go against evolutionary theory but takes it from a completely different point of view. This is called the Gaia hypothesis.

8

THE THEORY OF ONE

When Dawkins presented his selfish gene theory one section of the population very much disagree with this theory and that was the homosexual community. The foundation of the Dawkins's theory is that all genes are programmed to want to reproduce themselves. This means our basic instincts are to, "go forth and multiply". That is of course, unless you are gay. Homosexual relationships do not produce children. This has caused a big problem for the selfish gene theory, more so when some scientists have claimed to have found "gay genes". Because of this, supporters of Dawkins have made claims that homosexuality is not caused by genetics. Even fundamentalist Christian have since become supporters of the selfish gene theory as it more or less "proves" that homosexuality is unnatural.

The problem with this is that homosexuality is that it is not exclusive to humans. Same-sex activity has been observed in 450 species of birds and mammals. This includes the macho lion, where males have been observed to sodomise each other. So does this mean that, "The king of the beasts", is a queen after all? In species as diverse as the Japanese macaques, the mountain sheep, the giraffes and flamingo homosexuality is more commonplace than heterosexual behaviour. Unfortunately zoologist and ethnologists have kept quiet about this because even today animal homosexual behaviour is not seen as "natural". This is why in wild life films, although they like to show the violence of animals killing each other or having heterosexual sex, homosexual behaviour is still censored. The point is that it doesn't matter if homosexuality is caused by genes, environment or choice. If people and animals are involved in same sex relationship to the degree it interferes with their ability or desire to reproduce. Then it undermines the theory that the only purpose of life is to reproduce it's genes.

Then there is the problem that not all heterosexual people want to multiply. With the freedom that Feminism has given women some have made a deliberate decision not the have children. While other women who have problems in reproduction are happy to adopt children. If passing on their genes were the most important instinct in people, then these women would have no interest in bringing up other people's children. The same is true for men, not all men get to become fathers and many men today are happy being stepfathers. So do we then condemn these people as unnatural perverts because like homosexuals they don't have a powerful desire to reproduce?

This is true for other species of animals. It is true that some male lions will kill the young of pride he hasn't fathered, but not all lions do this. Other lions have been observed to accept cubs fathered by other males in the pride. So it is not a hard and fast rule that all males are obsessed by wanting to pass on their genes. This is true of females as well. Yes female animals have been observed to ignore young that have be orphaned. Yet there are many other cases of females mothering young that are not hers. There have even been cases of mothers of one species caring for the young of another species. As in the case of wild-children where human children have been cared for by female animals. So it seems that there are many humans and animals that are not conforming to Dawkins's theory. Perhaps we need to employ animal trainers for wild animals to train males to murder young that are not theirs and train females to ignore any young that is not hers. To make the theory work.

If there is a real problem with the selfish gene theory what is the alternative?

Mystics have for centuries claimed we are all one mind, one spirit. This concept has never caught on as it seems to go against all our personal experiences of competition and conflict with others. So is seen by ordinary people as to be a unrealistic fantasy. Then a scientist called James Lovelock developed a scientific theory that claimed the whole of life on this Earth is simply ONE ORGANISM. Which at first sight seem incredible but his theory answers many mysteries about the nature of life.

Back in the 1960s James Lovelock was employed by NASA to find ways a space craft could discover if there was life on Mars. So he started by examining the atmosphere of Mars to see it that would give a clue to signs of life. To understand this better he decided to examine the atmosphere of Earth and compared it with Mars. What he discovered was that the atmosphere on Mars was very stable and inert. Unlike Earth which had an unstable and dynamic atmosphere, because life itself was continually changing the gases within it. He then realised that you don't have to send a spacecraft to Mars to find out if it had life. You could do it by simply examining its atmosphere. Which is not what his bosses in NASA wanted to hear, because they needed a reason to convince politicians to fund a space mission to Mars. This resulted in him and NASA parting company, but he continued to develop his ideas further. As his studies of the Earth's atmosphere presented him with a number of scientific puzzles.

Every school child knows that there is a cycle where animals convert oxygen into carbon dioxide while plants convert carbon dioxide back into oxygen once again. But Lovelock took this concept even further, he looked at a mystery that no one had addressed, and that was although life began 3 - 4 billion years ago, the temperature of the Earth has changed very little in that time. The problem with this is that the sun 3 billion years ago was 30% colder, than today and has since been steadily heating up. The answer seems to be that 3 billion years ago the Earth's atmosphere had more carbon dioxide in it. Even though the sun was cooler the CO2 created a greenhouse effect and so keeping the temperature the same as it is today. Since then the levels of carbon dioxide have slowly fallen to keep the temperature of the Earth stable. So that's all right, problem solved.

Then Lovelock went on to ask a further question. How was it possible for the carbon dioxide to decrease over a period of 3-4 billion years AT EXACTLY THE SAME RATE THE SUN WAS WARMING UP. This is a real a problem, when you realise that by just making the Earth a few degrees colder can bring on an ice age. Also it only needs 10 degree increase or decrease in the earth's temperature to make the vast majority of life extinct. So how has the Earth kept in the very narrow range of temperatures to make life on Earth possible? There was no answer to this and to say it was just a lucky fluke was stretching credibility a bit too far.

Then Lovelock came across other amazing coincidences. At present 21% of the atmosphere is oxygen. Now oxygen is a very dangerous and volatile gas. If it was to increase to 25% (only 4% higher) and a fire was to start, through a lightening strike, it would be impossible to put it out. Even green and wet vegetation will continue to burn causing all vegetation on the earth to quickly burn up. Yet lower levels of oxygen would seriously effect the energy efficiency of animals. This means the oxygen levels on the Earth are about the most effective we need for life, without it increasing to a dangerous level. Yet life is continually taking oxygen out of the atmosphere and putting it back again. So how does life get it so right? In that it doesn't take too much oxygen out of the atmosphere thereby reducing the efficiency of animal respiration, or get it too high and create a worldwide disaster. What is more, life has been able to do this delicate balancing act for billions of years.

Lovelock realised that as it was life itself producing both carbon dioxide and oxygen and it was life that was regulating temperature and oxygen levels of the Earth, within the parameters to make life on earth possible. He was to find many more coincidences like this. Life also needs a chemical balanced world that is either too acid or too alkaline. Which is what we find on Earth, unlike both Venus and Mars who have environments that are too acid to support life. It seems that Earth has many forms of microorganisms that are working away to keep our world chemically neutral. He presented all his ideas in a scientific meeting about the origins of life but his ideas went down like a lead balloon. Only two scientists took a interest in his ideas, one being Lynn Margulis who had a background in Life science and was able to later help him to present and develop his ideas even further.

It took about 20 years for the scientific community to take his ideas seriously. (After all only theories that nature is very savage, brutal and selfish make sense. The idea that all life works in harmony, is the stuff of fairy tales) As the evidence piled up in favour of Lovelock, many scientists are now very reluctantly accepting his hypothesis, though he still gets his detractors, and guess who is one of his biggest critic? It is not a surprise to learn it is Richard Dawkins. A man, who tries to prove that life is basically selfish, is not going to be sympathetic to any idea that the whole of life is one organism.

Though Dawkins himself even admits that many species of animal do co-operate with each other for their mutual benefit, like the aphids who live in ants nests. The aphids get the benefit of being protected by the ants while the ants milk the aphids for food. Yet in when discussing life that helps each other he prefers to see it in terms of manipulation. He would rather use the word "bearers" instead of "carers" when writing about animals who care for the young. Hinting perhaps that bearers are suckers or losers. While the idea that any form of life could possibly give or help others because they love and care for them is completely ignored.

Another criticism of the Gaia hypothesis is that there is no very large brain laying around the place directing life and telling it what to do. Yet this problem is the same we have about social insects like Ants, Termites and Bees. They live in complex societies with different insects having very different roles, (like workers, queens, drone and soldiers). Yet what makes these nests and hives work is a mystery because these insects have minuscule brains and no obvious leader. (The queen is seen as the leader, but her role in directing what goes on in the nest is still a mystery). The Gaia hypothosis just treats the whole of life on this planet as a far bigger and more complex version of a beehive, with different species of animals, plants and microorganisms all having different roles in keeping the planet going. This is similar to the concepts of the Collective Unconscious that was put forward by the psychologist Carl Jung. Who discovered that the unconscious minds of his patients were remarkably similar. This means, we don't have to have an enormous brain lying around somewhere, to make the Gaia theory work. The whole of life can be the brain and intelligence of the planet.

If this is true then what is the role of human beings? After all we seem to be busy destroying the earth with thousands of species of animals and plants becoming extinct through the actions of men. Also we now have global warming where we are heating up the planet. Yet the planet has even got a bigger crisis than the meddling of a naked ape. As pointed out earlier the sun is slowing heating up, and life counteracts this by taking carbon dioxide out of the atmosphere. The problem is now carbon dioxide is down to just 0.03% of the atmosphere. So it doesn't take a genius to work out that the planet will not be able to take much more CO_2 out the atmosphere if the sun continues to warm up. So the strategy of using carbon dioxide as a means of regulating the temperature of the earth is coming to a end, as there is only a small amount of this gas left. This means life has to devise a new system in which to do this. So perhaps the creation of a clever monkey like humans with hands that can manipulate the environment, is part of this new strategy. Hopefully we will in time produce technology that can keep our planet cool, as the sun heats up. Or we can transport life from our planet to others planets or moons or even other stars with planetary systems. Admittedly at present we are not doing well, in that we are heating up the planet through industrial pollution. Yet even this may be part of the plan. In that an environmental catastrophe caused by global warming may make us human being realise the importance of looking after the planet. We now have the technological power to destroy the Earth, which we might do through thoughtless and irresponsible action. Because we still have a attitude of wanting to plunder and exploit the environment for our selfish gain. Once we wake up to the fact that to damage and destroy the world is to also to destroy ourselves. Then we may change our attitude and use our science and technology to save Gaia instead of trying to attack her.

Now an intellectual argument between Lovelock and Dawkins is not going have much effect on the lives of normal people. It only happens when these ideas are taken from the ivory towers of academic debate and are used by people like politicians and businessmen. We can see this clearly with the ideas of Social Darwinism that has been popularised by people like Andrew Carnegie. Which advocates competitive individualism and a market economy unregulated by government. I also have to say the Nazis used Social Darwinism as a justification for the genocide of "inferior" races. This then means that academic debate on the nature of life can be used as political tools in the hands of politicians.

So how have the theories of Lovelock and Dawkins been used? Clearly Dawkins' ideas are just another support for Social Darwinism, and conservative politics. While Lovelock's ideas have been taken up by the New Age movement. Though Lovelock himself is clearly not a New Ager in that he was a scientific adviser to Margaret Thatcher in the 1980s. He advocated then that Britain builds far more nuclear power stations and not worry about radiation contamination. He claimed that we receive enough radiation poisoning from the Sun so a little more is not going to harm us. (This was the position of many scientists until very recently. Then it was discovered that life has as much radiation poisoning from the Sun as it can cope with and even a small increase will greatly escalate the amount of cancers and other illnesses.)

So what effect has the Gaia hypothesis had on the public? Not a lot it seems, perhaps the idea that we are all one mind and one organism is too boring. Concepts like, "nature red in tooth and claw" is far more exciting and dramatic. While the Selfish Gene theory and Social Darwinism gives us license to behave as selfishly and badly as we like. If we were to think in terms that we are all One, we would have all the problems of caring about others and worrying about things like world poverty. Not a good idea. If we go down that route, we might think we need to take a more responsible attitude to the planet and all the life forms that live on it. When it's far, far easier to ignore all this and dull our minds with drink, drugs and consumer goods, to escape the suffering we create for others and ourselves.

The Gaia hypothesis also reflect many ideas in mysticism that we are all one mind, one spirit, but ideas like this only appeal to a minority of people. The problem for Gaia is that Oneness is a very feminine concept in much the same way as Social Darwinism is very masculine. So masculine competition is the foundation of Social Darwinism, while Gaia is about all of life co-operating with each other for the good of the whole. Feminists and other women see co-operation as being very feminine and the ideal they all want to achieve. Something they see as completely impossible while we live in a male dominated society.

Also the idea that life is dominated by masculine principles is the same as the concept, that a male god created our world. So it means neo-Darwinist and patriarchal religions like Judaism, Christianity and Islam have in one way a similar view of the world. While the Gaia theory says that the whole of life is dominated by the feminine. (So it is of interest that it was named after a Goddess). This means that a person's individual bias of wanting to live in either a masculine or feminine world, can greatly influence the religion or scientific theory they want to belong or subscribe to.

We all live in a masculine world that Feminists have pointed out is created by men for men. Just by reading history or reading today's newspapers we can see clearly how a masculine world operates. Where the three Cs, conflict, confrontation and competition is the name of the game. The problem is that the masculine world is the only world we know. Read any history books and you don't find it describing societies ruled by women, neither do you find equal societies. It is true that there are Ancient Greek and Roman stories of the Amazons but they are just myths, aren't they? So it is natural for us to assume that the masculine, patriarchal society is normal and natural.

Likewise if you read books about pre-history and the Stone Age you will also get the impression that men have always been the dominant sex. Which is used as a powerful argument against Feminism in books like *The Inevitability of Patriarchy.* Because if it was always the case that men were the dominant sex, even as far back as a million years ago, then we have to see Feminism as just a passing phase, a social experiment that will inevitably fail. Because the natural assertiveness of men will in the end win through and women will lose, and once again to be confined to the job of homemakers for their lords and masters. So it is only going to be a matter of time before we go back to a natural world, "where men are men and women love them for it". Right?

Now the foundation of this powerful argument is that women have never ruled society. If we find that this is not the case and women did once rule the world, and rule communities even today in many parts of the world, then the foundations of this argument is destroyed. Women ruling the world? Surely not! You show me a history book that says this! Well yes, in official history you will never find any reference to that very taboo word matriarchy. Matriarchy has been a taboo, in our world for the last two thousand years and more. Even today it is a very controversial subject within academic circles. There are many books about matriarchal or matrifocal societies and other books tell you that pre-history matriarchal is a myth. Yet there is a lot of evidence around that says that it did once exist. As we can see from the following examples

9

MATRIARCHAL SOCIETIES

In 1540 Francisco de Orellana led an expedition to the Amazon river and was the first European to do an extensive exploration of it. He reported finding along the riverbank large cities, towns and villages. He also somehow managed to communicate with the natives who told him women ruled them and they even showed him statues of these female rulers.

Then the Spanish managed to upset the natives and the first peaceful exchanges soon turned to open hostility. Where they were being to be attacked by the natives whenever they came to a village or town. He reported that female warriors led these attacks. When he got back to Spain the river he sailed on was named the Amazon after the stories Orellana told about these female warriors.

Yet 20 years later when the next European expedition explored the river they found no trace of the fabulous cities reported by Orellana or the Amazon warriors. As a result Orellana was to be labelled by historians a liar, and his stories of marvellous cities, female rulers and Amazon warriors exaggerated fantasies. This was to be confirmed in more modern time when it was realised that the soil in the rail-forests is very poor for growing crops. At present farmers are destroying the Amazon forest by the slash and burn method. They cut down a large area, then burn it and plant crops. Yet after a few years the soil is so depleted that crops no longer can be grown. So they have to go on to cut down another area and do the same thing.

For this reason modern experts claimed that an ancient civilisation to exist in the Amazon basin was impossible because all civilisations in the past have relied on intensive farming for food. So it seems to be that Orellana was clearly a liar because there was no evidence of any kind to support his stories.

Then very recently archaeologists began to find large earth mounds in the Amazon forests. It occurred to some of them that these mounds might be artificial and they began to dig in them and quickly found large amounts of pottery and other man made artefacts. Not only this, some of these fragments suggested they come from very large pots, far too large to be carried around by anyone. This then means that these mounds were the remains of ancient settlements. As the archaeologists explored further they found ancient roads, linking these mounds demonstrating a complex infrastructure of an ancient civilisation. If this was so, how did they feed themselves? Because, as previously mentioned, without intensive farming they could not feed a large population.

The archaeologists then noticed the soil in the mounds was very different to the normal soil of the rain forest. It was reasoned, that this ancient civilisation must have found a way to fertilise this normally barren soil. Tests were done on it and it was discovered the soil was full of charcoal. What become clear was this ancient civilisation used the slash and burn method, but instead of burning the vegetation they cooked the wood instead. (This is the method of making charcoal all over the world). The charcoal was then able to retain the nutrients in the wood. Not only that, this charcoal rich soil was full of bacteria, which fed the plants growing in it. So impressive are the trials that have been done on this soil. (In experimental plots, adding a combination of charcoal and fertiliser into the rain-forest soil boosted yields by 880% compared with fertiliser alone.) This has now been hailed as a solution to the world's hunger problem. It seems that this ancient civilisation found solutions to the problems of poor soil that modern science with all its sophisticated chemical fertilisers was unable to find.

This soil has been found in many other areas along the Amazon River. With ancient artificial artefacts within it wherever found. Showing a large civilisation and in all in the places where Orellana claimed he saw these cities and towns. So what happened to this ancient civilisation?

Scientists can only speculate, but it is known that the Europeans brought with them diseases that were unknown to the native population, like small pox and influenza. Not having any immunity to these diseases the native population was decimated. It means that the Orellana expedition brought to the native population these diseases, which would have wiped out most of them out very quickly. The civilisation collapsed and the jungle soon overgrew the cities and town. So by the time the next Europeans came to the same area all they would have seen was virgin jungle. The few survivors were then forcefully converted into Christianity and all knowledge of their ancient ways and stories ruthlessly destroyed. Though I have to say that it is not usual for civilizations to be wiped out by disease, civilization generally collapse through nature disasters like years of famine or conquest and genocide. Orellana questioned a native who told him that these female rulers had gold. We all know how gold mad the conquistadors were and with this knowledge reaching Spain they would want to come back to plunder this gold. Orellana did come back but was killed and his leaderless expedition returned to Spain, but it is likely that another expedition did go to the Amazon. If they had destroyed the Amazon civilization, plundered their gold and committed genocide they may not of wanted the world to know about this, so this expedition may have been written out of history.

This then means that Orellana has been vindicated. Though archaeologists as far as I know haven't been able to confirm that women ruled this ancient civilisation. Yet as everything else he reported has now been confirmed as correct, we can probably accept that was true as well.

The concept that women once ruled the world in ancient times is nothing new. A scholar called J.J Bachofen in the 19th century started it. He brought together all the evidence of matriarchy in ancient times then available, and very mildly suggested a matriarchal age in the past. He was strongly criticised for this by other scholars who dismissed and discredited his work. Yet in spite of this, his work was to inspire scholars like James Frazer who wrote his famous book, *The Golden Bough*, and more recently Joseph Campbell. It also influenced Karl Marx and Friedrich Engels who publicly praised Bachofen's work. As well as the psychologist Carl Jung who developed from it the theory that the ancient Great Mother, is a very important archetype in the collective unconscious. Other scholars in the early 20th century also wrote about matriarchy like Robert Briffault, who had pointed out that anthropologists then were very biased in their field studies. As they assumed that in all the Stone-Age cultures they studied they were all male dominated, and ignored any evidence when this wasn't the case. This didn't go down well with the academic community and again he was very heavily criticised. Yet his work was to inspire the anthropologist Bronislaw Malinowski who also found Stone Age communities they didn't fit the "normal patriarchal model. As did Margaret Mead who again was greatly criticised for making observations about societies that didn't fit into the patriarchal norm. Another anthropologist Eva Meyerowitz was to find evidence of matriarchal rule up to recent times in African tribes. While Evelyn Reed, in articles, lectures and her book, "Sexism and Science" was to savagery attack anthropologists for their sexual bias against women.

Jane Harrison another scholar also suggest matriarchy in ancient Greece, but managed to escape criticism by not being too explicit. Unlike Dr Margaret Murray a respected Egyptologist also received heavy criticism for writing that Witchcraft was an ancient Goddess religion that has survived up to the middle ages. These arguments were kept mostly within academic circles. Then in the 1940s the poet Robert Graves wrote his book, *The White Goddess*, which was the first attempt to bring this argument to the general public. Even though it was a very complex book. At about the same time Erich Fromm was bringing together the works of Freud, Marx and Bachofen. Where he pointed out that communism and socialism could only work in a matriarchy. Then on the wave of the Feminist movement of the 1960s and 70s Feminist scholars like Merlin Stone and Barbara G. Walker also continued to dig deep into ancient history to find more evidence of matriarchy in ancient times.

After the Second World War archaeologists started to make finds supporting the idea that there was a matriarchal age in the past. This evidence was again dismissed by academics but Feminist writers began to write about it. Like Elizabeth Gould Davis who was brave enough to directly claim that women did once rule the world, and Riane Eisler who kept strictly to Feminist dogma of equality. Yet we don't have to go to pre-history to find matriarchal societies, the shocking fact is that they exist in today's world. The biggest is the The Minangkabau people in Western Sumatra which numbers about 4 million people and is the largest and most stable Matriarchal community in the world today. There are also matriarchal communities in China, Tibet and Malaya, which is kept quiet as government officials find this an embarrassment. In Southern India there is a region called Keralal, which again is matriarchal and has a reputation of being a well run, stable and prosperous area. There is evidence of matriarchal communities that survived in Africa up until colonial times and even American Indian tribes that are still Matriarchal. The Basque people of France and Spain were matriarchal in historic times, but the Inquisition and the medieval witch-hunts finally destroyed this way of life.

There are legends that the Czech people were matriarchal up until the sixth or seventh century. Where it seems that after Libuse, the last matriarchal ruler, had died there was a patriarchal take over. In this legend the women fought back led by two women warriors called Vlasta and Sarka. After a very long and vicious war the men finally won and imposed patriarchy on the women. I have been informed that there are over 150 matriarchal communities all over the world, but we never hear about this in either the mainstream or alternative media.

Yet many Feminists are uncomfortable about this concept for three reasons.

1 Feminism is about equality; so many Feminists just see matriarchy as being the flip side of patriarchy. That is to say instead of men ruling the world, it is women doing it instead. Feminism has achieved a lot through just pointing out the unfairness and injustice of sexual bias in laws and customs. Which has resulted in men standing aside and allowing women to achieve equal opportunities in Western society. Start talking about matriarchy and this totally undermines the foundation of Feminism. As men can then claim that Feminism is not about equality but just "the thin end of the wedge" of female dominance. (Many men see it this way already, and don't really believe Feminists when they say, "we only want equality.")

2 Read any Feminist books, they are mostly about the horrors of patriarchy, and why it is wrong for men to dominate women. If there was an age in the past where women dominated men, then women will be as just a bad as men. (According to the women's Liberation Movement of the 1960s men and women are exactly the same. So if we accept this theory there shouldn't be a problem. Men have dominated women over the last five thousand years, so if women are like men, they will naturally want, "their turn").

3 There is also a fear of male violence among Feminists. Men in the past, and in Islamic countries today have dominated women through violence. In the 19th century in the West men were legally entitled to beat their wife with sticks if she misbehaves, and social custom encouraged this. (You weren't a "real" man if you couldn't dominate and beat up your wife). Yet over the last hundred years men in the West men seem to have seen the error of their ways through an appeal to fairness and equality. Start talking about matriarchy and women dominating society and

men might get angry with women and perhaps use violence to take back everything women have gained over.the last 100 years.

I can't say I would personally agree with this last reason, though I can understand women being frightened of male violence. Because just 4 hundred years ago the Church was still carrying on a murderous campaign of slaughtering millions of Witches, (mostly women). Also even today women are publicly executed and flogged in places like Iran, Afghanistan and Pakistan for minor infringements of Islamic law. Yet society in industrial countries has changed. After the Second World War the American military decided to interview all the returning troops to see if they could learn anything from their experiences. Most of these soldiers claimed that in the war they didn't kill anyone and only fired over the heads of the enemy. It seems only a small minority admitted to killing anyone. Which is not exactly the sort of image we have of GI soldiers in Hollywood films.

The Japanese military had similar problems. Japan ranks with Southern Ireland and Switzerland as being one off the most non-violent and crime free, countries in the world. Yet in the Second World War Japanese soldiers were even worse than German and Russian troops for brutality. So how did this happen?

It seems in the 1930s and 40s the Japanese military completely brutalised their troops. Older recruits at the beginning of their training beat up the new recruits. Then in the second year of training they were forced to do the same to the new intake. Later on many were made to kill prisoners of war, either as live dummies in bayonet practise or cutting off their heads. This total brutalisation made it possible for Japanese soldiers to kill without pity. Yet it is of interest that the Japanese military had to go this far into brutalisation to turn their troops into killers.

In very brutal societies as many third world countries, it seems men are so brutalised that they are far more likely to use violence against women to retain male dominance. Where men are less brutalised as in most industrial countries, then they are far less likely to resort to violence. Though I have to say the brutalisation of men in the West seems mostly to come from very violent films and video games. In that it helps to make violence acceptable to many young men. (Perhaps the makers of these films hope it will turn our young men into, "real "macho" men" who will put women back in their place).

Scientific studies have shown that boy and men who have been subjected to violence or fierce competition do have greatly increased testosterone levels. This can be increased to a level where sportsmen will commit horrific violence on the sporting field. A case in point is Australian Rugby. In the 1990s Australian rugby players developed what was called the pile-driver tackle. Where a group of players would lift a player of the opposing side off his feet and then drop him on his head. Neck injuries are the most horrendous injury you can get in rugby, where injured players have been left paralysed from the neck down. Also a pile-driver tackle has the potential to kill a player. So rugby laws had to be made to quickly stop this practice. Yet the question that was never asked is why were players willing to do it in the first place? They must also be aware of the physical damage that can happen by doing a pile-driver tackle. They also must be aware of the fact if they do it to the opposing side it will in turn be done to them. Yet reason and common sense didn't come into it and a law had to be made to outlaw his practise. This begs the question that if a loophole was found in the law that players could legally take a gun on the field of play and shoot opposing players to win the game. Would they do this?

So it means that when the testosterone levels are high in sportsmen they are willing to commit terrible injuries on the players of the opposing side. Surprisingly even watching competitive sport can increase the testosterone levels of men. So it seems that violent and competitions do make men even more violent. The less brutal and competitive a society is the less violent men become. This might be the answer to a very puzzling archaeological mystery and controversy.

10

A WORLD WITHOUT WAR AND VIOLENCE (YOU MUST BE JOKING!)

On Thursday 31 January 2002 at 9.00pm in Britain BBC Two the scientific TV program Horizon. Called, "The Lost Pyramids of Caral", the subject matter was archaeology (http://www.bbc.co.uk/science/horizon/2001/caral.shtml)

Now to anyone who didn't have an interest in science this program passed by unnoticed. Yet what this program was about is a very big shift in the understanding of our past and the true nature of human beings. To the degree that historians in the future will have to re-write history and sociologists will have to rethink all their theories about human nature. In fact what was discovered could bring about a colossal social, religious and political change in our future. Once the information about what was discovered fillers down to ordinary people.

As previously pointed out, most books about our ancestors in the Stone, Bronze and Iron age portray them as very brutal and violence people. It also seems that the further you go back in time the more violence and savage people seem to be. For this reason it was assumed that people who lived in prehistoric times were even more barbaric than the people in historic times. This has been the prevailing view by most archaeologists, anthropologist and palaeontologists up until very recently.

Now to most people academic theories are irrelevant to their normal daily lives, but the belief that we descended from savage barbarians effects us all. Because it assumes we are all deep down just violent brutes in modern clothing, and have to be kept in line through strict laws, moral codes and brutal punishment. This belief influences the nature of our religions, political systems and laws. It also has a unconscious effect on the way we treat others, because if we are to believe that the true nature of humans is barbaric. Then we learn to fear other people and assume the worst in them. Creating a vicious cycle of fear and hatred for other people.

This belief is not much different from the Christian belief that all people are born into sin. The implication of this belief, is that people can only be saved by obeying the very strict rules and moral code of the Christian religion. When scientists replaced priests as the "wise men" of our society all they done was to continue this belief in another form. In that we are no longer born into sin but we are given instead the equal negative belief that deep down we are all savage brutes.

This belief was spelt out on this Horizon program by Prof. C.C. Lamberg-Karlovsky of Harvard University, who said-

"I frankly find it difficult to conceive of the emergence of urbanisation complexity civilisation in the absence of degrees of conflict, or the presence of, warfare."

In other words he was saying it is natural for human beings to live in conflict, and he couldn't imagine any civilisation that didn't generate violence and war.

Proof of this belief was found by Dr Tom Pozorski of the University of Texas-Pan American and his wife Sheila who had previously discovered what was then thought to be the oldest city in South America. In the Casma Valley they had discovered one of the largest pyramids in the world, in fact it was so large that previous explorers had assumed it was just a hill. Wood on the site was carbon dated to 1500 BC and this at the time it made it the oldest city in the America. In the excavation they discovered carvings of warriors who were killing and mutilating their victims. To quote, Jonathan Haas of Field Museum, Chicago-

"Heads have blood flowing from their eyes and blood flowing from their mouths and then you have body parts so you'll have just the leg and you'll have a torso or you'll have feet and you'll have crossed hands".

So this find seems to confirm everything archaeologists believed about the early civilisations. That they were created by warlords who ruled by fear and created the first cities as fortresses against conquest by other warlords. This theory seemed to be validated until Dr Ruth Shady if the University of San Marcos, Lima, was to make a discovery that was to turn everything archaeologists believed about early civilisations, on its head.

Like Tom Pozorski she began to dig around what was thought to be hills in a place called Caral in Peru only to discover they were pyramids. As she and her team began to excavate the site she was puzzled the fact that there was no pottery on the site, (pottery is nearly always found in ancient civilisations) and finding only stone tools. This suggested this site was so ancient that it existed before the invention of pottery and metal. This was confirmed when some bags made of reeds found on the site were carbon dated. They were dated to 2600 BC so Caral was nearly five thousand years old making it as nearly as old as the first civilisation in Egypt, and was a thousand years older than any other civilisation in South America. This was to cause a sensation in the archaeological world and archaeologists from North America came to visit the site.

Jonathan Haas, "the world's leading expert on the warfare theory" began to search around for evidence of warfare. To his surprise he couldn't find any fortifications or any means the city could have defended itself. He began to look further afield to look for battlements in the hills around Caral and then in mountain passes where invading armies would have to travel though, but came up with nothing. Meanwhile Ruth Shady couldn't find any weapons of war or any carvings of violence in her excavations; so all this lack of evidence was undermining the warfare theory. To the degree Jonathan Haas had to admit-

"You seemed to really have the beginnings of that complex society and I'm able to look at it right at the start and I look for the conflict and I look for the warfare, I look for the armies and the fortifications and they're not there. They should be here and they're not and you have to change your whole mind-set about the role of warfare in these societies and so it's demolishing our warfare hypothesis. The warfare hypothesis just doesn't work."

It seems that archaeologists now accept that it was irrigation and not warfare is what started the first civilisations.

Another realisation about Caral is that what was true of this civilisation was also true for nearly the whole of South America at the time. Trading goods were found from the Amazon jungle at the other side of the Andes Mountains as well as from the coast. The picture that emerged was that Caral was the centre of a vast trading network. So if the people of Caral felt so safe that they didn't bother to look for ways to defend themselves. The same must of been true for most of South America, because in no way was Caral just an isolated city cut off from the rest of the world. It suggests that Caral lived in an age where warfare was completely unknown. The evidence is that the first civilisations in South America lived in peace for about a thousand years before we had warfare, violence, torture and human sacrifice.

The cosy picture painted by the Horizon program of unbiased scientists looking for the truth and finally finding it in the excavation of Caral is basically false. The archaeologists who strongly believed in the warfare theory and then were willing to admit they where wrong in the face of the evidence, or lack of evidence, in Caral, need to be congratulated. Yet this has not been the case for most archaeologists in the past. The truth is that the whole archaeological world for a period of 50 years has had to be dragged kicking and screaming into accepting the evidence, that the first civilisations live in a world where warfare was unknown. It was not just the evidence from Caral that made them ditch the warfare theory but evidence coming from Neolithic, Copper and Bronze age sites in Europe, the Middle East and China.

What happened in Caral at the beginning of the 21st century also happen 40 years previously in the 1950s and 60s in a place called Catal Höyük in Turkey. Unfortunately the way Archaeologists reacted to this excavation was very different.. An archaeologist called James Mellaart found in this location, the oldest city ever discovered, going back 9,000 years. Making it far older than the ancient Egyptian and Sumerian civilisations. Again the archaeologists couldn't find any evidence of fortifications or weapons of war. Nor any paintings or carvings showing images of violence, or for that matter any form of centralised government. What were found instead, were feminine images of childbirth, Goddesses and animal life.

This city was unlike anything discovered since. In that it had few streets, and most houses were built so close together that the only access was through the roof. This then means that to many people in the city to gain access to their homes they had to walk over the roofs of other people's houses. This was to greatly puzzle archaeologists.

It is impossible to understand Catal Höyük while we think in terms of a civilisation that had masculine values. Unfortunately what is not being considered is the possibility of civilisations those values were feminine, by mainstream archaeologists. In later civilisations we see the masculine values of war, power and status glorified in images and writings. In Catal Höyük we see images of the feminine values of childbirth, fertility being represented. So clearly women were the dominant sex in this community as it is their values that are represented and strongly influence the nature of the civilisation. As it is women's superior social skills of co-operation and communication that allows the city to function.

So disturbing was these findings that the whole site was closed down for thirty years by the Turkish Government. James Mellaart was criticised by many archaeologists for claiming that the people of Catal Höyük worshipped Goddesses. One of the most vocal critics was another archaeologist Ian Hodder. So it wasn't a surprise to find that when the excavations were reopened in the 1990s, it was the sceptic Ian Hodder who was put in charge. In the thirty years the excavation was closed down, the academic world kept quiet about the discoveries made at Catal Höyük. Though there was one archaeologist Marija Gimbutas who broke ranks and began to tell the world about implication of the findings. Not only have Catal Höyük but other Neolithic sites in Southern and Eastern Europe. She wrote about a peaceful world in ancient Europe that worshipped the Great Mother that was ended by violent Indo-European tribes that came from the North and invaded these peaceful civilisations.

Marija Gimbutas wrote books about the Neolithic excavations in Malta, Crete, Greece, Bulgaria, Romania, Moldavia and Ukraine, all these finds showed a world without war and violence and where the people worshipped the ancient Great Mother. It seems that when a society worship feminine deities, war and violence were unknown. But when societies worship male gods or both male and female deities then violence becomes commonplace. She was criticised and condemned by her colleges and it was claimed her work unscientific because it when against the fashionable warfare theories of the time. No other archaeologists at the time would support what she claimed, and she was dismissed as just a strident Feminist maverick of no importance.

Then similar finds began to be written about in the in Indus Valley Civilisation in Pakistan. (Although it was first discovered in the 1920s) Recently archaeologist have found its beginning goes back as 7,000 years making it again one of the oldest civilisations discovered. And again archaeologists couldn't find evidence of fortifications, violence and warfare, and it was a civilisation that worshipped horned Mother Goddesses. It was also claimed this civilisation was ended by a violence invasion from Aryan people from the North. Though his is know being disputed, as there is no evidence for this, as it came out of the imagination of 19th century archaeologists.

The first excavations of Neolithic sites started back in the 1940s. So why did it take over 50 years for archaeology to accept the evidence of an age in the past where warfare didn't exist? Controversies like this have happened before in science, new evidence and theories can take a long time to be accepted if they go against existing theories. The problem is that knowledge of a Golden Age of peace ruled by a Mother Goddess doesn't only just come from archaeology. They also come from myths and legends all over the world. What is clear there is a campaign to suppress and destroy all evidence about this Golden Age has been going on for thousands of years. The attack on Marija Gimbutas theories is only latest chapter in this crusade.

At Catal Höyük their are now Feminists and Goddess groups who are attempting to keep the archaeologists on the site honest. So when they attempts to dismiss evidence of a Mother Goddess culture out of hand they find passionate and articulate Feminists who are willing to contradict them. An example of this is a posting I found on the Internet in a Yahoo E-Group called Goddesssites.

Dear Diana,

That's great you enjoyed the site, it's so beautiful, and holds so much important history (herstory?) It's good they didn't make negative comments about the Goddess, I wouldn't really expect that. But did they mention the Goddess at all? The problem for me with the visitor's center was the ABSENCE of the Goddess, and the absence of what I would call "Goddess consciousness." Mellaart and other early archaeologists were congruent with the material they dug, in the sense that they were able to use language that explicated what they were looking at (peaceful, fertile, nurturing, egalitarian, spiritual, artistic, and so on) while the more recent archaeologists seem to shy away from anything remotely connected with "matriarchal" theories. By the way, matriarchal actually means "beginning with the mother," which makes it technically quite a good term for describing matrilineal, peaceful, mother-centered agricultural peoples of the Neolithic, although perhaps the term "matristic" used by Marija Gimbutas is more appropriate for our time. At the visitor's center there are two murals displayed—two versions of the same one—which happens to be the only wall painting from the site that was predominantly male. All the others are female-central and mostly Mother Goddesses and Double Goddesses. Interesting choice to represent the site, then, don't you think? In the display case showing the reproduction of the beautiful ivory-handled flint dagger, the artifacts are described as having to do with "hunting and war." This is a travesty, since the piece comes from the Neolithic and there is absolutely no evidence of any kind for war or violence. As I have written in an article recently, the knife is much more likely to fall into the category of knives that belong to midwives—for cutting the umbilical cord at birth. These knives were still used b shaman women in Siberia in the 20th century. Fortunately the museum in Ankara still has integrity and shows the finds from Catal Höyük as belonging to the ancient Mother Goddess cultures that are found all over Anatolia. It's too bad the team at Catal Höyük doesn't feel obliged to keep in step with local Turkish scholars and the way they see Anatolian history (and prehistory). I'm not trying to pick an argument, but I was really very upset when I went there. It was a place I had looked forward to visiting for such a long time—two decades at least—and it seemed criminal to me that no one seems to be monitoring what interpretations these "new archaeology" types come up with. There is a culture war happening right now—a concerted effort to block and erase certain approaches to ancient scholarship—and I believe this is quite political and dangerous for scholars of women's studies.

THANKS FOR LISTENING—VICKI NOBLE (VICKI NOBLE IS ALSO A WELL KNOWN AUTHORESS)

Also now there was now a younger group of scientists who wasn't so opposed to the theories of Marija Gimbutas. When Catal Höyük excavation was reopened and it suddenly became respectable to write about it. Richard Rudgley recently wrote two books and made a TV program called "The Secrets Of The Stone Age" that broadly supported Marija Gimbutas theories. So in recent years there are many people in the academic world who are now more accepting of the evidence that the first civilisations live in peace.

Richard Rudgeley comes straight to the point when he says, "The widely accepted view of the human story is wildly inaccurate." He then goes on to point out that because historians have ignored what happen during the Neolithic age it seems that to the general public that civilisations suddenly appeared out of no-where. Because we are taught that the people in the Stone Age were ignorant savages, who then suddenly created sophisticated civilisations like ancient Egypt and Mesopotamia. Then because orthodox archaeology gives no explanation to the public of how this suddenly happened, in this vacuum people outside science have invented their own theories. Like Erich Von Daniken in his book "Chariot Of The Gods", or the many theories of a lost continents like Atlantis, Mu and Lemuria.

The point he is trying to make is that if the general public was aware that Stone-Age people were not ignorant brutes and that civilisation didn't start with the Egyptians, but thousands of years earlier in the Neolithic age. Then we would not need aliens from outer space or lost continents to explain how civilisation got started.

He explains that the first large stone structures were not built in the Nile Valley but in the island of Malta. When the first archaeologists first excavated the Temple complex of Malta they assumed it was a crude attempt to copy what was built in ancient Greece, but when it was carbon dated it was found to be built 5,500 years ago. A thousand years older than the Great pyramid in Egypt. He then says that the comment of archaeologists hearing this news was that is was the wrong date in the wrong place. The reason apparently for this attitude for this is that Malta is off the beaten track. Which is strange because Malta is just off the coast of Italy and not that far from Ancient Greece and Egypt. A more plausible explanation is that the archaeologists didn't want to know that Malta had the oldest freestanding stone buildings in the world, because the Temples in Malta are Goddess Temples, with Giant statues of the Great Mother. Can it be, that the reason we have such a large gap in our history that Richard Rudgley complains about, is because it is an age when people clearly worshipped the Great Mother? As all the "lost Civilisations" that he writes about where all full of feminine images. It strongly suggests that his silence is simply male bias, in men who discovered these sites wanting males to be the ones who created the first civilisations and not women. Or is there more to this than that? Archaeology like most science is very expensive, so most archaeologists are either very rich individuals like they were in the 19th century, or they rely on funding from universities, governments or religious sects like the Roman Catholic Church. As in everything else in life, "he who pays the fiddler calls the tune". Archaeologists finding the "wrong" things or advocating the "wrong" theories, in the eyes of the people who sponsor them, could have there funding cut off.

The First person to do a "scientific" excavation on Malta was a Jesuit priest called Father Emmanuel Magri in 1903. His form of excavation was to rub off paintings on the walls of the largest Goddess temple in Malta. Then to dig up the floor of the Temple and what he discovered there mysteriously disappeared. In other words, his work was to destroy the site for its archaeological value. This is not unusual. In the 19th century European explorers discovered in Zimbabwe an ancient city that was built by African kings between the 12 and 16th century. Europeans at first carelessly destroyed all evidence that it was Africans who built this city searching for gold and wouldn't entertain the idea that Africans built it. Simply because if it was known that Africans were able to create civilisations in the past, it would undermine the right of European countries to colonise Africa. Because the justification of colonialism at the time was they were civilising the people of this continent, whom were called savages.

Not only did archaeologists keep quiet about the first civilisations of the Neolithic and Bronze Age period. They have also kept quiet about the Amazons. Some time ago I accidentally come across information that Western archaeologists have found graves of female warriors all over Europe. Yet they seem to think these finds are an "embarrassment", (where have we found this expression before?), and so they are never published. The only people who have let the cat out of the bag are archaeologists of the old Soviet Union. In the 1950s and 60s they have published finding graves of Female warriors in the Ukraine and Georgia.

Both the ancient Greeks and Romans have reported fighting Amazon warriors on the northeast coast of the Black Sea. This is where the Soviet archaeologists have discovered the graves of women with armour and weapons of war within them. So it seems from the Soviet finds we can say that the Amazons existed in the places the Greek and Roman historians said they did. Unfortunately the silence by Western archaeologists about their discoveries of female warriors is censoring an important chapter in human history. It seems that after the Goddess civilisations were invaded from the North not all women meekly submitted to this. Some it seems fought back and created Amazon armies and communities. Though it has to be said they were all finally defeated. This process of censorship is being clearly shown in the archaeology of what is called, "the holy land". The Bible gives an impression that the people of Israel worshipped Yahweh from the time of Abraham. It even suggests that the people in the Bible before Abraham like Adam, Cain, Able, Noah and Jonah also worshipped a male God. Yet modern scholars have found a hidden Goddess in the Old Testament. It seems there is 40 coded mentions of a Goddess called Asherah.

In support of this, archaeologists have discovered in Israel over 3000 clay figurines of Large Breasted women, some are pregnant and other are nursing children. There is a possibility that more have been found but when excavations are sponsored by Christian sects or Zionist organisations, then images of Goddesses are strangely not discovered. These statues it seems are of the Goddess Asherah, showing that the Children of Israel were worshipping other deities than Yahweh.

In the 1960s a young archaeologist found a inscription that read, "Blessed by Yahweh and his Asherah." It seems he was too frightened to publish this find until another archaeologist published a similar inscription he had discovered. The reason why he was so reluctant to publish his find is that archaeology has become very political in Israel today. This is because archaeologists are being accused by politicians of undermining the legitimacy of the Jewish people's right to own modern Israel. Because the legitimacy of the Jews owning Israel comes from the truth of the Hebrew Bible. Start proving that the Bible is not accurate and it undermines the Israelite's case.

It seems that Asherah was openly worshipped in Israel up until a series reforms between 721BC and 609BC when by royal command Yahweh became the only God that was allowed to be worshipped. Though in this period some later Kings backtracked on this reform so it seems there was in this period a religious power struggle, that the worshipers of Yahweh finally won. Though the ordinary people were still worshipping Asherah in the privacy of there own homes. As shown in the images archaeologists found in ordinary people's home after this date. Also in this period the Hebrew Bible was written to create the belief that the Jews had always worshipped Yahweh. This rewriting of history was so successful that people even today are shocked to learn that the Jews once worshipped a Goddess.

The success of the Jewish ruling class in rewriting their own history seems to have inspired other rulers of other nations to follow suit including that of the rulers of the Roman Empire. When the rulers of Rome decided to create a religion to unite the whole of the Roman Empire they chose a Jewish sect called Christianity. They followed up this by destroying all knowledge of ancient history burning down libraries throughout the Roman Empire and attacking educated men and women. The Moslems also done the same thing in adopting their own version of Judaism called Islam and also tried to destroy all ancient knowledge. Yet it seems some ancient knowledge did survive like the legends of a Golden Age of the past.

The Golden age is written about by Hesiod the 8th century BC Greek poet, in which he says : "they lived like gods, free from worry and fatigue, old age did not afflict them, they rejoiced in continual festivity." " All the blessing of the world were theirs: the fruitful earth gave forth its treasures unbidden."

The Golden age would probably be before humans began to use agriculture. Now there is some evidence that people then lived better lives. Modern nutritionists are coming to the conclusion that human beings are healthier on what is called, "the Stone-Age diet". This is because this is what our bodies have been used to over millions of years of evolution. Then came agriculture, which gave us a far greater supply of food, but it also brought about a change in our diet that also brought about diseases caused by dietary deficiencies. The same is true with the modern Western diet today in that we are now eating foods like margarine, refined flour and sugar that are completely new to our bodies. Also it seems we didn't really benefit from agriculture in the way we should. Because with the increasing food supply the human population became larger and larger, which was all right while they had good harvests. Then suddenly when where there was famine, the population was too large to find food for everyone to eat and there was mass starvation.

Hesiod goes on to talk about the Silver age.

"After the Golden Age came the Silver Age, during which lived a race of feeble and inept men who obeyed their mothers all their lives."

Clearly he is talking about the Neolithic age confirms this age was ruled by women. Clearly Hesiod had contempt for these men who were dominated by women.

Then there was the Bronze age which he says.-

"The men of the Bronze Age were robust as ash trees and delighted only in oaths and warlike exploits. 'Their pitiless hearts were as hard as steel, their might was untameable, their arms invincible."

We now see the rise of the warrior who ruthlessly conquered the peaceful matriarchal world.

After the Bronze Age Hesiod talks about a Heroic age which declines to the Iron Age which is the age that Hesiod lived which he says is a period of misery and crime. "When men respect neither their vows, nor justice, nor virtue"..

Yet the myth of the Golden Age doesn't only come from Ancient Greece. Probably the most ancient religion that survives today is Taoism in China. Again in the Tao-Te-Ching it talks about a Golden age in the past, and the slow deterioration to our present world. We even have a Golden Age Legend in the Bible in the story of the Garden Of Eden that probably came from Mesopotamia. Though the story was rewritten to blame women for the fall from grace and claim it happened as a punishment from God for disobeying him. Hinduism also has a Golden Age myth similar to the Greeks where they write about an eternal cycle of Golden, Silver, Copper and Iron ages. They claim that when our present Iron age finishes, then a new Golden Age will dawn.

Now that archaeologists are unwittingly proving that the ancient Golden Age legends are not myth but historical fact. This could bring about world wide political revolution. For the last five thousand years we have lived in a world of violence that has resulted in wars, conquest and genocide. We also live in a very unfair and uncaring world where the majority of the world's wealth are in the hands of only 3% of the world's population. Today in spite of all the advances in modern technology we still live in a world where billions of people live in poverty. Yet world wide the common people are forced to accept this because we are told there is no alternative. We have always lived in an unfair and uncaring world of violence and war and so nothing can change. Yet what archaeologists have been finding over the last 50 years in the earliest civilisations shows us there is an alternative view of our past. Which means that these finds are becoming highly political.

11

WHY THE HAND THAT ROCKS THE CRADLE, IS NOT RULING THE WORLD

When Dr Ruth Shady began to make know her findings at Caral the local people were proud that the earliest civilisation found in America was in Peru, but they were also very puzzled. The question that she is frequently asked is: "Why did our ancestors have the capacity to build such an important city, and we live so poorly and don't have the ability to do similar things?". The only answer she is able to give is: "the society was organised with a population that worked to do things collectively for the collective good." Though she didn't go on to point out that whereas today everyone works for the benefit of the ruling elite who keep the wealth of the country in their own hands.

The Peruvian government is now feeling the political ramifications of these finds. Already they have cut her funding making it very difficult to continue her excavation or preserve what she has already discovered. Universities in USA have offered to fund the site, but their condition is that they themselves will take over the excavation. So it seems there are political moves to sack Dr Ruth Shady and put someone in charge who will toe the political line. Which could mean censorship of what is being discovered.

So it seems ancient discoveries are very political. If it became common knowledge that thousands of years ago people lived in peace and equality, then people world wide will begin to ask the same questions that the Peruvian peasants are asking today. This is turn could create new political and religious movements that will challenge our present ruling elite. Because if in the past we lived in a world of peace and equality then why can't we do the same today? This is why archaeology today is becoming increasingly political, as it is questioning the way our world has been ruled for the last five thousand years. The stability of any ruling elite is a belief that life is better now than any time in the past, because if the people are to believe that life in the past was better. It would create great unrest as they will want to recreate the better conditions of the past. So the leaders need to be able to tell the people, "you never had it so good." This is what the ruling elite have successfully convinced the people over the last couple of thousand years through censorship and destruction of all knowledge of early civilisations. Now this is changing, there is evidence that people in the past where able to live in peace and equality that is unmatched by any country today. Then if this knowledge was to become common knowledge, people will ask why can't we do the same today? Which could cause a worldwide revolution that could undermine all governments all over the world. It is no wonder there is a attempt to censor all the archaeological finds from the Neolithic age.

As I have pointed out before many Feminist are uncomfortable about the findings of the Neolithic age to the degree that some are as critical of the concept of pre-historic matriarchy as many male chauvinists. Even women like Riane Eisler and Marija Gimbutas have claimed that the people in the Neolithic age lived in a age of sexually equality. Which is a very politically correct Feminist line.

The problem is that we have no writings from the Neolithic age has been satisfactory translated. So we know nothing about the social system of that era. This means there is not real proof that people then lived in a matriarchy, patriarchy or an equal society. (Though the fact they worshipped Goddesses and lived in a non-violent society is more likely to suggest matriarchy or equality.)

The suggestion of sexual equality in the Neolithic age does present a few problems for men. It means that when women had power they used it to create a equal society. Yet when men later had power they used violence to dominate society and women. This then makes men out to be the "bad-guy", while women come out of it being paradigms of virtue. So many men would be very resistant to ideas of pre-historic equality, as it puts them into a very bad light. It seems to prove the children's saying, "What are little boys made of? Snakes and snails and puppy dog tails. What are little girls made off? Sugar and spice and All things NICE." For this reason, many men would prefer the opposite extreme where women did rule men harshly in those days and preferably walked around in black leather and carrying whips in which to beat men.

Another problem with a equal or matriarchal society is how did women prevent men from competing with each other and with women? A clue to this is what I mentioned in the last chapter. If men live in a society without violence and competition then their testosterone levels greatly decrease. So men in these societies would be more amiable then than in the later very brutal patriarchal societies. Problem solved then. Just keep men away from violence and competition and everything will be all right. Except how did it happen that these peaceful non-violent men of the Neolithic age suddenly became the brutal savages of the Bronze and Iron ages?

Marija Gimbutas suggests this happened through invasion. In that violent patriarchal tribes from the North conquered the peaceful matriarchal communities. That doesn't solve the problem because how did these Northern tribes become violent and patriarchal? A possible explanation is that life in the North was so harsh, it brutalised the men. Raising their testosterone levels and they became violent and competitive with women. Resulting in them dominating women through violence. That explanation sounds reasonable enough but there is another explanation that comes from the myths of Pandora and the story of Adam and Eve.

Pandora was the Ancient Greek's Eve, in that she was the first women and lived in a Golden Age like that of the Garden of Eden. She was given a jar or box and one day she opened it to find out what was inside. Then from it out come all the plagues of illness, envy, spite and revenge that have been with us ever since. This at first sight seems to be a absurd and fanciful tale and a attempt to blame women for all this ills of the world. Yet if we look at modern research on the Stone and Neolithic ages we find it is a metaphor of what could have happened.

When palaeontologists and archaeologists began to discover the remains of humans during the Stone Age they were surprised to discovered in carved statues and wall paintings there was far more images of women than men. At first they didn't take the feminine images seriously and female statuettes were routinely discarded as just fertility images or Stone Age pornography. It was only because some people in the art world got interested in these statuettes that we know about them today. As palaeontologists found they had a profitable sideline in selling female statuettes to art dealers.

Yet the surprise of scientists that Stone-Age people seemed to be more interested in making images of women rather than men has a lot to do with the Judeo-Christian attitudes. For the last two thousand years it has been accepted by the main religions of Christianity, Islam, Buddhism and to some degree Hinduism that god is a male. We have then been so brainwashed into believing this, that it is hard for us to think of a Creator that is not a male. Including it seems scientists whom many profess to being unbiased and logical atheists.

Yet it was not always like this and from the evidence coming from the Stone and Neolithic Ages, it seems people then naturally assume our Creatix was a women.

When humans first became self aware they began to ask themselves, "what created the world?" It then would be natural for them to assume that the intelligence that created our world would be feminine. Because if we look at animal and human life we find that life is created within the bodies of females. In fact it must have seem to our ancestors that women had great magical powers to create life like this. So it would be logical for them to assume that the whole of creation was born from the body of what they called, "The Great Mother".

This belief it seems gave women great power and status in human societies, because if the Creatrix was female then all women were created in the image of the Great Mother. This then made women very sacred and holy because it was only women who could create in the same way the Great Mother had done. This is seen clearly in the many images found in Stone Age and Neolithic sites that show images of the sex-act, the genitalia of women represented as V or slit symbols and the very many naked images of women themselves. The picture that comes from these ancient times is that people then regarded the sex-act, menstruation, childbirth and breast-feeding as all being very sacred, because they were all part of the process of creating life.

Some palaeontologists have speculated that people in the Stone Age were unaware that the sex act produced childbirth. So women suddenly producing children would be seen as a wondrous miracle where men had no input. They also went on to imagine that when men realised this role in conception, he no longer worshipped women as magical beings and took over the role of Creator himself. To support this theory we do find in Ancient Egypt that the God Atum created the world in a act of masturbation. The problem is that we do find the sexual act portrayed in Stone-Age art. So the people then, may not be as daft as we assume they might be. Also the input of men in the act of creation can be over in two seconds, (wham, bam, thank you ma'am). Which is not anywhere equal to women carrying a foetus for nine months, the pain and drama of childbirth itself, then the ability of the women to feed the newborn baby from her breasts. Not to mention all the mysteries of menstrual, which was seen as something very holy and sacred in matriarchal societies, and something as unclean and taboo in later patriarchal societies.

So we can see from this that the ancient religion of the Great Mother would be a very feminine religion and empathise the feminine virtues of compassion, caring, nurturing, loving and creativity. This is supported by the fact that in the first civilisations of the Neolithic age, warfare and violence against other people was completely unknown. We only begin to find weapons of war, fortifications and images of violence in the later bronze and iron ages. Where it seems people began to worship male warrior gods.

It seems that men started to began to dominate our world about five thousand years ago through violence and conquest. They then also created male dominated religions that made the Creator a male and claimed that the sexual act; menstruation, childbirth and breast-feeding were all unclean, sinful and taboo. Even today few women dare to breast feed in public. While back in the 1950s and 60s male doctors all but banned breast-feeding claiming that cow's milk was better for the child! It was only later scientific research showed the obvious fact that that human milk was best for human babies. As it had been discovered that mothers pass on their immunity through the breast milk. Unfortunately there is still resistance because mothers are not encouraged to keep breast-feeding too long, and to switch to cow's milk as soon as possible. In spite of the fact that the research shows that mothers keep on feeding their immunity to disease to the baby right up to time the baby is weaned.

Some Christian women, even now will after birth still go to priests for a cleansing ritual to clean them of the "sin" of childbirth. Children also go through the cleansing ritual of baptism, which originally was to clean them of the sin of being, "born of women". So we can see through patriarchal attitudes an attack on the importance of women's roles. As Feminists have pointed out so often, child rearing is the most devalued work in our society. When some Feminist in the 1960s and 70s suggested that women should be paid to bring up children they were laughed at and ridiculed. After all bringing children and caring for them is clearly not as important as the work of a general who make plans to wipe out whole cities with nuclear weapons, or politicians who tell the public lies, to get votes.

So this is the difference between matriarchal and patriarchal religions. The feminine Goddess religions were about the celebration of whole act of creation from the sexual act to giving birth and breast-feeding. So it empathised the maternal instincts of women of compassion, caring and love. The masculine religions on the other hand have throughout history have been about the glorification of violence. Where religious wars have been commonplace and still go on even today. The irony of this is that in Christianity, Jesus preached love and compassion yet Christianity has been one of the world's most violence religions, throughout it's history.

This has been the great tragedy of the last five thousand years. While humans believed that the world was created by the Great Mother, the feminine maternal instincts of compassion, nurturing and love became the ideal for everyone. Then people began to question this belief and accept that our Creator could be male and female. This allowed people to accept masculine principles and instincts of competition and aggression. In time this was allowed to grow until it turned into violence, and conquest. Creating the world we know throughout recorded history of war, oppression, poverty and suffering.

So we see a similar story to that of Pandora's Box. Some Feminists have commented that because Pandora and Eve are blamed for bringing all the ills into the world these are anti women stories. Yet blame also implies power. Suggesting that in the past women did have power and gave it away.

In societies that worshipped the Great Mother, women would be the superior sex because only women had the magical power to create life. This would then make men the inferior sex who would have no real power or status except to serve women. It then must have occurred to many women that perhaps this was a bit unfair. So we find that the Great Mother then has a son, this son soon becomes the lover or brother of the Great Mother and they became co-creators. This probably reflected on the growing status of men in society as women allowed men to have equal rights.

The anthropologist Eva Meyerowitz discovered the way one African tribe change over from matriarchy to patriarchy. Living in Ghana she got friendly with the Akan people and learnt their history, which she wrote in four books. It seems in the past they were once a matriarchal tribe ruled by a Queen. Then over time some Queens allowed their sons more power to rule men's affairs. Slowly over time if the son was more assertive than his mother then the son would take more power to himself. While on the other hand if the Queen was more assertive then things stayed as they were. So in this way the power of women in the tribe was slowly eroded over many generations. Then when the British came they only dealt with the men and ignore the Queen and the power of the women. Which confirmed to the men they didn't need a powerful Queen and she was overthrown in colonial times and all the power given to the King.

In some ways this research confirms the ideas of Steven Goldberg that women are not assertive enough to allow men to slowly take over. Yet women did rule in the past suggesting in this tribe women were once far more assertive in the past than they are now. Suggesting that the patriarchal age came into being not only because of men's aggression but also of women's apathy in allowing it to happen. This apathy could only come about through women not realising that men would create a world of conflict and suffering if they ruled the world.

So it is probably true that equal rights between men and women is possible, in the change over from matriarchy to patriarchy. Anthologists have studied Stone-Age culture who have practised this in modern times. Perhaps in a hunter/gather community this wasn't a problem but in an age of agriculture, it sowed the seeds for its own destruction. People who have become dependants on their crops to feed themselves become very dependant on having a good harvest most years. One bad harvest is not a real problem if grain is saved from previous years. Three or more bad harvests in a row is a real problem and can destroy a civilisation.

In situations of starvation people can become very selfish and violent. Archaeologists have even found cases of cannibalism being practised in very bad drought conditions. Starvation created a true situation of the survival of the fittest. This means that men being bigger, stronger and more aggressive will have a big advantage over women in taking what small amount of food that is left. So men will gain dominance over women through violence. Then once the drought is over it is doubtful if men will give up their dominant position and continue to dominate women.

Now this wouldn't of happened if women still retained a strong sisterhood. They could of stuck together and ganged up on the men in starvation conditions. Ensuring it was them and their children that was fed first, an example of this was written by Paul Vallely a Christian aid worker.

In visiting many refugee camps he was used to them being taken over by the local alpha males who run them like a Mafia, where food was used to as a weapon to give the alpha males greater power over the population, and if the food aid charities objected, they were threatened with violence. Yet in a place called Tendelti in the Sahara desert he found something different. This was a refugee camp of ten thousand people most of whom were women. (The men had either died in wars or were still fighting wars). The women organised the food aid in a very different way, in that they gave the small amount they received equally to the children. While the adults lived on mokheit and the other scant famine foods in which the desert people turned to at times of desperation. It seems that without alpha men in the camp it greatly increased the survival chances of all the people within it. The above shows what women can do if they organise themselves into a strong sisterhood. They will put the welfare of the children first and try to share what food they have fairly. Unfortunately if the sisterhood is broken down through patriarchy or equality, women then become very vulnerable to the violence and dominance of men.

The story of Pandora's box and Adam and Eve suggest that once women were the dominant sex and people then lived in a non-violent Golden age and later Silver age. Then women decided that making men the inferior sex was unfair. This is represented by Pandora opening the box or Eve tempting Adam to eat from the tree of knowledge. The very act of doing this suggests that Eve was in charge.

Unfortunately in giving men equality resulted in him eventually becoming competitive with women and dominating society through violence. This resulted in our present world of violence, injustice and poverty. As the Bible points out this was a tragedy for both men and women as Adam found that outside the Garden of Eden were he had to, "work by the sweat of this brow". In other words in a masculine world of winners and losers there are few winners and many losers. So the losers in a patriarchal society which includes both men and women found themselves having to work, not only to support themselves, but the ruling and warrior classes and the patriarchal priesthood.

The problem is that whatever theory you subscribe to does seem that women will always have problems in the long run in trying to tame men. If women are able to create a society where violence and competition is unknown and it brings down the testosterone levels of men. Or they convince men that the Creatrix is a woman and so all are Goddesses in the same mould. It doesn't always mean that men will always be like this. There is always a chance that a natural disaster may happen and in the fight for survival, men's testosterone levels may rise again.

While men are naturally aggressive and competitive there is always the chance that this aggression will break out into violence and brutality. So is that it? Does it mean that although women can tame men, in the end men's instinctive competitiveness will break through and we will be back to the violent world we have seen over the last five thousand years.

The question is, is it natural and normal for men to be violent and brutal? The evidence from the whole of recorded history, with its countless wars, genocide and torture and would be a resounding "Yes". Yet five thousand years is a very small period in the four million years humans have lived on the Earth. Were men always very brutal and violent during that period? Most palaeontologists would probably say, "yes" to this as well. Unfortunately most palaeontologists are men and seem to be very chauvinistic men at that. So we will have to accept some bias in this assumption. There is another way to look at our early ancestors that shows us in a completely different light. Recently I learnt of surprising statistic. It seem that of all the British soldiers that experienced military action during the Falklands War, more of them have since committed suicide, than died during the conflict. There is an even more shocking statistic about the Vietnam War. Where THREE TIMES as many ex-soldiers that saw action, have since committed suicide, than died in the war. Though this figure is hotly disputed there is still an agreement that it is still a very large number. So if men do get very traumatised by war where many kill themselves afterwards. It begs the question, if war and violence is normal and natural for men? It is true some individual men enjoy war and enjoy killing as we see in the case of serial killers. Though there is still a high suicide rate in men who have committed multiple murders. So it seems that men can be made into killers through brutalisation, but do they really want to be like this?

If killing traumatises men, it also begs the question whether all the wars and massacres we see in history is also normal and natural for men. As previously pointed out the Japanese military had to brutalise their troops in the Second World War to turn them into trained killers. The German army also brutalised their young men in the same war, to again make it possible for them to kill without mercy.

So we are back to the nature verse nurture debate. Is violence and male dominance over women only possible by the brutalisation of men? Or is it "all in the jeans" and men are naturally programmed by their genes to be violent and dominant over women? I would personally think it was the third option and that it is a bit of both. We can see clearly that if you brutalise men that will become violent and will dominate others less violent then themselves, like women. So men do have this potential, which is probably programmed in his genes, but without this brutalisation it seem that men are not naturally violent. Nor do they naturally dominate women. As we can see today in Western societies where men are less brutalised then they were in the past, and seem far less inclined to commit violence on women.

So was this true in the Stone Age, which makes up 95% of human existence? Were men violent brutes then, or were they able to live lives of peace and harmony in those days. We cannot know because we have no written record of those times, but their is evidence coming from the behaviour of one ape that throw a very different light on the behaviour of early humans.

Since Darwin, it has been accepted that humans have evolved from apes. The general public know about four different species of ape, Orang-utan, Gorilla, chimpanzee and Gibbon. You will see all these apes featured on wild life programmes on TV. Yet there is one other ape that doesn't get the same coverage, and that is the bonobo. Along with the chimpanzee this ape, the closest species to us. So we can learn a lot about our ancestors by examining the behaviour of both apes. Interestingly people are comfortable with the behaviour of chimpanzee because the males are very violent and brutal. (Just ordinary, good o' macho males) Yet they are not so comfortable about the behaviour of bonobos and this is because they are the, "the make love not war, ape."

12

MAKE LOVE NOT WAR

The bonobo was first discovered by Europeans in 1929 and was considered then to be only a subspecies of the chimpanzees. More recent research has shown it to be very different from the chimpanzee. Being more lightly built and having longer legs, it has the body structure more like a human than any other ape. But the main difference is in the way it behaves, which is very human.

Back in the 1960s professor Leakey in trying to understand how early humans behaved decided that a insight in this could be gained by observing different species of apes in the wild. He decided that women were better observers than men, so he used women like Jane Goodall observing chimpanzees Diane Fossey studying Gorillas. The result of this brought about a revolution in the study of apes, and many new things were discovered. Like chimpanzees were able to make tools, as up until then scientists believed that only humans could do this. Also it was discovered that gorillas were gentle and peaceful creatures, as it was formerly believed that gorillas were dangerous and aggressive animals. All the other apes were observed in the same way, with the bonobo being only intensely observed in very recent times.

One of the first surprises about this ape is that it is very sexual in its behaviour. Like the human female the bonobo female can still have sex even when her body is not ready for fertilization. It also indulges in homosexual sexual behaviour with both sexes doing this and can copulate face to face. (Though the orangutan has also been observed to do this as well).

In many other animals and apes aggression between males and against females is quite common. Most animals overcome this aggression by having a strict hierarchical system where everyone knows its place. With the animals with lesser social status giving way to those with higher status. The animal's place in the system is controlled by its strength and aggression. So fights only break out when a animal of lesser status wants to achieve higher status in the pecking order.

The bonobo does have a similar system but aggressive behaviour between them is far less than other animals because of the way they use sex. In a article by Frans B. M. de Waal, it compares the different behaviour of chimpanzees and bonobos when two females and a male come across some food. In the case of the chimpanzees the food was bananas. Their behaviour was very straight forward the male chimpanzee fed first until he had enough and he then took away as many bananas as he could carry. Then the dominant female fed herself, and the subordinate female it seems got nothing. In the case of the bonobos it was sugar cane, and their behaviour was more complex. The two female started by indulging in sex by rubbing their genitals together. While the male bonobo displays his erect penis to them, but they ignore him. Then the two female fed together equally and only when they had finish was the male allowed to feed.

This is it seems is normal bonobo behaviour where there is a possibility of a dispute, the first thing they do is to have sex together which seems to defuse the situation. In this situation the natural aggression of the male seems to work against the male bonobo in contrast to the way it helps the male chimpanzees. As the female bonobos are less aggressive it is easier for them to bond with each other, which they reinforce through sexual play. It then makes it easier for them to gang up on males, who although do also bond together through sex, are still more aggressive towards each other. This makes them less able to co-operate and work together in the way the females can. Which suggests that the bonobo could also be called, "The Sisterhood Is Powerful" apc.

As the bonobo males are bigger than the females they stand a better chance in a one to one situation but even here they can lose out. In a conflict say over food, the female will immediately have sex with the male, the sexual bonding defuses the natural aggression of the male and they will share the food equally. It also has been observed of a male who had found a large fruit and a female immediately had sex with him and he afterwards gave her his fruit. Which seems to be the first case observed in the animal world of prostitution. Female bonobos will also encourage males to help in looking after their children in return for sexual favours. Which also sounds very much like human behaviour.

So this it seems is how the slogan "make love not war" can work in practice, by having disputes settled by sexual bonding. Comparing the bonobo's behaviour with that of the chimpanzees' can assess how effective this is. Both animals share 98% of the genetic makeup of a human and we were all the same animal as little as eight million years ago. In fact of the body structure of the bonobo looks very similar to that of a australopithecine, a early pre-human with similar length arms and legs. From this it is speculated that the bonobo is more similar to our common ancestor than either the chimpanzee or the human. With the human later growing longer legs and a more upright stance while the chimpanzee growing longer and stronger arms to climb trees. As our body is shaped by our behaviour over evolutionary time, it is reasonable to suggest that how the bonobo behaves today is more like how our common ancestor behaved in the past.

The behaviour of the chimpanzees is of the traditional patriarchal society. Chimpanzees only have sex to fertilise the females when they are on heat. This is the ideal of the patriarchal Christian Church who has tried to enforce this type of behaviour for hundreds of years. Claiming that sex only for the sake of pleasure is "sinful" and should only be used for conception. So it is strange that the Christian Church has never held up the chimpanzee as a ideal of moral virtue!

Chimpanzees tend to bond through fear and mutual protection, with a group of males holding on to a territory against other groups of males. There seems to be sometimes war between these different groups over land, resulting in males getting badly injured or even killed. The effect of this is there is always more females in a community than males as so many males get killed through violence. As the males have to stick together to fight off the territorial ambitions of other groups of male, they bond closer together than the females. Males not only show aggression to other groups of males but to each other, as they will charge each other or show off their strength to try and intimidate each other to gain more status in the pecking order. Aggression is also shown towards females who being smaller than males have to give way to them in all disputes.

In contrast the bonobo society nearly all aggression is defused through sexual bonding. It has been observed in zoos that if say a cardboard box is thrown into the enclosure and more than one bonobo shows interest in it. They will then briefly mount each other before playing with the box together. Or if one jealous male chases away another male near a female. The two males will then reconcile with each other by engaging in scrotal rubbing together. The same will be true if two adult females have a dispute over the behaviour of one of their children. They will reconcile by rubbing their genitals together. Male bonobos rarely fight each other over status. A male bonobo stays attached to his mother all his life and his status in society depends on the status of his mother, whom he will look to for protection from any aggression from other bonobos. Even though she may be smaller than him in size.

In human behavioural studies it has been noted that people who live in very stressful situations like extreme poverty, war, prison, an aggressive family or neighbourhood, tend to become very desensitised and so they are far less affected by fear and pain. In Hellabrun, Germany, in the World War Two there was a zoo, which housed both chimpanzees and bonobos. One night the city was bombed and the bonobos died of fright from the noise while the chimpanzees were completely unaffected. Demonstrating how desensitised chimpanzees have become living in their brutal patriarchal society, and how sensitive bonobos are, living in a more peaceful matriarchal world.

Apart from the fact that chimpanzees do not get married or "pair-bond". Its society is very much like a normal human patriarchal society. And until bonobo behaviour was studied properly, chimpanzee behaviour justified the patriarchal society as being "natural" for humans. So it is of interest that when primatologists first started to study bonobos in zoos during the 1950s the first findings were completely ignored by the scientific establishment until the 1970s. Even today most people are unaware of the behaviour of the bonobo or even that such a creature exists. The reason for this silence is because the bonobo's behaviour undermined all our patriarchal beliefs about human and pre-human behaviour.

If the bonobo is a very sexual ape than it has to be said that so is the human. Though chimpanzees only partake in basic reproductive sex, bonobos share all kinds of sexual pleasures, including cunnilingus, fellatio, masturbation, massage, bisexuality, incest, body-licking, sex in different positions, group sex, and French kissing. Also like humans in love, copulating bonobos often look deeply into each other's eyes.

Although patriarchal societies have attempted to enforce sexual relations in the confines of marriage, many human have always had urges to want more than this. So in all patriarchal societies none have been able to prevent prostitution. While in secret and sometimes quite openly both men and women have had relationships outside of marriage. In very recent times with the decline of the patriarchal society, marriage is breaking down in Western countries. Which has resulted in many people frequently changing sexual partners, having "one night stands", joining sex-clubs, going to sex-parties, advertising for sex in contact magazines or having "open" relationships. So why do many people have the urge to have sex with many different partners? To the degree that the patriarchal society with all its laws, religious and social censure fail to stamp this behaviour out. The only reason could be is that before the patriarchal society took control with all it laws to restricting people's behaviour. People's behaviour must of been very similar to that of the bonobo.

Bonobos like humans also tend to eat food in the company of other bonobos in big dinner parties. It seems that when fruit is in abundance bonobos will collect the fruit for a large community feast. Then will eat it together, in a big banquet after the high status females have eaten first. This is very unlike the chimpanzees that will generally hide food from others and eat alone. Another interesting point is that human couples have romantic evenings together. This involves sharing a meal together, either at a restaurant or sometimes at home, then having sex together. Which is also what bonobos couples do, though they tend to have sex before the meal and not afterwards.

It is well know that many couples when they have a "flaming row", they will afterwards "make up" by having sex together. To the degree that some couples claim that they enjoy a turbulent relationship because they greatly enjoy the making up afterwards. This then is similar to bonobo behaviour of using sex to defuse a conflict.

So like the bonobos, humans do associate conflict and food with sex. In times of war it used to be that when a conquering army takes a town or city, all the women and even sometimes the men are raped. This behaviour is generally seen as an expression of power over conquered people. Which is probably true but looking at bonobo behaviour their could be another reason for this. Perhaps it is a form of unconscious reconciliation by rape. Soldiers in warfare can become through extreme fear, very aggressive in battle. Even disciplined troops have been known to slaughter defenceless civilian populations after a battle, because of this fear induced aggression. So rape may defuse this situation, making possible for the soldiers to calm down and prevent a killing spree.

In the past when people used to worship Goddesses which is a indication of a matriarchal religion. The later patriarchal priests condemned the priestess of Goddess temples as being prostitutes. When the Romans first conquered Britain many of the Celtic tribes were still ruled by Queens. Their behaviour was seen as being very scandalous by later writers, as some of these Queens would openly have sex with large numbers of different men. So it does suggest that the old matriarchal societies were far more sexual than the later patriarchal societies. Which does suggest that a matriarchal society could perhaps be as sexual as a bonobo society. With people bonding together through sexual behaviour, allowing people to be more intimate with each other. Which will in turn will create a more intimate, caring and loving community.

War has been "normal" throughout recorded history, where there has never been a time when there hasn't been a war going on in some part of the world. Many people have written about the senseless suffering of war, and have looked unsuccessfully for ways to prevent future wars. The study of both the chimpanzee and bonobo societies shows there is a alternative to war. In the non-sexual chimpanzee society, conflict and war is normal. In the very sexual bonobo society conflict is rare. So because of the study of these different ape societies we find that the slogan "make love not war" is not a joke but does in fact work.

It is of interest that Frans de Waal who has written books and articles about the bonobo was criticised by Dawkins for "bad science". Which is understandable because observations on the bonobo undermine completely his belief that we are all basically selfish. Perhaps it would be "good science" to ignore the bonobo completely and only concentrate on the chimpanzee. It is of interest that Dawkins also criticises the anthropologist Margaret Mead. Her crime being that she observed human nature in a positive light. Also the fact that she was both a famous scientist and a feminist at the same time upset many of her male colleges.

It then means we humans have a choice. As pointed out previously both the chimpanzee and bonobo are the closest species to us, and we can clearly see similarities in their behaviour to ours. The behaviour of the chimpanzee is very similar to a patriarchal society in that it is very violence and relatively non-sexual.

In contrast the bonobo live in a very sexual world where both males and females bond together through many different forms of sexual play. So it means we all get to be laid and with multiple partners and can experiment with heterosexual and homosexual sex play. We even would get to try things that are considered to be kinky. The bonus is that by bonding through sex we won't have to fight wars any more. Is it that easy? Well probably not, as human society is far more complex than that of the bonobo. Yet we can see many similarities with bonobo society.

1. Over the last hundred years in the West women have gained equal opportunity, and guess what? As women have gain more status, power and freedom, our society has become more sexually liberated at the same time. Is that a coincidence?
2. Patriarchal societies create oppressive laws and customs not only to restrict women's freedoms but also women's sexuality. In fact patriarchal Christians have declared that sex is dirty and sinful and can only be used for reproduction. Which is what chimpanzee do.
3. Goddess religions in the past were called an abomination by patriarchal priests because they openly used sexual rituals. Goddess priestesses were condemned by patriarchal priests as temple prostitutes. Was this just sour grapes by patriarchal priests because they weren't getting laid? Or had they worked out the connection between sex and intimacy versus war and sexual frustration. It is of interest that even today many sportsmen will not have sex before an important sporting event because they believe sex will weaken them. Doctors claim that this is a myth because sex only weakens a person temporary. So having sex the night before is not going to affect any sportsman physically. Yet coaches ignore this advice, so perhaps sex will lessen men's aggression and this is why it will weaken men. Some coaches have even banned wives and girlfriends when going to sporting events in other countries. Does this suggest that even the presents of girlfriends and wives undermine the sportsmen's aggression?
4. In the Neolithic age we find many images of sexual expression as we find the presents of Goddess worship and non-violence. Is this just another coincidence?
5. The famous psychiatrist Sigmaund Freud discovered at the beginning of the 20th century that most of his patients were suffering from mental illness because of sexual repression. So it seems that suppression of sexual desire can not only make men violent but also it can cause female hysteria.

This concept was taken even further by the controversial psychiatrist Wilhelm Reich, who has been dubbed, "A scientist with attitude" He was originally a disciple of Freud but Reich took Freud's theories to the extreme, claiming that our whole society was insane because of sexual repression. This was a step too far for Freud whom was very aware that his theories were controversial enough already. He wanted social acceptance and scientific respectability for them and didn't want to alienate everyone by taking it too far. This wasn't a consideration for Reich who was willing to, "rush in where angels fear to tread".

He created a storm in Austria in the 1930s by trying to encourage young girls to have sex before marriage and teach them about contraception. This in a society that then rigidly believed that it was a sin and a social disgrace for a woman to have sex before of marriage. He was forced to leave Austria and went to Germany in 1933, where he wrote a book called *The Mass Psychology*

Of Fascism, which linked fascism with sexual repression and insanity. Which didn't exactly go down a storm with the Nazi party and he had to flee Germany in disguise. He then went to Copenhagen and managed to upset the Danish Communist Party and other left wing intellectuals. (They claimed that his book *The Mass Psychology Of Fascism* was counter-revolutionary). The Danish government had him thrown out of the country and about the same time, the Congress of Psycho-analysis, also expelled him for his views and opinions. He ended up in USA where he continued to make waves and upset people. Then after the Second World War he was sent to prison where he died and the FBI destroyed his papers and laboratories. To make enemies of the Nazis, the Communists and USA authorities, is quite a feat, and he probably died in prison wondering, "was it something I said?"

The irony is that he was put into prison by a country that proclaimed freedom of speech. All right, he clearly didn't read the book, *How To Win Friends And Influence People,* and some of his theories and research was very wild and controversial.. Yet why did the authorities need to destroy all his research papers and try to burn all the books he had published? After all he had lost all scientific credibility by chasing UFOs in the Arizona desert, and trying to shoot them down with something called a cloudbuster. All right, perhaps he did go potty towards the end of this life. Yet his earlier work was just a logical extension of Freud's work.

Saying what Freud dare not say, for fear of upsetting too many people. What probably upset the authorities so much was the fact that Reich was brave or foolhardy enough to claim that the whole of our society was insane because of sexual repression. Which although sounds like a extreme position, is valid when we realise that the whole of human kind became very close to committing global suicide during the Cold War. We must remember that USA was gripped by the McCarthyism at the time Reich was put into jail. So the last thing the authorities at the time would want is a psychiatrist claiming that they were paranoia in wanting to persecute communists. More so if he was to comparing them to Nazis in the way they persecuted people.

Oppression, genocide, war and male violence in general is justified through the concept of good and evil. The concept is one of the biggest con tricks ever invented. This can be illustrated by a story about an encounter between Lady Astor and Joseph Stalin. Before the Second World War Lady Astor was a member of a party of British MPs who visited the Soviet Union and were made guests Stalin. Lady Astor being a very out spoken woman verbally attacked Stalin for the millions of peasants that had died, because of his policies of the collectivisation of agriculture and forced industrialisation. He listened to her patiently and then explained that it was very unfortunately that all these people died, but it was needed if the Soviet Union was to become an industrial country and was able to efficiently feed itself in the future. He clearly didn't see anything wrong with what he was doing, and believed it was necessary to make the Soviet Union a modern prosperous country.

The point is that to many people Joseph Stalin was one of the most evil men in history. Yet he didn't see himself like this. He honestly saw himself as a good man who was attempting to do the best for his country. Likewise the same can be said of even worse tyrants like Hitler and Po-Pot the Cambodia dictator. Hitler felt justified in the genocide of the Jews and Slavs because in his mind they were a evil and inferior race. This means that in his mind he was a good person, fighting what HE had decided was evil. The same is true of Po-Pot who slaughtered millions of his own countrymen and women who didn't share his ideal of a perfect society. What is clear is that all these men believed very strongly that, "the ends justified the means". So in their minds war, violence, torture and genocide were all acceptable in creating, what they believed was a better future for their countries.

I remembered once reading about a prison governor who relating his long experiences dealing with prisoners explained the surprising fact, that most criminals see themselves as good people. It seems that criminals tend to blame society, the police or the system for their crimes. To be fair, there is some justification for this, as the majority of criminals come from the poorest and least educated sections of society.

This then means that if we divide the world up into good guys and bad guys. We find it is very much a matter of opinion who is who. For instance in the conflict in Northern Ireland the Roman Catholic assume it is the Protestant para-militaries and the police who are the bad guys. While the Protestants assume it is the IRA. With both sides claiming that the other side are the evil and they off coarse are the good guys. It makes peace talks between the two sides very difficult, if not impossible. The IRA and the Protestant terrorist groups are also in a strange collusion, because they are justified in their existence and actions by the behaviour of the other side. As both sides can point to the atrocities done by the other side to give credence to their violent behaviour. This keeps a cycle of violence going in perpetually.

This is true for every war ever fought. With both sides claiming that they are the good guys while the other side is off coarse evil. This was brought out in the open in the Xmas of 1914 during the First World War. The British and Germans in the trenches began singing Christmas carols with each other, and then calling out to each other over no-mans-land. In the end some soldiers came out trenches and began to talk with each other and organising football matches against each other. When they began to talk British and German soldiers ask each other.-

"What are you fighting for?"

"For freedom and my country," came the replied, "what are you fighting for?"

"The same."

Exchanges like this caused many of the soldiers to ask the obvious question,

"Why are we fighting each other?"

Unfortunately no one came up with a sensible answer to this question. The incident greatly worried the politicians and military leaders on both sides as it threatened to turn the whole war into a farce. (Which is what war is, although it is a very tragic farce). In the end "normality" was restored and both sides went back to murdering each other. The problem this highlights is that war is easy if you believe the people you are fighting are bad or evil. Once you realise they are just human being like yourself, then this greatly undermines the moral justification for wanting to kill them.

The result of condemning someone as evil is that it de-humanises them. Once it has been agreed that someone is evil then it becomes acceptable to hurt, torture and kill them. For instance the justification of Europeans to massacre and steal the land of the native people in the Americas and Australia was that they were "savages". Which is just another de-humanising word like bad and evil.

In many action and adventure films, books and TV programmes the concept of good and evil comes across very strongly. A villain is established; who behaves in an appalling manner and this gives the hero the justification to commit violence and murder on the villain. Some commentators claim that these stories are just harmless fun. Yet as any advertising executive knows, people are greatly influenced by what entertains them. So in the end it becomes just another way to indoctrinate people, that hate and violence is perfectly justified.

Even intelligent and academic people can be seduced by the concept of good and evil as in the case of the Christian author and academic C.S Lewis. He wrote a trilogy of Science Fiction books to explore religious themes. I read the first one, *Out of the Silent Planet* and I thought it was very good book but the second one *Journey To Venus* shocked and horrified me. In it, he had a hero and a villain travel to Venus, where they find a Garden of Eden complete with a Venusian Adam and Eve. (This was written before and spacecraft flew to Vesus, to show what a inhospitable planet it is.) Both men then set about influencing this couple's beliefs. Initially, the villain was successful; the Venusians listened to him more than they did the hero. Eventually the hero became desperate, believing there was nothing but misery for the Venusians if they followed the villain's ideas. His solution was to beat the villain to death with a rock. The logic being that his actions were justified because the man was evil. Yet it was an appalling message to give to the Venusians, if you can't win an argument, kill your opponent! C. S. Lewis was a respected academic. He wrote children's books, which are still hugely popular, and a number of books on religion, as well as his novels. Yet it's clear that illusions about good and evil were able to blind even an intelligent man like him.

The concept of good and evil also prevents us from solving problems like crime. The "macho" solution to crime is that when you catch a criminal you then punish him. (it is far more likely to be a him than a her). Yet prisons are known and the "university of crime", in that they are more likely to confirm a man into a life of crime than cure him. This happens for four reasons.

1. In going to prison a criminal gets to mix with other criminals where he learns better ways to rob and steal from other prisoners. He also gets to make criminal contacts, which he will probably use once he is released.
2. In mixing with other criminals he gets to believe that crime is a 'normal' way of life for him.
3. Once a man has a criminal record it is much harder for him to get a legal job. So he is more likely to drift back to a life of crime even if he has intentions of going straight.
4. Although in theory criminals are not longer punished. Being put into a over crowed prison can be hell, which results in criminals becoming brutalised. So they learn to hate the society that put him into prison. Teaching a man to hate society and then releasing him back into the community, is not a good idea.

Prison should be about rehabilitation. This has been put forward as early as the 19th century but even now in the 20th century many politicians and prison governors still only pay lip service to this concept. In many Western countries today prisoners are still not properly educated and get no support or help to become productive members of the community.

Although it is natural for people to want to punish criminals more so if you are personally a victim of crime. Revenge is certainly not the answer and it only makes a bad situation even worse. This is clearly illustrated by happened in Tihar jail in India.

In the 1980s Kiran Bedi was a very successful female tennis star, but she then abandoned her jet-set life to become the first female officer in the Indian police force. She rose swiftly through the ranks and her success made her enemies of some of her superiors, who firmly believed that a women's place was in the home. So to bring her down a peg or two they gave her the poison chalice, of one of the toughest jobs imaginable. They made her the governor of Tihar jail.

To quote, Tihar Jail in New Delhi is the size of a small town. It was designed to hold three thousand people. Instead, it holds ten thousand men, women and children. The desolation of the surroundings reflects the dire poverty of the inmates. There are no means of occupation, education or recreation, and the prison is a breeding ground for the very crimes it was designed to punish. Drugs are endemic, prostitution flourishes, corruption breeds and violence and fear lurk in every corner. Remand prisoners, including women with their children, can languish here for up to ten years before their cases come to trial, sharing overcrowded cells with petty thieves, murders and addicts. Under a succession of male governors, mob management barely maintains the status quo, and the problems are more than the staff can handle. Inmates are sometimes shot at random by prison officers out of control.

So in July 1993 this small Indian woman stepped into the hell of Tihar prison. Yet she had the self-confidence to adopt a very feminine strategy to govern the prison and quickly changed everything.

She fired the worst prison officers, then began a radical restructure of the prisoners day. She introduced a complaint box for inmates to air their grievances. She initiated drug rehabilitation, health care, yoga therapy, prayer meetings, music, arts and crafts sessions, adult literacy and physical fitness programmes. Idleness was banished, every hour of the day was positively accounted for, and she achieved this by motivation and encouragement, not by the 'compelling force of law'...To men and women used to the rule of the stick and the gun, the arrival of Kiran Bedi was like a gift from the Gods.

She even called in a famous guru S.N. Goenka to teach the prisoners meditation.

The authorities who appointed Kiran Bedi in the expectation of destroying her saw her turn every obstacle to her advantage, winning the trust, respect - and love - of both prisoners and officers. She was given the Magsaysay award for public service, and although her time at Tiher was short-lived, the changes she instituted had a lasting effect. Prisoners who leave the jail do not usually return.

Punishing prisoners is the masculine solution to crime while rehabilitation is the feminine way. In the West both methods are used. With politicians and newspaper owners trying to whip up hatred by the general public against prisoners. So they can once again use the masculine methods to brutalise prisoners. Although in theory politicians claim that prison is for rehabilitation, they tend to starve the prison service of money so prisons are vastly overcrowd and don't have the staff or resources to rehabilitate the prisoners properly. This has resulted in Britain in recent years of some prisoners being locked up 23 hours of 24 hours in a day.

Yet the ideas of reforming prisoners instead of punishing them goes back to the early 19th century.

Elizabeth Fry (1780-1845) came from a wealthy Quaker family, and enjoyed the benefits of a very academic education, which was unusual for women of those days. In 1812 she began to take a interest in the plight of prisoners and visited London's Newgate prison for women and was appalled at what she saw there. Prisoners were crowded into single cells where they had to eat, sleep and defecate. Typically a woman's children would accompany her to prison, where they lived in destitute poverty, obtained clothes, alcohol, even food by begging or stealing. To tolerate this hell many prisoners only begged for alcohol and sat around in a drunken stupor stark naked.

Other prisoners who were unable to beg or cared for by families or charities simply starved to death. Children often remained in the prison until their mothers died or were executed. They clung to their mothers and watched as they were led to the gallows and hung.

The attitude at the time that prisons were places of punishment and that the inmates were evil, so this perfectly justified this appalling treatment. Elizabeth Fry didn't see it like this and set about using all the influence of her position of wealth and privilege gave her. She started by providing basic food, clothing and medicine for the prisoners. She then turned to education, ministering to the prisoners and establishing a small school. Recognising that occupation was essential to self-esteem and dignity, she convinced the wardens that the school should be run by the prisoners themselves. She also provided materials allowing the women to sew, knit and make goods for sale, in order to buy food, clothing and fresh straw for bedding. In 1817 she enlisted the help of ten friends to form the Ladies' Association for the Reformation of the Female Prisoners in Newgate.

Somehow her work did prick the conscience of the nation. She soon found herself in the role of a prisoner adviser and was invited to other prisons to advice on measures for improvements. She was also asked to give evidence on prison reform before a Committee of the House of Commons in which she advocated compassionate treatment of prisoners. It says something for her personality that in a age when women were suppose to keep quiet, her views and opinions were listened to and some of them became in time encoded in the laws of England.

She was even invited to Ireland, France, Belgium, the Netherlands and Prussia to give advice to prison officials and reformers in these countries. Her work planted the seeds that prisons are place for reforming and not punishment.

Her ideas were tried out by a prisoner governor called Alexander Maconochie on Norfolk island in 1840-44. Norfolk island, which was halfway between Australia and New Zealand, was in many ways the British version of the more infamous French, Devil's Island. Where the prisoners were kept in harsh and degrading conditions to punish them for their crimes. Maconochie instead bravely tried reforming prisoners instead of punishing them.

After receiving contradictory stories about his reforms the authorities sent out a commission. His report was very favourable but Maconochie was still dismissed by a new Colonial Secretary. Yet his success can be measured by the fact that of 920 prisoners he released only 20 were re-convicted.

Back in Britain he was to obtain support from many people including Charles Dickens and became a very controversial figure. Because then people believe in a evil criminal class, the idea that criminals can be reformed undermines the concept of evil and the justification of punishment. Also it makes people also ask questions like, "why are people criminals". If we ask questions like this, then we have to look at the unfair hierarchical system that gives some people great wealth, power and privilege and others only poverty and brutality, because the overwhelming numbers of criminals come for the poor and unprivileged sections of society. So it is not surprising that most, "good" people come from the upper and middle classes and most "bad" people come from the working classes. (The word villain come from the middle ages and originally meant villager. So this word gives an insight about what the upper classes then felt about the common people).

This then is adding insult to injury. Not only do he rich and powerful keep the vast majority of wealth and power in their own hands. On top of this, they condemn the poor as being bad and evil, while they of coarse are good people. Punishment and vengeance are the masculine solutions to problems. That is to say you overcome violence with violence. In other words, "two wrongs make a right". In this situation the person with the biggest stick wins. Yet violence has another side to it in that it ensures that men have dominance over women.

Aggression, competition and violence are the ways that men can always get the upper hand over women, whereas a non-violence and non-competitive community gives all the advantages to women. This has been clearly shown in primate studies.

In many species of primates like chimpanzees, orang-utans and hamadryas baboons male violence against females is commonplace. A female can expect an assault from the larger males on average once a week and can be seriously injured about once a year from these assaults. Observations of these assaults suggest that males do this to gain sexual access. This behaviour is very similar to that observed of men in badly run prisons. If a naïve and attractive looking young man is put into prison he will find himself being assaulted by older prisoners, who want to have sex with him. If caught on his own in a group he may find himself being raped. He quickly learns from this he has two choices. He can continue to be assaulted and raped, or if he wants to stop this he has to align himself with a protector. This would be a bullyboy or alpha man in the prison who will give the young man protection in return for sexual access. It was from this form of relationship the contemptuous expression "sucker" or "bum" come from, in referring to people at the bottom of the pecking order. It is also the origins of the sayings like, "get your arse (ass) over here", or "get your arse into gear", which are very dominant assertions to man about to be buggered. There is nothing about consent or consideration of other people's feelings in any of these sayings. The passive male's response about this form of relationship is the statement, "your just a pain in the arse"(to me).

This expression is similar to, "your a right pain in the neck" in reference to someone who is too demanding. A way a person can get a neck ache is through giving cunnilingus. (This happens because to lick a women's clitoris while she is lying on her back, the man is forced to hold his head back. If this goes on for too long he can get a neck ache). So a man could say that about a women who is too demanding in wanting him to give her long sessions of oral sex. Now this is unlikely to become a common saying in patriarchal times. So it must be a very ancient, going back to a time when women were the dominant sex.

In primate behaviour we can see a strong connection between sex and power. In many primate species, when two male confront each other and one back down he turn his back and allows the winner to demonstrate his superiority by mounting him. Which is also the behaviour of homosexual men in that the man who "takes it up the arse" is seen as the submissive member of the relationship. In Japanese macaque monkeys females have been observed to mount males and rub themselves against the male. As the female is the dominant sex in this species it is a demonstration of the dominance of the female. Again we can see similar behaviour in human beings. In the dominatrix scene some of them wear strap-on dildos and bugger their clients. Who are willing to pay for this privilege.

Male violence takes away the female's right to choose who which males she wants to mate with, in any species where males fight among themselves for the right to mate. The strongest male also uses violence against females to keep them under his control. So violence becomes a way of keeping women, "in their place".

We can see this pattern in human traditional patriarchal societies where husbands are encouraged to assault their wives. In many Islam countries they claim that a man has no "honour" if he doesn't exercise his right to beat his wife. This custom also give him the right to have sex or rape his wife whenever he wants to without contraception, and so taking away the women's right to refuse to have children.

Also in these societies boys are also beaten, the idea being to "toughen them up". Child abuse is needed to make "real men" out of boys. The way it works is that if a child is abuse enough then they only way he can cope with it is to learn not to feel anything. This then makes him not only unaware of his own pain but the pain of others. In fact more than that it teaches him to hate, so he can become a "good" soldier and kill without pity, and become a "good" father and husband and in turn beat his wife and children without mercy.

Yet not all primates are like this. Many species are female dominated like the bonobo ape, Vervet monkeys, macaques, olive baboons, patas, rhesus monkeys, grey langus, capuchins, prosimians and Lemus. In all these species the females form a powerful sisterhood, where if one female is assaulted or intimidated by a larger male, then all the females in the area will be quick to defend their sisters and drive the male away. The exception is the Lemus were female dominance seemed to be bred within the species.

So these studies show that in all primates including humans male dominance over females is only possible through male violence. While female dominance came about through a powerful sisterhood. So it seems from primate studies we have we have two choices.

1. We can behave like chimpanzees, and live in a violent; male dominated, and sexually repressed society.
2. We can behave like bonobos and live in a non-violent, female dominated and sexually liberated societies were anything goes.

So which type of society is natural for human beings? It could be that both types of societies are natural for us as we can partly see in the work of Desmond Morris. Whom has attempted to examine human behaviour from the point of view of a zoologist.

13

WHAT TURNED ON, OUR STONE AGE ANCESTORS

Desmond Morris wrote his famous book "The Naked Ape" at the time of the sexual revolution of the 1960s, and reading through it today in the 21st century, we can see how, in many ways, this book is dated. Yet some of the ideas in the book are still revolutionary as he attempts to explain human behaviour through the eyes of a zoologist. Unfortunately his book is greatly influenced by the conventions of the patriarchal society. So although in some parts of the book he gave very invaluable insights, his patriarchal biases limits the conclusions he comes to. Like most academics of the time he mostly ignores the role of women in evolution.

We can see this in the chapter on sex as he tries to put forward the reasons why human beings "pair-bond". Which is a way to explain in zoological terms why people get married and men go to work, because in the "man the hunter" theory it is men who "brings home the bacon" or the Mammoth. He also rationalises that because humans have a far longer childhood than other animals, it needed women to stay at home to look after children. This was because human culture is far more complex than any other animal so children need longer time to learn. So it needed a man to provide food for the mother and children.

Hunting of course provided this food. As men had a poor hunting bodies, that is to say they didn't have great strength, canine teeth or large claws, they needed their intelligence and ability to co-operate with men to be successful. He notes in other primates and animals that the males do not co-operate very well as they are competing for food, sex and status. This is because the male are competing with each other for the right to mate with the females. So for men to co-operate to the degree that they can hunt successfully this competition had to be broken down. Resulting in each man having his own woman who he looked after and therefore didn't have to compete with others over who could penetrate her. He ignored the fact that many non-Christian cultures don't have pair bonding, where men could have more than one wife.

In recent times the "man the hunter" theory has come under attack. In the excavations of very early humans the bones of animals can still be found, giving the impression to palaeontologists that early humans were carnivores. Then critics of this theory have pointed out that in Africa where humans first evolve, in the Stone-Age communities that still exist there, the vast majority of the food produced comes from the women's gathering. Rather than the man's hunting. Women also do not stay at home but are quite happy to carry their young children with them as they gather food.

The problem with excavations is that the bones of animals tend to be preserved while the remains of vegetable matter soon rot away. Giving the false impression that early humans only existed on a diet of meat. So there is now doubt about the "man the hunter" theory. It is true that in colder climates where the growing season is far smaller or non-existent, hunting became essential for survival, but humans don't really need to hunt in tropical climates, where humans first evolved.

Today in the 21st century there is some doubt whether humans are natural "pair-bonders". In the 1960s when "The Naked Ape" was written marriage was still the normal behaviour of most people. Now with the majority of marriages failing there in some doubt today whether marriage is normal for us all. Marriage has been enforced in the past through laws, religious taboos and social customs. Without these social restrictions today people are now questioning why they should get married. With the result is the increase of single mothers, who are not interested in living with a man, and prefer to bring up their children on there own. Which is the more the normal primate behaviour of the chimpanzee and the bonobo our nearest genetic relations.

Feminists have also pointed out that marriage is a patriarchal institution enforced because it allows men to know who their children are. So they are able to pass on their inheritance through the male line. Without marriages that restrict women to one man, a woman would be able to have sex relations with many men and would herself be unsure who is the father of her children. In other words it is an artificial restriction imposed on women by men, and not natural human behaviour as suggested by Desmond Morris.

It is true that the gibbons "pair-bond" to the exclusion of other gibbons, but are more distant relations to us than the chimpanzee, bonobo and gorilla. Every type of ape (including the human) has a very different social organisation and why they are different no-one really knows.

Where Desmond Morris does break new ground is in his attempt to explain why women have breasts and why unlike other primates we have large exposed lips on our mouths. He points out that other female primates have their genitals on show to give the males "visual stimulus" when she is on heat. Which would of been also true of our ancestors when we still walked on all fours. Then when we began to walk upright, this caused a problem in that the female genital region is no longer easily seen.

What the male used to see when we were on all fours was her bottom and the red lips of the vagina region. So when we started to walk upright because men would be still looking for this visual stimulus, the only thing he would see would be her bottom, and he would be stimulated by this. So women with larger bottoms would have the advantage, as it would be a larger sexual stimulant. This would put evolutionary pressure for women to have far larger buttocks than men. Unfortunately, the problem would still remain that the man wouldn't see the women's vagina from behind when standing upright. Yet can see it from the front. This would encourage face to face copulation, (which more modern research has shown is something both the Orang-utan and the bonobo are able to do). He points out that when female primates are on heat the vagina area colours up to give a strong visual signal. Without these visual signs men would be looking for similar signs on women. So women with larger than usual red lips on her mouth would become attractive to men, as men will see this as being similar to the red lips of the vagina when they used to see when humans were on all fours. (Which might be one reason why we have oral sex, and many men have the desire to put their penises in women's mouths). Likewise women with fleshy chests would also became attractive to men from the front as it reminds them of women's buttocks. So it suggests that women have end up with breasts, large buttocks and red lips because of sexual selection. As women who have these attributes, are more likely to mate with men.

Even today this is still true where women paint their lips red and know if they have large breasts they have a better chance of attracting men. Desmond Morris backs up his claim by pointing out that the mandrill and gelada baboons mimic the colours of their sexual area on their faces and chests. Which makes sense for these primates, because they spend a large part of their time sitting upright

In the same chapter he points out that compared with other primates the penis of a man is very much larger then any other primate. (The average size of a penis of the largest ape, the gorilla, is smaller than a human's little finger). In his attempt to explain this he is on more shaky ground. He also points out that in other primates, female don't seem to have orgasms and after the sex-act walk away as if nothing had happened. He explains this that if women were to do the same, then because she walks in an upright position the seminal fluid would, under the weight of gravity, flow back out of her vagina. So she needed a reason in which to lie down for a while to allow time for the fluid to fertilise her. So an orgasm that leaves her exhausted for a while would have this effect. So far makes sense and he goes on to point out that it is the stimulation of the women's clitoris that allows the women to have an orgasm.

Desmond Morris reasoning then breaks down because he claims that it requires a large penis in a man to stimulate a women's clitoris. Unfortunately more modern sexual research has shown that a man with a small penis is as just as able to bring a woman to orgasm as a man with a far larger one. What he seems to have missed, and it was probably his patriarchal bias that caused this, was that when humans were on all fours to some degree the penis is concealed. When men started to stand upright his penis is very much on display. Now if large breasts, buttocks and red lips on a woman, are a great sexual stimulation to a man. Then it would mean that a penis would also be a strong visual sexual stimulation to a woman. So like men being stimulated by very large breasts, the larger the penis the stronger the visual affects it will have on women.

This is confirmed by the mating behaviour of birds like peacocks and birds of paradise. The male bird in these two species has developed extraordinary, very large and colourful feathers. It seems that the evolutionary pressure for male birds to develop these feathers come from the female bird who picks which male she wants to mate with. It seems that the female bird picks her mate on the basis of who has the most colourful feathers and so over evolutionary time the most successful male birds in mating has been those who have the largest feathers.

For Demond Morris in the 1960s such a theory would have been unacceptable. Because even though women's liberation did get started then, it still wasn't acceptable that women could enjoy the sight of completely naked men. Also the patriarchal bias dictated that it was men who always ruled society and took the initiative in all things. So for women to pick men, only with large penises, with this resulting in men evolving even larger penises because of this. Means that there was a time in the past when women could choose their sexual partners.

Now clearly this doesn't happen in patriarchal societies and it is noticeable that in most of these societies the genitals are concealed. Even in very hot climates where people wear very little. It is of interest that in some tribes in New Guinea where men openly display their penises, it is the men with the largest ones that have the highest status in the tribe. This suggests that the women are the dominant sex in the tribe or were in the recent past. Because it strongly suggests that it is women who have the final say in which partner she has sex with. This is such a concern for men in these tribes, that they will tie weights to their penises in an attempt to stretch them or to push hollow tubes of wood over them to make them look longer. Which gives a clue as to why in patriarchal societies the genitals are covered. The more ambitious and aggressive men in a society would have problems if his status were only governed by the size of his penis. So these men had to bring in laws and taboos for a cover-up to ensure that more well endowed men couldn't challenge them for status and power.

So it means for men to grow large penises it needed a society in the past where men had their genitals on display, and for women chose their sexual partners, to the degree that it is mostly well-endowed men who have sexual intercourse with women. In our patriarchal society we have men who expose themselves who are called "flashers". Many women find this behaviour offensive and threatening and can be frightened by it. The reason for this is because women fear these men will come after them and try and rape them. So to have a situation where women are not afraid of "flashers" and are even willing to choose her sexual partners on the size of his penis.

Means a woman has to be very confident that she is in control of the situation and the man. Also women in a patriarchal situation can be frightened by men with extra large penises because they fear it could hurt or damage them. So for a woman to approach a well endowed man for sex means she is confident she can dictate to him if she wants it inside her, and can order him to withdraw it if it physically hurts her. In other words she has to be in control of the situation, unlike the situation in strict patriarchal society where a wife was unable to refuse her husband sex.

In the patriarchal society women have always dressed to attract the man with red lipstick or low-cut dresses. Even when dress codes dictated that women cover-up, as in the Victorian times, women then started to wear bustles, which greatly exaggerated the size of their buttocks. Even today women wear tight jeans, to show off the shape of their bottom and vagina, or skimpy and high-cut swim wear to show themselves off to men. It is true some men have done the same as we can see with codpieces in the past or the padded tights of male ballet-dancers. (So it is of interest that male ballet-dancers have the reputation of being feminine or "wimps"). But it is mostly the women who have attempted to dress in a sexual way rather than men. In recent times this is starting to change some men are now attempting to look sexy in the same way. As they also wear tight jeans and tee shirts or wear skimpy bathing suits when swimming. Which shows that they are putting out a signal to women that they want to attract them and even for them to take the initiative.

Many of the ancient Gods in the past like Pan did have very large penises, and in many pagan religions and even in Hinduism today the penis was, and is still, worshipped. Societies where the penis is worshipped and openly displayed by men is going to create large problems for men who are not well-endowed. In a strictly patriarchal society where it is covered up and women are only suppose to have knowledge of the penis of her husband this is no problem. Today when there is more sexual-freedom, men are having relationships with women who will openly talk about having had sexual relationships with many other men before. This creates a problem for men in how they "measure up" whether his girl friend or wife had sex with men who were bigger than him. Even though sex therapists and agony aunts have tried to reassure men that "size doesn't matter", no one is really persuaded by this. Because although technically size doesn't matter, as a visual stimuli it matters a lot.

In recent times because of the advances in plastic surgery many women who can afford it, are having their breast sizes increased. Likewise some surgeons are also claiming to be able to do the same for men's penises, and this is also becoming popular for men who can afford it. (Though there are still worries about the safety of these operations). Also for a number of years sex-catalogues have been selling vacuum pumps to increase the size of the penis. Which men still buy although there is some doubt as to whether these devices really work. So like the New Guinea tribesmen who tie weights to their penises, men in Western societies are starting to become obsessed with the size of their penises. Many men today with small penises can feel inadequate and even depressed about it. Women who want to humiliate men know that one of the best ways is to suggest their too small to satisfy them. Men have an instinctive feeling that penis size is important to women. In the Stone Age it probably was, and as women become more sexually liberated, it might turn out to be just as significant in the future. Just imagine how interested men would be if doctors found a safe, cheap and reliable way to enlarge their penises? Most men would be very tempted. In the recent past penis size wouldn't of mattered too much if a man's wife had to be faithful to just her husband. In that she is not in a position to compare her husband's penis with other men. Today with sexual liberation most women get to compare the penis sizes of many men. The very fact that men do worry about the size of their equipment to the point of getting very depressed about it, points to a time in the past when this was very important to men's status and importance. Suggesting a matriarchal society where women choose their sexual partners, so the hang-ups about size must be instinctive feelings coming from this time.

If this were a problem today then it would have been one in the past when people worshipped "well-endowed" Gods and walked around completely naked as the early ancient Greeks did. As this would only be a problem for men and not for women, it points to such a society being either equal or dominated by women.

So what this seems to suggest is that thousands of years of patriarchal rule will through sexual selection cause women to have larger breasts and buttocks. While matriarchal rule will again through sexual selection cause men to have larger penises.

So what does this tell us about our early ancestors? The large breasts of women strongly suggest a patriarchal age, while the large penises of men strongly suggest a matriarchal age. Or does it suggest both and men a women were equal then? This will mean an equal society where both men and women choose their sexual partners and the result would be a free-for-all. You may have an elite group of large-breasted females mating with males who have big penises, but what will the rest of the population do?

They'll be mating with each other as well. So there would be no survival advantage in having either large breasts or a large penis. The reason why a peacock has such enormous tail feathers is because the peahen finds them sexually attractive, and it is she who chooses. If the peacock had a say in the matter then there wouldn't be such a strong evolutionary pressure to develop such ridiculously large feathers. This means that this kind of evolution can only happen to the male if the female alone does the choosing. The same goes for male-dominated societies where the alpha males only select women with large breasts. The offspring of these women will be more likely to survive, protected by the alpha males. So it needs one sex doing the choosing to exaggerate the sexual characteristics of the other sex. If both sexes are doing it, then survival remains dependent on other factors.

This could suggest that a sexually equal society has never happened in human history. Where the only time we had equality is when we were changing from a patriarchy to a matriarchy, as is happening now, or vice-versa, at the end of the Neolithic age. Which I admit is not what Feminists would like to hear. Though even Feminists admit that equality is very difficult because we live in a masculine society, designed by men exclusively for men. There's little provision even today for women who have both a career and children. If a woman has children she has two stark choices. Pursue a career while simultaneously caring for her family, which is enormously stressful, or leave work for a number of years, thus reducing her promotion prospects. The alternative is, the woman has a househusband, but that can't be called equality, because the male then has to sacrifice his own career, for her. We also live in a highly competitive society that favours aggressive men rather than co-operative women. If we change our society so that the feminine virtues of co-operation and caring are rewarded, this would help women, but it would severely disadvantage the average man. Because as shown in the war between Capitalism and Communism, men respond best under the very competitive environment of Capitalism and didn't do so well in a Communist system. Where competition is not encouraged. Equality between the sexes becomes very difficult to sustain over many generations. What helps men, disadvantages women and vice-versa.

14

MEN AND WOMEN GET TO BE SEXUALLY INCOMPATIBLE

Back in the 19th century and early 20th century it was commonly believed that respectable women didn't enjoy sex. Then with the rise of women's Liberation in the 1960s women came out and claimed that they were capable for enjoying sex as much as men. Since then women's sexuality has been openly discussed to the degree that men are becoming aware that women probably can enjoy sex, as much, if not more than what men can.

The 19th century belief was that women do not enjoy sex, fitted in nicely with the belief that men had always been the dominant sex. This is because in evolutionary terms if this is true, then there was no need for women to enjoy sex because it was assumed that men initiated all sexual encounters. Men being the dominant sex were at liberty to have sex with women or their wives whenever they felt like it. (Women up until very recently were not legally able to refuse their husband sex). This means in evolutionary terms there was no need for women to enjoy sex, as she didn't have a say in the matter. So even if women had no sexual desire, women can still have children, because she plays the passive role.

The acceptance today that women do enjoy sex, shows that in the past women must of had a choice about whether they wanted to have sex or not. Because having sexual desires means that women have a drive to initiate sex. Certainly today with far fewer patriarchal restrictions on women they are showing they are capable of being assertive and even dominant in wanting sex. These desires don't come out of nowhere and suggests that they come from behaviour that was once commonplace. Before women were controlled by patriarchal laws, customs and taboos.

This then presents a very different picture of our Stone Age past than what palaeontologists have led us to believe. We now can go back four million years, to the first humans, compared with the four or five thousand years of recorded history. This means that 99.9% of human existence is unknown. So we can see that what happened in the Stone Age is far more important in making us what we are, than recorded history.

It always has been assumed that men have been the dominant sex, so all images we have of the Stone-Age is of man being the dominant and brutal hunter while women have been the submissive and brutalised slave. Millions of years of brutal men and brutalised women would make it unlikely for women to enjoy sex because it would have no evolutionary advantage, if men were at liberty to rape women. So the fact that women have a clitoris and sexual desires and can have an orgasm suggests that in the Stone Age women were not as submissive as portrayed, because in evolutionary terms something that is not used ends up disappearing. So it means that women's sexual desires and pleasure must of been an important aspect of the mating between women and men during the Stone Age. Which suggests that the development of women's sexual desires means that in the past women were capable of initiating sex as much as men are.

This could suggest the relationships between women and men were equal during the Stone Age. Because if both sexes had an equal desire for sex then it suggests that sex only came about when both partners wanted it. Unfortunately it is not that simple, as women's sexuality is more complicated than this. What has become very clear in recent years is that not all women can enjoy sex through penetration. This is because the clitoris is located near the outside of the vagina and with many women the clitoris is not stimulated by a male penis inside them. To make matters even more complex, it seems that the timing of sex seems to be different for most men and women as well. Most young men it seems can become aroused and ejaculate far quicker than most women. This has caused real problems in the sexual relationships in recent times.

Back in the 19th century sex was easy for men. No wife was able to legally refuse sex from her husband. So he could have sex whenever and however he wanted to. As it was believe that women didn't enjoy sex he didn't have to worry about her feelings, as foreplay then was unknown, as was the female orgasm. He was a liberty to put his penis in his wife and not worry if she was aroused and lubricated. As it was his wife's duty to lie back and endure any pain she might have from having his penis in her dry vagina. Anyway it usually didn't last too long, as most men can come within a few minutes.

In the 20th century sex has become far more difficult for men. Women demanded that men give them foreplay so their arousal will lubricate their vagina. So the man in a aroused state had to wait, until she was ready, then when he was inside her he then was told to delay his ejection until she reached orgasm before he was allowed to come. Unfortunately many men have been unable to manage all this and as we can see with the popularity of the drug Viagra, impotency has become commonplace among men in modern times. This is because in foreplay, some men loose their erections while their wives or girlfriends are slowly aroused. If a man gets past this hurdle he then has to control when he ejects. Not all men are able to do this, if he ejects too early he is accused of being a selfish and if he has to hang on for too long he again can lose his erection. While other men they find they can keep on pumping away as long as they like they will never bring their partner to orgasm, because her clitoris is not stimulated by the movement of this penis. All this has undermined the confidence of many men sexually whom today are considered to be failures if they cannot give their wives an orgasm with their penises. Resulting in many men buckling under the pressure, and becoming impotent.

So to protect their partners some women have to fake orgasm. The irony is that in the 19th century a good Christian woman if she has a orgasm had to suppress this feeling and pretend she didn't have it, because "respectable" women didn't enjoy sex. While in the 20th century when social customs change, women who didn't have orgasms with their husband had to "fake it" for the sake of his ego, or because she could be accused of being frigid.

What many women have discovered is that to enjoy sex it is far easier for them to masturbate themselves than to have a man's penis inside them. This is also true if a man wants to give a woman sexual pleasure, for many women he is far more likely to do a better job with his finger or tongue than with his penis. This then means for many couples if a man wants to give a woman sexual enjoyment it would be far better if he forgets about his penis and his own sexual pleasure and gives his partner oral or manual sex.

Does this mean that nature has played a cruel trick on the human race? In that women and men do not seem to be sexually compatible. Human beings seem to be set up sexually to make it difficult for men and women to mutually enjoy sex together. It is far easier for the man to enjoy sex if either he or his partner is worried about her sexual enjoyment. The same is true if a woman wants to enjoy sex it is far easier if the man gives her what she wants and not worry about his physical enjoyment.

Certainly sex between homosexual couples seems to be far easier than between heterosexual couples. This is because two men or two women together have very much the same attitude and feelings about sex as each other. While women and men seem to live on different planets not only are they physically incompatible, for reasons I have mentioned, but are incompatible emotionally as well. Men think about sex in terms of power, pleasure, a quick ejaculation and little emotional involvement, while women think about sex in terms of love, romance, unhurried sensual pleasure and personal feelings.

This then could point to men and women having homosexual relations in the Stone Age, like that of the bonobo. In that women formed a strong Lesbian sisterhood. The position of the clitoris does make it very easy for lesbian women to enjoy sex with each other. Also if Stone-Age lesbians did began to fashion dildos and use them on each other, (Dildos have been found in Stone-Age excavations,) this would mean in evolutionary terms women's vaginas would become used to having long sex sessions as she wouldn't be in a hurry to orgasm. The same is true for men. It is a strange fact that men's anus can lubricate in the same way as a women's vagina lubricates when sexually aroused. So in evolutionary terms homosexual sex play must of been very commonplace in the four million years of human history. To make these physical changes in our sexual make up.

Homosexuality was prominent in some civilisations in historical time like in Ancient Greece where it seems that as one time homosexuality was more commonplace than heterosexuality. Because of this in Sparta the women formed a strong lesbian sisterhood that allowed them far more freedoms and power than in any other part of Greece. Unfortunately this freedom and power in the end worked against them.

Although Sparta was a military State where the young boys were trained to be soldiers from a very early age. The freedom given to it's women, was in complete contrast to its neighbour Athens. Which although was the birthplace of Democracy, the men completely subjugated their women. Although Sparta was a very successful military state and defeated Athens in 404 BC, it seems its military downfall was caused by the freedom it gave to its women. In Athens and other Ancient Greek states women didn't have control over their own bodies. So they couldn't refuse sex from their husbands and were forced to have large numbers of children. In Sparta on the other hand women had complete control over their own bodies and could refuse her husband or any other man sex, (it seems the Spartan women even had the freedom to openly have sex with other men). This then means they were free to decide how many children she wanted to have. As the result over many years as the population of the surrounding Greek states grew, the population and in Sparta declined. Resulting in Sparta being heavily outnumbered when other Greek states, finally ganged up on her.

In modern times we still have the same problem. Western counties where women have greater freedom, have stable populations while inhabitants in countries where women are still subjugated keeping on growing at a alarming rate. Fortunately the Western countries are very powerful both economically and militarily and so are not likely to be conquered by a much larger military force in the foreseeable future. Like what happened to the Spartans.

Though this could be the problem for female freedom in the future. In any Feminist or matriarchal country the population will be stable and even decline. While in patriarchal counties the population will keep on growing. This then makes it very difficult for patriarchal and matriarchal countries to live together, because matriarchal countries will be under increasing pressure of immigration or conquest from patriarchal countries. Because patriarchal counties will need somewhere for its surplus population to go, and they will want live in the less crowed matriarchal countries.

So in the long term the concept of female freedom is a worldwide issue. Because while there are countries where women do not have control over their own bodies, the population of these countries will continue to grow. Which means in time they will import their culture and beliefs into countries where women have greater freedom through immigration or conquest. It is true at present immigrates that go to Europe and North America tend to be converted to a more Western lifestyle after a generation or two. Yet the pressure is still there, and we have the possible danger of the whole world going back to a extreme form of patriarchy through the population explosion in patriarchal countries. In other words what happened to the Spartans could also happen to Western countries if their population rate declines too fast.

All this seems to show that the Feminist ideal of sexual equality is very difficult on both the personal and global levels. If this strange state of affairs is brought about through evolution then what is this telling us about our ancestors in the Stone-Age? If Stone-Age men and women were equal in status with each other, then the sexual timing of women and men's orgasm would be very similar. They would take about the same time to get aroused, in that it would take the same amount of time for a man to get an erection, as it does for a woman to be lubricated. While the clitoris would be in a position to be stimulated by the penis when a man penetrates a woman. The fact that these things don't often happen, suggests that equality between the sexes wasn't very common during the Stone Age.

For women's sexual organs to evolve through millions of years where many women today can only enjoy sex, with a partner stimulating their clitoris with their finger or tongue. Means that women had to be able to control men. To the degree that men were willing to give up any idea of sexual enjoyment with women and only concentrate on her enjoyment, for thousands of generations. Or women had other women as sexual partners instead of men.

What we don't know about the people of the Stone Age is whether they linked the sexual-act with childbirth. Some academics claim that human being have only discovered this in the last few thousand years in civilised times. Yet recent research has discovered that human beings in the Stone Age were as far more intelligent than was previously thought. In fact some skeletons of Stone Age people has shown they had larger brains that the average person today. The more scientists find about Stone-Age people the more sophisticated and intelligent they become, so there is the possibility that human beings worked out the connection between sex and childbirth a half-a-million or a million years ago or more. It has to be remembered that in Western countries a birth control pill was only discovered only in the 1960s. Yet the Aborigines of Australia who had a Stone-Age culture before Europeans settled there, had knowledge of herbs that would also prevent women from having children. This means we know of one Stone-Age people who were far in advance of Western knowledge about birth control until the 1960s. Thus suggests that if in the Stone Age women knew about the connection between sex and childbirth it would make sense of why women then and now have evolved to a state where they have separated sexual pleasure from conception.

If there were matriarchal societies in the Stone Age and women also had worked out how to have sex with a man without having a child. What women could do is to order their male sexual partner to stimulate their clitoris and not to penetrate them. Or alternatively they would order the man to hold back their ejection and withdraw after she has an orgasm or if he cannot hold back any longer, if this practice continued over many thousands of generations. It would increase the length of time it would take women to orgasm because having men under control it wouldn't matter how long she took. Also if women regularly practised having men stimulate their clitoris with either a finger or tongue. They again wouldn't be in a hurry to orgasm and may even try to delay it so they can enjoy the pleasure for a longer period of time.

So we can see that having matriarchal sex with women in control with over many thousands of years can physically change women. As many women will start to get all their sexual pleasure from clitoris stimulation rather than penetration. So they will evolve to a degree where it doesn't matter if their clitoris is not stimulated if there is a penis inside them. Because they only time they will want penetration is when they want children. Or if women did prefer penetrative sex then they would train men to withhold ejaculation. This has been practised by men in historic times in Chinese and Indian through the religions of Taoism and Tantra. Where men learn to have sexual intercourse without ejaculation. The reason they give is that they claim ejaculation weakens a man's spiritual energy. Yet it also has to be admitted that it gives women a great advantage during sex. In that she can take as long as she likes in coming to orgasm. Suggesting that if was probably a woman who invented this concept. It is of interest that Tantra worships the Goddess Kali, while Taoism worships the Tao, which in the Tao-Te-Ching is called, "the mother" or "the mysterious female". So Taoism and Tantra practices that give women all the advantages in sex also worshipped Goddesses. Strongly suggesting that both these religions originated in a ancient matriarchal society.

It is of interest that scientists have found that in Neolithic times and even back in the times of the old Stone Age people then were obsessed with creating calendars, the most famous being Stonehenge and the many stone circles found in Britain, Ireland, and France. Yet scientists have discovered markings on bone that clearly show Stone-Age people keeping track of the phases of the moon 30 thousand years ago. So why was Stone-Age people so obsessed with time and the phases of the moon?

A obvious reason would be that Stone-Age women probably worked out that their menstruation period roughly fitted in with the phases of the moon. They also may have worked out from this when they were fertile and when they weren't. This would mean that they might have worked out the best time when they would allow men to ejaculate inside them to have children. This suggest that men having been trained to withhold ejection, when given the chance to ejaculate inside a woman would probably come very quickly. This is because the women would be more interested in conceiving than sexual pleasure, when she wanted to conceive. So the man would want to come quickly in case she might change her mind. This certainly would be a consideration in a society where there is no marriage, as the women may have other sex partners lined up if he didn't perform quickly enough.

In many patriarchal cultures even today the clitorises of young women are removed. Perhaps the original reason for this is the knowledge that sexually active women are dominant woman. So men attempted to make women more submissive by removing their clitorises. This suggests that when this practice was first started off in the ancient past, men were aware that very sexually active women were also dominant.

If this is true then were the patriarchal and matriarchal ages equal? With both women and men ruling at about the same length of time. It is of interest that women are far more sensual than men in sex play. For thousands of years men have dominated women and used them as sex-slaves. Yet if a man goes to a very submissive prostitute even though he can use her however he likes for his own pleasure, in the end most men seem to be more concerned in ejaculating quickly, than any sensual pleasure she can give him.

Yet it has been shown in recent times when the roles are reverse and a woman can buy sex from men they have a very different attitude. A woman can enjoy hours of sensual and sexual play and massage. While although men can enjoy sex play and being massaged they soon get tired of this. This has been discovered in massage parlours where men soon get aroused when being massaged by a young woman and he quickly wants to ejaculate. This might be because women have in the past have enjoyed men giving them sexual and sensual pleasure far more than women doing the same for men. So men are not used to receiving sensual and sexual pleasure from women and only want a quick orgasm, while women in the past through many thousands of years of matriarchal rule are used to men giving them unhurried sexual and sensual pleasure.

This then suggests that patriarchal rule by men are in evolutionary terms were fairly brief. After a patriarchal age women would know the reason why they must keep men under firm control. Because if all patriarchal ages are the same then both women and men will know how much conflict, fear, hatred and violence is caused when men rule society. So a warning would be passed down from mother to daughter never to allow men to get into a position of power again. Yet over many thousands of years this warning would become weaker and may even be forgotten, or just dismissed as an exaggerated myth. So some women will take pity on men and decide that it is unfair to treat men like slaves and give them equal rights. This then allows the competitive nature of men to be reawakened and soon men are ruling society through fear and violence. Until all people, including men, get fed up with the patriarchal world of suffering and go back to matriarchy again.

So there is probably a matriarchal/patriarchal cycle, but as women have a greater capacity to enjoy themselves sexually when they are in the dominant position then men, it suggests the patriarchal ages are far shorter than the matriarchal ages. As it seems from their behaviour women have had far more experience of dominating men sexually.

15

SHE WHO MUST BE OBEYED

Now there is a big mystery about the 20th century that no one seems to comment on. Throughout the last five thousand years of history it has been accepted that men are the dominant sex. This was true up until the end of the 19th century when women all over the world had less rights than a slave. Yet a hundred years later at the end of the 20th century women in the West have equal opportunity? What suddenly happened in the 20th century than women have gain more rights and power than they had over the last four thousand years?

In answer to this question people look to the work of the Suffragettes, women's Liberation Movement and Feminists. Yet to be frank women have had it easy. If we say compared the Feminist struggle with say with the civil rights struggle of black people in USA, there is no comparison. The savage violence that black people have had to endure is incredible, with white lynch mobs being able to hang black people without fear of the law, and even today the vast majority of the prison population in USA are black people, as they are the poorest sections of the community.

It is true some Suffragettes and Feminists have been victims of violence but it has not been in the same league as endured by black people, or even trade unionist fighting for workers rights. So why has it been the case that men have successfully kept women in virtual slavery for thousands of years have suddenly caved in to Feminists demands, and gone belly up, without hardly a fight? Though I have to say this is not true in many Moslem countries where Feminists have been beaten up and murdered.

If you take a cork and hold it underwater it is very easy to hold it down but it will only stay there while you keep holding it in that position. If at any time you arm gets tired or you get fed up with keeping the cork underwater, and then let go, the cork will automatically rise to the top. This concept gives a good metaphor of what is happening today in the politics of female power.

For anyone who has read the history of patriarchy over the last five thousand years what it very striking is the great efforts needed to keep women powerless. Up until the end of the 19th century, there were laws to ensure that women couldn't own any property or wealth. As the law stated that her father or husband owned everything a woman had. The law also make it very difficult for any woman to inherit property. Women were also barred from all jobs and professions except being a housewife, servant or prostitute. So women were unable to acquire any wealth of power in her own right. Husbands were also encouraged to dominate their wives, and women had to swear to obey their husbands when they were married. The law even gave husbands the right to beat their wives with either a stick or whip.

In other cultures the laws oppressing women were even stricter than in the Western world. It was traditional for the Somalis people of Somalia, Kenya, Ethiopia and Djibouti for a bride to start married life with a flogging from their husbands. It seems the newly wedded husband would wait for her in the bridal chamber with a whip in his hand. This was also true with the Sifon people of Tibet, who traditionally would again start of married life with the husband whipping his bride. In many places like Sicily, Ethiopia and Eastern Europe where it was commonplace for men to choose their bride through kidnap and rape. A young man would pick out which girl he wanted to marry and then with a few friends kidnap and rape her. The girl was then force by social custom to marry her rapist. This went on in Sicily up until the 1960s and it still goes on in Ethiopia.

In India there is the custom of "Suttee". This is where when a husband dies his wife is put on the funeral pile to be burnt alive. So what are the origins of this very barbaric custom? It seems that in the past women would frequently poison their husbands, so to discourage this all women were made to die with their husbands. So the Suttee tradition was created by a brutal sex war between men and women in India, which men finally won by simply being more violent than women.

In China there was the tradition of foot binding. Again this is a very strange custom, but the end result is that women were left crippled. So this tradition suggest that at one time men were so frighten of they women that they had to cripple them to be able to dominate them.

Yet we are taught at school and in our history books that men have always been the dominant sex going back to early Stone Age. The irony is that if it is natural for men to be the dominant sex why do then men had to create very oppressive laws and customs against women? If it is natural for men to be the dominant sex then they shouldn't need any laws, custom or propaganda to keep their place as the dominant sex. For instance they only reason way we have laws against stealing is because many people do steal. If people didn't steal there would be no reason to have laws against this behaviour. The same is true of all customs and traditions. The custom of marriage with people swearing to be true to each other is only needed because people do tend to have sex outside of marriage. If pair bonding was completely natural for human beings then we wouldn't need customs like marriage, enforced by laws and social censure. This then means that oppressive laws and customs to keep women in a subservient position suggests that it is not natural for women to be the submissive sex. If it was natural for men to be the dominant sex then there would be no reason for men to have oppressive laws and customs to keep women in bondage.

If you think about it, from the time the original Aryan invaders conquered Matriarchal communities in southern Europe to the start of Christianity and Islam was about 3,000 years. This means the Patriarchs needed 3,000 years of brainwashing all men and women into believing that our Creator was a male, that sex, childbirth, and menstruation was sinful or dirty and that women was inferior to men. This suggests that women were held in such high regard in ancient times that the original patriarchal invaders with all the advantages of violence and intimidation still took thousands of years to overcome the power of women.

If we compared this with what is happening today, where women in a position of complete powerlessness in the 19th century, has in just over a 100 years gained near equality with men. Through the undermining of the patriarchal religion Christianity we can now see women rapidly rise to power once again. So it is like a holding a cork underwater. It is easy to hold the cork down, but once you let go the cork rises to the surface. Patriarchy could only keep women down while it was actively suppressing them, and when the pressure was release we know find women are naturally moving back to ruling society once again. This suggests to me, that it is probably natural for human beings to be ruled by women.

Not only has women gain political power over the last hundred years but the relationship between men and women are also changing rapidly. With the undermining of the many customs, beliefs and social conventions that men are the dominant sex, the personal relationships between men and women are rapidly changing. It is now more commonplace for women to openly claim they are the head of the household and we even now have househusbands. While sexually attitudes are also changing, from very tiny beginnings during the early 1970s the FemDom sex industry has grown strongly and steadily.

It has been patriarchal religions like Christianity and Islam that has been in the forefront oppressing women. Even today extreme Islam countries try to force women to wear facial screens and discourage female education. Restrictions like this wouldn't be needed if men didn't fear the power of women. In the past Christianity used extreme violence against women. In the infamous Witch hunts of the medieval age the vast majority of millions of people who were tortured and burnt alive were women. Suggesting again a real fear of women becoming too powerful.

It was only the decline of the power of Christianity in the Western world through the rise of science that took away the oppression of women. With the ending of oppressive laws and customs throughout the 20th century women have quickly gained near equality with men. I know to us a hundred years might seem a long time but in historical terms it is very quick, for such a far-reaching social change. If this rate of progress for women was to continue during the 21st century then clearly women will be ruling the world within a hundred years.

It has been claimed that, "the hand that rocks the cradle rules the world". Now at first sight this seems to be a stupid saying because it a woman's hand that rocks the cradle and women are clearly not ruling the world, and never have done in recorded history. Yet it is still quoted because within it is a kernel of truth. Patriarchal religions and oppressive dictatorships like Nazism and Communism know that it is very important to brainwash children from a very early age. The Roman Catholic Jesuits boasted that, "give us a child for the first seven years and we have him for life".

Children up until the 20th century were basically brutalised in the Western world. It was normal for parents and schoolteachers to cane, birch and whip children. Favourite saying then were, "spare the rod and spoil the child", "children should be seen but not heard" and "if you see a child look guilty. Hit him. You may not know what it is for, but he does". Children were brutalise even as babies. Male "experts" wrote, that a crying baby was being wilful, and mothers where encouraged not to pick up crying baby. They were also told a baby that cried too much was to be put in a room and lock the door to let it cry itself to sleep. Then infants the moment they began to walk and talk they were subjected to physical punishment. (Boys in general were punished more severely than girls.) This was done not only to teach children discipline from a very early age. It was also done to make, "real men" out of boys. In other words by being brought up in a environment of violence, the children naturally became violent themselves. They then make good soldiers and they are able to kill without pity and they are more likely to, "keep women in their place".

Then as the 20th century progressed, women not only gained power over their own bodies but their children as well. Female child experts and more moderate child male experts like Dr Spock began to write books on child care. The development continued to the point that today what was normal for children in the 19th century, would be seen today as child abuse.

Children in the past were subjected to sexual abuse as well. That man who the "whistle blower" was surprisingly a young Sigmund Freud. In the past men have got away with child sex abuse scot-free. Then in 1896 a young Sigmund Freud presented a paper entitled "The Aetiology of Hysteria". In this paper he said he had discovered that the neuroses suffered by his patients stemmed from sexual assaults and violence they had suffered as young children, with most of these assaults coming from their own fathers, brothers or other male relations in "respectable middle class" homes. This paper went down like a lead balloon and his colleges put great pressure was put on him to suppress his paper. Which was singled out from all the other papers presented in Vienna in 1896 to not be published in psychoanalysis's Journal "Wiener Klinische Wochenschrift". Moreover no discussion of his work was allowed. In the end Freud caved in. (he wasn't a Wilhelm Reich). To save his career Freud did suppress his paper and then came up later with other theories like "Penis envy" and the "Oedipus complex" to explain neuroses. Which hinted at child sex abuse but never openly said it. These theories explained how the abused child felt and how it will affect them later. Unfortunately because these children were in reality were abused, but this fact was censored, this meant that the blame of the neuroses was put on the abused and not the abuser.

Now child sexual abuse is out in the open and not even Roman Catholic priests find they can get away with it. The result is that now children are being far less sexually and physically abused in the Western world. This lack of childhood abuse is causing men to be far less assertive, while women are becoming far more confident in themselves. So what is happening today was predicted back in the 19th century. When it was claimed that if you didn't "harden" (brutalise) boys they will become wimps.

The degree Western men have become wimps can be seen, as previously mentioned, in the number of suicides of soldier after both the Vietnam and Falklands wars. There are probably similar figures for the first Gulf war but the "Gulf War Syndrome" obscures these. (This is going on in spite of the extremely violent film; TV programmes and video games young people are encouraged to watch.) To some people today, it is terrible that our young men are losing their, "manhood", but if we want to live in a world of non-violence and peace, this is a very good thing. It is of interest that the most violent group of men in USA and UK are those of African decent. Black people seem to have been left behind in the reform of child rearing as many young black children are still routinely beaten by their parents. So it is not surprisingly that young black men still tend to be very violent. Though it also doesn't help that more black people are unemployed or work for low wages, than any other ethnic group in Western societies.

If you watch sport or action adventure movies you might be forgiven for thinking that men are really strong creatures. Well I'm afraid to tell all you "macho" guys out there, but compared but for its size and weight the human animal is just about the weakest animal in the world. Arnold Schwarzenegger is a weakling compared with an average adult chimpanzee.

In most animals it seems that the males fight over the right to mate with the females. We see this clearly animals like cattle and deer where the males head butt each other until the weakest male backs down and the strongest mate with the females. We also see the same behaviour among cats and dogs and other carnivorous animals where it is the strongest and most aggressive male is more likely to mate. Now the advantage of this according to Darwin's theory of evolution is that the strongest and fittest males will mate and past down their genes to the next generation. So this means that the weaker males are eliminated from the gene pool of any species. This seems to work very well with many species of animal but there are exceptions like us Human beings and bonobos.

What is remarkable about us as a species of animal is how weak we are. An average male chimpanzee is about three times as strong as the average man, even though he is smaller in statue, while the gorilla is about four times the strength of humans. This is also true of any other animal of about our size. A deer, dog or big cat of about the same weight as a human can run 3 to 5 times faster than the average human. While one blow from a big cat or large ape will kill even a very strong man.

So why has the Human become so weak compared with other animals of a equal size? Does this suggest that some time during Human evolution the need for males to compete with each other to mate with females no longer became a important for the survival of the species? This can be seen clearly in the relationship between the Neanderthal man and the first modern Humans over 40 thousand years ago in Europe. The skeletons of the Neanderthals showed they were far stronger and more heavily built than modern Humans living at that time. Both species had about the same size brains and both used tools. Yet it was the Neanderthals that became extinct and not the physically weaker modern Humans. So it seems that the increased intelligence and tool making ability of Humans made the need for physical strength no longer an important aspect of survival.

The relationship between the Neanderthal and the first modern humans we can see in two species of chimpanzees today. The Congo River in Africa is one of the largest rivers in the World and is in some places it is over 10 miles wide. The result of this is that the chimpanzee living on different sides of the Congo River have evolved into two different species. Living on one bank is the normal chimpanzee you see in other parts of Africa but on the other bank is the bonobo. In spite of its name it is not really smaller but is more lightly built than the heavier and stronger Common chimpanzee. Bonobos males like humans do not compete with each other through fighting for the right to mate with females. This is what makes both species physically weaker than chimpanzees and other animals of a similar size.

It is a curious fact that in all the Lemur species of Lemur on the island of Madagascar the female is the dominant sex. It has be observed many times by biologists, That if a male lemur approaches a female before she has finished feeding, he is swiftly put in his place. Female lemurs drive males away from food until they and their young have eaten and will even jump at them, bite them or cuff them. Then the male will retreat and give a submissive call.

Unlike with bonobos this behaviour is not re-enforced by a powerful lesbian sisterhood. It seems to be a part of male Lemur's genetic behaviour. It has also been observed that when adult males begin issuing submissive signals to adolescent females, the young females are taken by surprise. After a while they figure out what's going on and enjoy it, demanding that the adult males play with them. It also seems that young females also play more than males, a behaviour commonly linked to dominance in young male mammals.

The theory put forward by the biologists observing this behaviour is that it is caused by the extreme weather conditions on Madagascar, which makes it very tough for the wild life living there. During four months of the year, the island experiences torrential downpours that nourish the lemurs' food supplies of leaves and fruits. The other eight months of the year tend to be cold and dry. During these dry spells, lemurs rely on low quality foods like bamboo pith. Overall, survival is very difficult, more so for the female, than the male. Pregnancy and providing milk for infants require energy. So Lemurs cannot afford the luxury of males assaulting females, pinching female's food or even feeding before the female and her young. This means having males who are very submissive towards female is a very important consideration for the survival of the species. Lemur groups with alpha males would quickly die out because only the males would survive. This is because they would hog the short supply of food in the dry months, and the female and young would be first to die. While in female dominated groups even if only one male survives a bad year he is still able to fertilise all the females in the group. So survival pressures have made Lemurs on Madagascar matriarchal.

Scientist now believe that the Neanderthals died out because of the changing climate of Europe at the time of their extinction. But the mystery is why it was the Neanderthals that died out and not the first modern humans. As the bones of Neanderthals show they were physically far stronger than humans. This suggests this was brought about in evolutionary time by Neanderthals males fighting each other in a test of strength for the right to mate, with only the strongest males reproducing. This makes the species far stronger than humans. Who because of their weaker body strength it shows that the male humans were not fighting each other for dominance and right to mate.

If we assume that the physically powerful Neanderthal had a similar society to present day chimpanzees, then females being at the bottom of the pecking order would have to always give way to males in disputes over food. Now this wouldn't be a problem when they had food in abundance. Yet we know during the ice age because of times of rapidly changing climates, food became very difficult to obtain at certain times. So it would only be the alpha males who were allowed to feed and survive. The females and their children being at the bottom of the pecking order would be the first to die, and even if some survived they would be so undernourished that they would be unlikely to be able to give birth and feed their young. This means that in times of scarcity the evolutionary strategy of only allowing the most strongest and most aggressive males to breed would work against the Neanderthals, because although the alpha males would survive they would be incapable of breeding a new generation.

On the other hand the weaker modern humans that no longer had this evolutionary strategy. Their weak and slight bodies suggest they would be more like the bobobos with female at the top of the pecking order. It would then be more likely the alpha females that would survive in times of scarcity. The deaths of the lower order males wouldn't be such a problem because it would only require a few males to survive to continue the breeding of the species. In that one male can father hundreds children of different mothers. It wouldn't even matter if the male dies after he has done his job, of fertilising the females, as the caring of the children he fathered would be in the hands of the mothers. This then means that in the changing climate conditions which brought about the extinction of the Neanderthals, it would be humans a matriarchal society that would be more likely to survive.

It is true that in recorded history we have lived in a patriarchal society and this may of come about because of agriculture and the abundance of food that this created. While humans lived conditions where survival was difficult. It would mean that matriarchal tribes would be the one who would survive and continue to breed. Certainly in the time of the Ice Age and the changing weather conditions made survival for all animals difficult. Then once the Ice Age had ended and the climate settled down into a stable pattern and human intelligence found ways to acquire an abundance of food. Like when humans began to grow crops and herd animals. Then the advantages of living in a matriarchal society for survival declined. This would allow patriarchal tribes ruled by alpha males to be created. They in turn make war on their more peaceful matriarchal neighbours who would be defenceless against organised male violence. In these conditions of abundance of food put females on the lower end of the pecking order as patriarchy would no longer be a threat to the survival of the tribe. This allowed men to indulge in their favourite pastime of war with other tribes, and so over a few thousand years the whole world would become patriarchal through this violence and warfare

So the study of bobobos gives support to the work of Mariji Gimbutas. It also gives a reason why Neanderthals became extinct and not our ancestors.

What is clear is that men can only become the dominant sex by enforcing through violence and propaganda oppressive laws and customs against women. This means that it is not natural for men to be the dominant sex if men have to brutalise each other to become violent and dominant. If we get rid of all these artificial laws and customs created by patriarchal men and follow our natural instincts then we may end up with a equal society. Or we might end up with a female dominated world.

16

THE AQUATIC APE

Scientists have for a long time puzzled over why humans are so different from other animals. In the early 20th century it was simple, it was because humans developed larger brains than any other animal. So because men had bigger brains, they could figure out how to walk on two legs, how to speak and make tools. The problem with this theory is that the elephant, and most species of dolphins and whales have larger brains than us. So a theory was developed that intelligence relied on a brain v body weight ratio. There was no scientific proof that this theory was correct, but then you can't have another allow another animal to be more intelligent than man, can you? More so, if you are the one making up the rules. It was the same when I.Q. tests were invented, also in the early 20th century. The first time they tried it out they discovered according to the tests, women were smarter than men. So of course the tests must be wrong. They had to fiddle about with I.Q. tests until they came up with the "correct" results that made men smarter then women. After all women had smaller brains than men and were too emotionally unstable to vote. So they couldn't possibly be smarter than men.

These men also decided that it was hunting skills that made man so intelligent. It must be this, because hunting is very much a "macho" pursuit. It couldn't possibly be anything to do with gathering because that is a female thing. As in the Stone-Age communities that have survived into modern times it was observed that men do the hunting and women gathered food. So it must be hunting skills that made men so intelligent. It also made man number one on the food chain. (In no way does man what to be number two, that is to say a plant eater and have carnivores feed off him). And it confirmed he was always ruthless and aggressive as well as the superior sex. So from this, the Great White Hunter theory was created.

Then in the 1960s a scientist called Alistair Hardy noticed that the blubber around a seal was very similar the fat around a human. Now fat is commonplace in all aquatic animals but rare in land mammals. This is because fat is a better protector against the cold in water than fur, while fur is a far better insulator for a land animal than fat. From this Hardy began to wonder if we were once an aquatic creature. (Hardy as it turns out wasn't the first scientist to make this observation, but he was the first scientist to publicise it). He also wondered if it would make sense of why we are also the only primate that is hairless. He notes that other hairless creatures like dolphins, hippos, pigs and manatees are aquatic or semi-aquatic animals. Being hairless only makes sense if you spend a large amount of time in water or swamps, where hair can get wet and drag you down.

This theory immediately received the thumbs down by the scientific community. A typical reaction came from Prof. Emeritus Phillip Tobias FRS, -

"Ever since Sir Alister Hardy put it forward in 1960, it has been scorned, derided, made fun of. Nobody has really taken it seriously. You either burst into guffaws of uncontrollable laughter or you tap your head in respect of the person speaking it."

With reactions like this, Hardy dropped it like a hot potato. (He was street wise enough to know that to advocate an unpopular theory would ruin his scientific career). Fortunately it was taken up by the Feminist, Elaine Morgan, who has since developed it further. As she is a journalist and screenplay writer, she had to intellectual freedom to write about the theory without fear of jeopardising her career. If she had an academic career it would of been ruined by the hostility of other academics to this theory.

The beauty of the Aquatic Ape theory is that it explains so much about how humans evolved from being so much different than any other ape.

For instance bipedalism, the great white hunter theory claims that man walked on two legs to see above the high African grass on the savannah. The problem with this theory is that you also have large numbers of grazing animals eating this grass. So these conditions don't last for very long and would only be a temporary situation every year.

Yet in the past there was another ape, which was biped like us. This was the long-extinct Oreopithecus, known as the swamp ape, which means it was also probably a aquatic ape. Scientists have found it had a pelvis like ours, making suitable for bipedalism. In modern times the two primates that are able to walk upright are the proboscis monkey who lives in the mangrove swamps of Borneo. (This is a real swimming primate and some have been found by fishermen swimming in the ocean.) Also the bonobo who lives in forests that are seasonally flooded every year. Both species wade through the water in a similar way to human beings, so this suggests that bipedalism in primates come from living in flooded or swampy areas.

Although there is another primate that stands on two legs and that is the sifaka or leaping lemur of Madagascar. Unlike some species of ape like gibbons or chimpanzees who use long powerful arms to swing among the trees. These lemurs are leapers and will use long powerful legs to leap from branch to branch or even from tree to tree. Some have been observed to leap as far as 30 feet from one tree to another. The problem for these Lemurs is that when they come to the ground their legs are so long that they are unable to walk on four legs. This means they are forced to stand upright and jump or skip along the ground, so why couldn't of this happened to humans? Because like Sifakas our legs are too long of us to comfortably walk on all fours.

The bonobo like many primates have almost the same length of arms and legs. The chimpanzee developed from a bonobo like ancestor to become a swinger, resulting in long powerful arms, to swing through the trees. So it would be logical that humans evolved from the same ancestor to become a leaper. To leap through the trees which resulted in the development of long powerful legs. Which would force humans to walk upright when they had to walk on the ground. This could happen simply because of the types of trees these apes lived in. Some found themselves in trees where it was easier to swing through them, developing the chimpanzee. Others found themselves in trees where it was easier to leap from tree to tree, developing the hominid type ape. While others were living in trees where there was no advantage in becoming a specialist leaper or swinger, resulting in the bonobo. This would then give a great advantage to the hominid ape when they came to ground. Because walking on two legs it would have its hands free to pick up things it might need to carry, or develop tool-making skills. Bonobos and chimpanzees have been observed to use tools but are restricted by the fact they also use their hands for locomotion either on the ground or in trees.

This occurred to me years ago when I saw a picture of a sifaka and read why it could only stand upright on the ground. Being young and very naïve I couldn't understand why scientists had overlooked a obvious reason why humans had become bipeds. It is only now being much older and wiser, I realise that scientists are not going to be interested in such a explanation, because it doesn't in any way support the Great White Hunter theory. Anyway lemurs are highly suspect because the males as so wimpy that they give way to female in all disputes. Clearly male lemurs lack moral fibre, and so not "real men", so the least said about these creatures the better. We wouldn't want yellow belly male lemurs contaminating the "macho" Great White Hunter theory, would we? So hopefully they will go away, if we forget about them. Which is what they might do, as some species of lemurs in Madagascar are considered the most endangered of all species of primates.

The Aquatic ape camp also wouldn't be interested in the leaper idea because again it doesn't in any way help their theory. So anyway, to continue to explain this theory. Human being have voluntary breath control, which is unusual for land animals but commonplace for aquatic mammals. Voluntary breathing is need for aquatic mammals because they need to hold their breath to stay underwater for long lengths of time. The adaptations resulting in this has also allowed humans to speak.

At one time scientist believed that only humans had language. (Because man is so much smarter than any other animal, right?) Then a maverick scientist Dr John C. Lilly put forward the research that showed that both dolphins and whale also can communicate through sound. Not something that egoist male scientists wanted to hear, so he was either ignored or savagely criticised. Then up popped a husband a wife scientific team, the Gardners. Who also wasn't a team player either and badly let the side down by training a chimpanzee to speak using deaf and dumb sign language. Again they were savagely criticised by other scientists who had to redefined speech to "prove" that this chimpanzee wasn't really using language. Perhaps the Gardners were a bit naïve in choosing a female chimpanzee. Had they of trained a male chimpanzee instead, mentioning just how violent and "macho" he was, they may of got more acceptance. It is true that working with adult male chimpanzees is dangerous because of their great strength and aggression. Yet if you want scientific acceptance you have got to do things like this. If they had paired a male with a female chimp this would of established pair bonding, which would of gone down well. Then mention the violence that the male chimpanzee dishes out to the female. Perhaps even have the male chimp sign, "I like bashing females". Now this would of been very popular, as it establishes he is an O.K. guy. There would be no talk about him not really using language if he said intelligent and sensible things like that.

So it seems that language is not exclusive to humans. Apes don't speak, simply because they don't have the vocal ability to do so, not because they are stupid. This is not true of dolphins and whales whom like humans have a large brain and the ability to take conscious control of our breathing. So it seems our ability to take conscious control of our breathing has also resulted in a far greater variety of the sounds we can make, compared with other apes. It is this greater variety of noises we can make, which has resulted in the formation of speech.

Other human characteristics that support the Aquatic Ape theory is that we sweat salt and water from our skin glands. Which for a land animal is a waste, more so in a hot country like Africa, as water is very scarce at certain times of the years. So sweating water is a very inefficient method of keeping cool for a tropical animal. Salt, is also scarce for land animals who will travel a long way to find salt licks. Yet sweating salt makes a lot of sense to aquatic animals that need a way to get rid of an excess of salt in their bodies when swimming in the ocean. Humans can also get rid of excess salt through their tear glands, again something common to aquatic animals but not land animals.

Also being naked is not a good idea in the hot African sun. (Even black people can get sun burnt, or skin cancer from too much sun). Fur protects the skin from the deadly effects of the sun and is also a far better insulator than fat for land animals. This is because a land animal can shed fur in the summer and grow it again in the winter. It can also fluff up fur in the heat, to allow the air to get to its skin to cool down. Or bring the hairs closer to the body, trapping the air in the fur to allow better insulation, in the cold. Fur also makes it far easier for animals to adapt to very cold conditions. In the 19th century when the first zoos were created in Europe they attempted to house tropical animals in heated rooms, but the animals quickly died. So they tried leaving the tropical animals outside and they quickly adapted to the cold by growing thicker fur. It was found that even Russian zoos have no problems in caging tropical animals out in the open, as they grow fur thick enough to adapt to the Russian weather.

It is true that some animals like bears, grow a layers of fat around them for the winter when they hibernate. The trouble is that humans don't hibernate, not even the Eskimos, who for thousands of years endured dark arctic winters living in Igloos.

So it begs the question: what is a tropical animal like human beings walking around using a layer of fat as insulation? Because another disadvantage is that it is unnecessary weight for us to carry around. If you want to stay alive either as a predator or a plant eater on the African plains, speed is a big advantage. So lightness and strength is very important for most animals the size of humans. It seems the only advantage of the fat we have around our bodies is that fat is a better insulator in water and it gives us buoyancy. This then makes it easier for us to float and swim in the water.

We also have large oil glands in our skin. Again this is of little use to a land animal in that they only need enough oil in their skin to keep out the rain. Aquatic animals on the other hand have very large oil glands to make their fur or skin, waterproof. Our oil glands are as large as that of a aquatic animal, rather than a land animal.

There is an old saying that oysters make you brainy. There is some truth in this as brain tissue needs an adequate supply of Omega-3 fatty acids. Which is found in abundance in fish oil but is very scarce in the food found on land. So living on food from the sea would be a big advantage in helping humans to develop a large brain. Some people also have vestigial webbing between their fingers and toes. Which suggests that at one time the webbing was more pronounced giving us an advantage in swimming.

Just how aquatic humans are, can be seen in the very modern sport of "free-diving", that is to say diving without the use of oxygen tanks. When scientist observed people doing very deep free-diving they found that there heart beats would go right down until is was barely beating. The lungs were crushed until they had little more space than a drink can. While what little oxygen left in the body is used to just keep the heart and brain going. In other words human body behaves in exactly the same way in a deep dive without diving gear as a whale or dolphin. Free divers now go deeper than the rescue divers that tried to save the crew of the doomed Russian Kursk submarine. The Norwegian divers in this rescue bid had to spent five days recovering in a decompression chamber. While a free diver do not suffer from bends at all. It seems that the first moment cold water hits the face of a human diving in the water the human body starts to behave like a aquatic animal.

Which makes it more than capable of dealing with the problems of deep diving. On August 17, 2002- a new Freediving World Record has been set by Tanya Streeter, at a depth of 160m/

525ft in a total dive time of 3 minutes and 26 seconds. This dive shatters the previous women's No Limits World Record held by Canadian, Mandy-Rae Cruickshank (136m/446ft) and even surpasses the men's No Limits World Record of 154m/505ft held by Frenchman, Loic LeFerme.

There is a lot of other points that have been put forward by Elaine Morgan like the fact that human legs are very similar in shape and mechanic function to that of a frog. Which is adapted to make it easier for both frogs and humans to swim better. Some mothers today have, water births where the mother gives birth in a tub of water. Apparently birth like this is made a lot easier for mothers suggesting that at one time in our evolution this was commonplace. Also it has been found that newborn babies can float and swim straight away after birth. Whereas with other apes, like a new born chimpanzee or gorilla, it will quickly sink and drown, if not rescued. Water births are not just some new-age fad. There is a tribe in Indonesian called the Suku laut, or the "Sea People", who live a semi-aquatic existence. The Sea People spend up to 10 hours every day in the water, they give birth in the water, and the children dive before they walk and the people harvest all their food from the sea.

So how did our ape ancestors become aquatic? It seems that for a ape that can use it's hands to pick up things from the ground and wade through water, shell fish and edible seaweed would be a very easy way to obtain food. Unfortunately if too many apes take advantage of this, the shallows will quickly become over fished. Forcing them either to mover further along the coast, or to start to dive under water further out. Clearly at first it they would just quickly duck their heads under the water, to collect shellfish deeper than a arms length. Then in time becoming specialist feeders their bodies would adapt to going further and further out to sea.

So you can see there is a very strong arguments for the Aquatic Ape theory. Yet most male scientists still resist this theory. To quote the Anthropologist Prof. Leslie Aiello

"Until there is actual evidence to support a serious aquatic involvement, I don't think that we're going to be able to say that that's at all a contender for a theory for human evolution."

There is no actual evidence of the man the hunter theory, but this hasn't stop scientists presenting it to the public as fact. In recent times they are backtracking they now call it the savannah theory and acceptance that early humans might of scavenged for food instead of hunting. There is even a acceptance nowadays, that the mighty hunter might be black! Elaine Morgan now has the confidence to declare that the Man The Hunter theory is defunct. Yet she is clearly puzzled that with all the weight of evidence she can present for her theory, it is still not widely accepted in the scientific community. As we can see from the quotes from two other scientists.

"It is difficult to see how all the points assembled to back the Aquatic Theory can be explained away." - Dr. Desmond Morris, author of 'The Naked Ape'

"The aquatic hypothesis... cannot be eliminated yet." - Prof. Glyn Isaac

Now this begs the question: Why does this theory need to be, explained away or eliminated? Or for that matter why is the Aquatic Ape theory so popular among Feminists but extremely unpopular among male scientists? Is it because of a very strong gender bias in comparing the Man The Hunter theory with the Aquatic Ape theory?

Apart from the fact that the Aquatic Ape theory doesn't in any way support the ideal of man the mighty hunter, another big problem with this theory is that women are more adaptable to water than men. Because women have less body hair than men, and have more body fat. So what is the problem with that? The trouble is that when we look at modern day communities that still dive for shellfish we find that women have a distinct advantage.

There is a group of islands between southern Japan and southern Korea where before the tourist trade got going, the main source of food and income on these islands was shellfish and edible seaweed. Which is harvested by female divers.

To quote, a Korean travel guide:

Women have dominated this profession because they are physically better suited for it than men, women possess a higher percentage of subcutaneous fat, which insulates them from cold, allowing a longer stay in the water. Thus, it has long been customary for Cheju-do's men to mind the children at home while the women work, culling shellfish, seaweed, and sea urchins from the seabed, on which many of the island's inhabitants depend for subsistence and livelihood. Ranging in age from 10 to 60, these women divers can plunge as deep as 45 to 60 feet and stay underwater for as long as three to five minutes without the aid of breathing equipment. The average dive, however, lasts about 30 seconds at a depth of 15 or 20 feet."

The Cheju-do women are referred to by some Korean commentators as Amazons, because they are far more assertive than ordinary Korean women. In the extremely "macho" society of Korea, these women and their "weak" husbands are an embarrassment, and for this reason knowledge about Cheju-do customs were once kept quiet.

The Japanese islands have a similar story to quote, the late Jacques Cousteau

For 1500 years in ancient Japan, as well as neighbouring Korea, these women have traditionally dived for pearls. At least 30,000 of their kind remain. Today they mostly dive for food. Wearing only a loincloth, they have begun to wear masks and snorkels within the 20th century. They dive both during the warm summers and the cooler winter months when temperatures can reach 50° F. They plunge to depths of 20 to 80 feet – sometimes 100 – to gather food, in the form of shellfish and seaweed, which they place in a net around their waists. They learn to dive around puberty and do not stop till they are about 60 years old. They are known to dive right up to the point of childbirth and having given birth, resume shortly after, nursing their infants between dives! A similar group of women once dived in the wave tossed waters off Tierra del Fuego. (Islands at the most southern point of South America). *They descended completely naked, through waters averaging 42°* F *to collect clams and crabs for food.*

The Japanese and Korean women divers did experiment with modern equipment like scuba gear, but it was soon found that using such equipment would quickly over fish the area, so scuba equipment was banned by the authorities.

There is also some reports of women divers in other parts of the world. In Barents Sea, palaeontologists and archaeologists have for a long time been puzzled why such large amounts of shellfish shells have been found in Palaeolithic sites without any evidence of fishing gear and boats. This would only be a puzzle for male scientists who are blind to the role women play in ancient communities. Before the 1920s when the Russian authorities began to use modern diving gear and motorboats equipped with dredges, there was still a local tradition of using professional women-divers similar to that in Japan and Korea. Even in these cold waters on the coast of Siberia these divers would continue diving in the cold autumn months. (Needless to say when they adopted modern equipment the area was soon over fished and fishing in the area was banned in 1960).

If male divers had been doing this job these scientists wouldn't of had no problems in putting two and two together. They would of praised the male divers about how tough and macho they were, given it wide coverage, but because they were women, the fact was ignored.

It is perfectly possible for women to swim in these waters without a wet suit. In the sporting world we are used to men outperforming women, yet there is one sport where women are now outperforming men, which is the sport of marathon open water swimming. In the 21 miles across the English Channel, the first women to do this was Gertrude Caroline Ederle of USA. In 1926 she broke the record of the fastest man by one hour and fifty-nine minutes. In spite of having to battle through heavy seas in the second half of her swim. Since then the record for the fast channel swim has been held at different times by both men and women. In 1987 Lynne Cox of USA, (who also held the fastest time for swimming the English Channel for awhile), swam the across the Bering Strait, from the U.S. to Soviet Union with water temperatures at 38-42 degrees Fahrenheit, without wearing a wet suit. She done it wearing only a normal swim suit, cap and goggles. At this temperature most normal men will freeze to death in the water within 20 minutes.

The censorship by patriarchal authorities of women divers many be responsible for the mermaid legend. Once a Dutch ship was wrecked on Cheju island's coast. Subsequently, its crew was detained for 13 years. One of the seamen, Hamel, published a record of their experiences upon his return to Europe, describing the 'haenyo' (women divers) as mermaids. Which is interesting because being on the island for 13 years he must of known they were ordinary women. So why did he write that they were mermaids? In may be because in those days a story of mermaids was more acceptable to people than female divers. After all, the Korean authorities at one time forbade and written record of these divers. The official version of the mermaid story is the sailors have mistaken animals like seals and dugongs as mermaids. Which is a typical patronising attitude from academics towards uneducated working class people, in assuming they are stupid. I personally find it hard to believe that experienced sailors couldn't tell the difference between a seal and a women swimming in the sea or sitting on rocks. Korea and Japan the authorities have tended to keep quiet about women divers up until recent times. Because it undermines patriarchal beliefs, to have assertive women doing a physical job better than men. So the same was probably true in other parts of the world. The patriarchal Jews went as far as to ban shellfish as a taboo food. Was this because in those days women divers were still collecting them from the sea? Had not female divers in Japan and Korea survived up until modern time we today wouldn't know nothing about them. There is other evidence that women divers were still commonplace all over the world in the recent past. For instance in the 19th century peal industry, some of the European traders were horrified to find the locals using women peal diving. To the degree that in the Torres Strait islands they banned women divers.

Because of the patriarchal conspiracy of silence, sailors would be shocked suddenly coming across women divers. To these very patriarchal sailors used to their own women being very submissive, shy, retiring and modest. To suddenly see naked, (They probably were naked as the bathing suit was only invented at the end of the 19th century and clothing is a hindrance in the water), athletic and confident women going about their work would be something completely outside of their personal experience. As we can see from this following sighting in Britain.

"A SCHOOL MASTER OF THURSO IN CAITHNESS, William Munro, wrote in a report in THE TIMES on September 8, 1809 that twelve years earlier he had been walking along Sandside Bay shore when he saw what he first thought was a naked woman, sitting on a rock and combing her light brown hair. The face was plump, with ruddy cheeks and blue eyes. If the rock where the woman sat had not been so dangerous for swimmers, Munro would have assumed it was human. After a few minutes it dropped into the sea and swam away. Others had seen it too.."

He clearly states is that he saw a naked woman, sitting on a rock. Yet it is reported as a mermaid sighting. Probably in isolated fishing villages all over the world women divers may of been used up to fairly recent times. Because people living on the edge of survival couldn't afford to ignore a important food resource like shell fish and edible seaweed. In traditional mermaid stories from Europe there is stories of fishermen marrying mermaids. Now, if it was to a women with a fishes tail this would virtually impossible, so in some of the stories the mermaid obtains legs by magical means. Yet if we take a more sensible view, that mermaids are women divers then there is no problem with this. Most women divers were probably married to fishermen anyway.

They would also have to keep this tradition secret because of patriarchal condemnation of women doing men's work. There would be a even more deadly reason to do this, churchmen in the past have condemned mermaids as pagan. Now this is a real threat, because the Church in the middle ages had murder millions of women as Witches. It seems that country people in the times still had many pre-Christian beliefs, which was stamped out as pagan during the witch-hunts. (The word pagan comes from the word peasant). This includes women healers who practised the ancient art of herbal medicine. (There was no problem about educated men giving out herbal medicine, they were called doctors, so that was all right, but a women doing this was condemned as a witch). To protect themselves, one of the ways of keeping the tradition of women divers secret, would be to invent stories of mermaids. Then to tell strangers who did see them, that it was a mermaid that they saw.

So why was it that women become more aquatic than men? A possible explanation is that wading in the water was also a protection from predators, who are unlikely to try and swim out to catch a ape who can stand upright in the water and can walk out as far as it's neck. To this ape the water will come a safe haven in much the same way a tree is, so instead of climbing a tree to escape from a predator it can run into the ocean instead. In fact a beach is a difficult hunting ground for predators as there is not much cover a large cat can hide behind to stalk their prey. This then would make shell hunting more popular among females if she is pregnant or breast feeding a child as she is protected by the water she is wading through. Even when the child is too big to carry, the mother can leave the child on the water's edge and then quickly snatch it and take it out to deeper water if she sees a predator coming down the beach. So there is a lot of advantages of female apes becoming marine food gathers. Though not so much for male apes, who would be bigger and stronger anyway and don't have the burden of trying to save a helpless baby from a predator as well. So it would cause a division of labour of men gathering on land while women gathered in the sea.

So the Aquatic Ape theory seems to be very much appeal to women, and this also may be why many male scientists don't like it. Instead of having a great white hunter, coming home from a hard day of hunting to be greeted by his adoring wife, who will submissively wait on her lord and master hand and foot. We now have women who are the breadwinners and it is the men who have to look after the home and children! Well, we can't possibly have that can we? More so if you realise that it is claimed by Elaine Morgan that it took a 6.5 million year for humans to evolve into a semi-aquatic animal. Does this mean that men were under the women's thumb all this time? It couldn't be possible be that our male ancestors were a bunch of yellow belly wimps, can it?

Large deposits of shellfish shells have been found in South Africa in early human sites. Proving that shellfish was being eaten by early humans. Also very early hominids like Homo erectus had very thick tooth enamel and powerful jaws. Which it is speculated that they were needed, to break open nuts and shellfish with their teeth. Later on they would of used stones or clubs to do this, which may of been the first use of tools for hominids. Yet most male scientists still do not accept the Aquatic Ape theory and still cling desperately to very watered down versions of the Great Hunter theory, or prefer to have no theory at all.

This then means that it is possible to make out a case that human society was dominated by women from the time when we were still a ape to the end of the Neolithic Age. We can briefly summarise this in the following points.

1. The skeleton of the bonobo ape is very similar to the australopithecines oldest discovered is 3 million year old and the australopithecus ramidus which dates back to 4,4 million years old. The teeth of these primates show that they were vegetarians, which is another blow to the man the hunter theory. So as the bonobo ape lives in female dominated communities can we also assume that the australopithecines was the same? Now I am sure that male chauvinists scientists will correctly claim that you cannot make such a assumption on such slender evidence. Yet we know that if these skeletons were more like that of a chimpanzee than a bonobo. These same scientists would be very quick to claim that humans then had exactly the same social structure as male dominated chimpanzee communities.
2. Then we have the Aquatic Ape theory that shows that humans went through a Aquatic period in their evolution. The bones of the australopithecines were found at the edge of ancient sea, which means the this ancient human could of used this sea as a means of obtaining food. It is true that many bones of ancient humans have also been found inland, but what we don't really know is whether any of these hominids were our direct ancestors. There has been many species of hominids in the past yet only one species, the modern human, has survived into modern times. It seems that because of the aquatic adaptations to our bodies it was only the aquatic species that survived. If we accept that Aquatic Ape theory then we also have to accept that "macho" hunting had little to do with our evolution. Also that because women's bodies are more adaptable to aquatic life it was women and not men who became the main, "bread winners".
3. As we move forward in time to the more modern humans that came into existence about 200,000 years ago. What we find compared with other animals of a similar size is that we are incredibility weak. In fact far weaker that apes like chimpanzees and gorillas and other hominids like the Neanderthals. As evolutionist point out one of the main reasons why a animal becomes very powerful and strong is the competition between males who have a test of strength and aggression for the right to mate. The fact that the modern human is so weak compared with its nearest species except the bonobo, is probably because there was very little male competition for the right to mate with females, among our ancestors. This points to women selecting which males she wants to mate with instead of men. Suggesting a situation where women were either equal to men in status or the dominant sex.
4. Of the many species of hominids it was only the modern human that has survived. This was because of periods of rapid changing weather conditions during the last ice age. When many large species of animals became extinct. Even we were probably nearly wiped out

because genetically it seems that all humans today had only one female ancestor about 200,000 years ago. In the survival of any species, women are far more important than men. This is because one man can father hundreds of children, while a women is very limited on how many children she can have. More so in the state of stress and starvation, it is important that a women is reasonably well fed to nourish a baby. So like the lemurs in the island of Madagascar, communities that give preference to alpha males are less likely to survive than communities that give preference to females.

5. Then in the Neolithic age we find evidence of people worshipping Goddesses and no evidence of war or violence. Which changed dramatically when in the bronze and iron ages where the use of weapons of war, fortifications and the worship of male warrior gods became commonplace.

Taking all the evidence from above it would seem that women have always dominated human society up until five thousand years ago. I have to say that is unlikely. The point is that what you read in this book readdress the balance of sexual bias scholarship, archaeology, zoology, biology, anthropology and palaeontology, which claims that man was always the dominant sex.

Ever since I went to school in the 1950s to now all I have ever read in mainstream science is that we have always lived in male dominated societies. It was only by reading a book called, "The First Sex", by Elizabeth Gould Davis in the 1970s that opened my eyes to different possibility. Since then I have taken a interest in this subject and soon found that to get any information on anything that suggests human beings were once dominated by females, very difficult to find. The truth is that the general public is only given one very sexual biased point of view.

This is because of very egocentric academic males who very much want to believe that men have always been the dominant sex. The problem is that the censorship about the possibility of women rule or even sexual equality, gives the general public the illusion they only have one choice and that is patriarchy. Which wouldn't be a problem if men were doing a wonderful job in ruling our world. The trouble is that men do a really terrible job of doing this. I would even go as far as saying that, it would be difficult to do a worse job of ruling our world, than what men do.

If we accept that in the past we didn't always live in brutal and violent patriarchal communities. It means we can if we choose create a more peaceful and caring world ruled by women.

17

MASCULINE AND FEMININE CYCLES

We live in a sick, sad world, which needs to be healed. The first thing needed in process of healing is an acknowledgement that there is an illness. For instance with alcoholics or drug addicts attempts to cure them are a waste of time until they acknowledges they have a real problem. Then the healer needs to convince them that they have a workable method that will bring genuine healing.

So the first hurdle is the universal admission that we do actually live in a sick world. The problem is that we are taught from childhood that the world we live in is "normal". We have all been brought up from childhood to believe war, crime, violence and hatred is customary for human beings. If we think about it a bit deeper we find that all the major religions of the world has failed to make our world a better place. Communism and Socialism with the ideal of equality also seems to have completely failed. The only thing that seems to have worked is Democracy, which it is clearly a step in the right direction. Yet even Democracy is being undermined by corrupt, two faced politicians who seem to be incapable of telling the truth.

So the message that comes to us from history and the media, is that the world of conflict, hatred and violence we live in is simply human nature and there is nothing we can do about it. The reason why we seem to be incapable of making our world a better place is because we are caught in the trap of a masculine cycle of fear and violence.

We stand on the brink of two possible futures, either a masculine or feminine destiny. These two possibilities come through two very different cycles. The masculine cycle began with the end of the Neolithic age. Somehow women lost control of a handful of men who became very violent. The male cycle probably began with men who find they can obtain power over other people through violence and aggression. Probably at first they were simply outcasts who survived by robbing people moving between towns and villages. Then in time some of these men formed groups and become bandits. They would be joined by other men who would be drawn by the attraction of power over others, through violence. In time these groups would become so large that they were able to take over towns and villages and impose on the people a protection racket. "you give us what we want and we leave you alone". This would be in effect the first taxation. Then different bandit gangs would then start to fight each other for territory. Until one bandit leader got on top and conquered other bandit gang and he would become a king.

The bandits would exploit their power over the people and probably would steal whatever they wanted. As well as rape and kidnap women and use them as sex slaves. Understandably the people would get angry with this behaviour and perhaps rise up and against the bandits. Some of these revolutions would fail and the people would find themselves receiving even worse treatment than before. Other revolutions would succeed but the people will find that even getting rid of the bandits, will not allow them to return to their previous life of peace. If the revolution is led by men they will become as violent as the bandits and will end up behaving the same, once in power. If the revolution is led by women they will become Amazons and still have to learn warfare to defend themselves from attack from other bandits. In the end the Amazons died away probably because violence is not as natural for women as it is for men. So in the end women will be subdued by male violence.

This violence is very similar to what we observe in apes like chimpanzees and the male hamadryas baboons.

As female chimps come into season males start to become attractive to them, but many females can be choosy and only prefer certain males. Males who are not chosen by females counter the females right to choose by aggression and violence, by repetitively attacking the females he wants to mate with. Jane Goodall who has observed this behaviour claims that alpha males train the females he wants to mate with through intimidation and fear. So she will be too frighten to refuse him when he wants to mate with her.

A graphic account of this was observed by the Japanese primatologist Mariko Hiraiwa-Hasegawa. She was observing two chimp communities she called M and K group. One day she discovered the alpha male of M group called Ntologi with four of his side kicks attacking a lone female from K group and her three year old child. With the help of a companion Hiraiwa-Hasegawa attempted to beat the male chimps off by beating them with canes, but the powerful males ignored them. Then her companion threw a rock at the males and this had the effect of making them backing off. (Had the male chimps had instead attacked the two humans they wouldn't of stood a chance against the powerful chimpanzees). The life of the female was saved although she and her child were covered in blood and badly injured. A year later the same female had another child and was again attacked by the Nitologi and his henchmen. This time her baby was eaten alive by them. After this the female defected to M group and mated with her baby's murder. Probably because she couldn't no longer find safety in F group for herself and her children. A post script to this, was that Ntologi himself was later murdered by his second in command, so he could take over the position of the alpha male. While Hiraiwa Hasegawa herself have given up observing chimpanzees because she was so appalled by their behaviour, that she learnt to hate them.

Male hamadryas baboons are also very aggressive. They kidnap females to become part of their harems from a young age and maintain it through continuous threats and intimidation. Usually by biting the back of the necks of his females. Which is a real threat as hamadryas baboons have large razor-sharp canines. So he is capable of killing or bad injure the female if was to bite hard. The males frighten the females so much that they will not stray too far from them, so that even a stare by the male will so frighten the females they will run back to the male. They are so under the control of the male that they will never refuse sex when they are into estrus.

The behaviour of humans in extremely patriarchal societies is very similar. It use to be that the alpha male, the king or local lord, could have as many wives he wanted. Even when Christianity come into force and man were suppose to have only one wife. Many lords still had conjugal rights to all the peasant women working on his land. In places like Sicily, Ethiopia and Eastern Europe it was commonplace up until recently that if a young man wants to marry a girl, with some of his friends he would kidnap her and then raped her. After that there would be social pressure put on the girl to marry her rapist. This was only stopped in Sicily, when one young women in the 1960s was brave enough to take her rapist to court and have him charged with rape. In doing so she had to not only resist social traditions but also the Mafia. So we can see that this behaviour is not far removed from that of the hamadryas baboon.

We can see a contrast in the behaviour of the bonobo. Milwaukee County Zoo had a group of bonobos and they attempted to train them in the same way they train chimpanzees and other animals. The bonobos reacted by becoming extremely non co-operative. They would scream loudly at the zoo keepers and urinate on them if they come into the pen. Then a female keeper took over and she adopted a system of kindness and positive reward. The behaviour of the bonobos changed and they became very co-operative and easy to work with. So it seems that bonobo females will not accept force and intimidation. Yet this is not the attitude of the male bonobos.

In zoos it was found that bonobo males were frequently assaulted by females who would gang up on a single male. To the degree of having fingers and toes bitten off and in one case a female bit off male's penis! It seems that this is normal behaviour in the wild but the differences is that the male can run away, but in a zoo he has no form of escape. So it seems to be normal behaviour for female bonobos gang up and assault lone males to show them, who is the boss. (They also assault male zoo keepers who come into their pen).

Scientists have not been slow to compare primate behaviour with human behaviour. Where domestic violence between men and women is commonplace. In the past in the Western world it was once "normal" for a husband to beat his wife with a stick. In the Islamic world even today a man is "dishonoured" if he cannot dominate his wife by beating her up. In China as late as the 20th century was the tradition of foot binding which left women nearly crippled. Which is very similar to the behaviour of some male chimps who will not only beat up the female he wants to mate with, but cripple her as well, so she is unable to run away.

So sadomasochism is part of the primate sex war between males and females. Males dominate through violence and the female have to become masochistic to be able to stay sane in a life of brutal beatings and rape. Patriarchal societies also enforce the custom of marriage that forces a women stay with a man and breaks up any chance of women creating a powerful sisterhood. Bonobos and other female dominated primates re-enforce the sisterhood through lesbian sex. Which even today is discouraged by patriarchal custom. Female macaque and rhesus monkeys also mount males and rub themselves against them as a sign of dominance over the male. Which is again similar to human behaviour, it seems some men will go to a dominatrix to pay them to bugger them with strap on dildos. Is this a unconscious desire by these men to want women to dominate them once more?

One of the reasons why male chimpanzees and humans continue to use violence and intimidation against females and other males, is because it works. If people and female chimps adopted the attitude of, "Give Me Liberty Or Give Me Death" (Patrick Henry, 1775). Then this behaviour wouldn't be able to continue. Though admittedly his is a lot to ask of any person or creature. Yet again some women have done this. In certain parts of Pakistan and India some mothers will murder their female babies. Some feminists have seen this as a sign of extreme patriarchal brainwashing on women. But other feminists have pointed out that another reason for this could be that these mothers do not want to bring up daughters in the very brutal patriarchal world they live in.

Feminists have point out that a women to gives in to a violent husband and cares for him and has his children is betraying the next generation of women. This is because her sons will think it "normal" to beat up their girlfriends or wives while her daughters will think it "normal" to beaten up by men. Also she is allowing his violent genes to be passed on as well. This then allows this behaviour to continue generation after generation. So like the female chimpanzee or hamadryas baboon if she gives into male violence it encourages males to continue to use it. Though it has to be admitted that very few women are able to stand up to male violence on their own. It was only by Feminists setting up Women's Refuses where women subjected to violence could go to, that allowed women to tackle male violence in recent times. This then is the advantage human females have over female chimpanzees, they are better able to communicate with each other and organise resistance to this behaviour.

In extremely patriarchal countries male dominance is enforced by male violence. Not only against women but men also fight each other for supremacy with violence as well. It seems to be the more violent a society becomes the more men dominate it. A example of this is Afghanistan. Up until the 1970s it was a country that had lived in peace for nearly a hundred years. In that time it began to become slowly Westernised, in that the women were allowed education and all the Islamic restrictions against women were slowly eroding away. Then it was invaded by the Soviet Union. Even after the Soviet Union left in the 1980s war still continued between various warlords. The result of over 20 years of war has been that women's rights have been taken away and Afghanistan has now one of the most harshest laws and customs against women. Even the recent invasion by USA hasn't changed the attitudes of brutalised men towards women, and is still a country mostly ruled by violent warlords.

So the masculine cycle is created by male violence. The effect of male violence is to brutalised men and increasing their testosterone levels. While women become more submissive, to counter male violence by appeasing men. Which undermines women's confidence and self-respect.

The antidote for male violence is peace. Like with capitalism the end result of companies competing with each other is a monopoly where one company comes out on top and competition comes to a end. The end results of competition between warring warlords and states is empire. Where one leader ends up coming out on top and imposes peace, by force. This brings about a time of peace where the testosterone levels of men go down as they become less brutalised by the decreasing violence. Unfortunately peaceful countries then become open to invasion by other states who are still fighting among themselves. This is not a problem while they continue to do this but when they become united under one strong leader, this leader becomes a conqueror. Because finding he has a united army of battle harden fighters he will invade peaceful states on its border. This is what happened to China when it was invaded by the Mongols.

In 1206 Genghis Khan united the warring Mongols under one ruler. These men used to fighting among themselves found it easy to conquer other surrounding countries, who had been at peace for many years. The Mongols invaded not only China, but India and Europe as well and ended up with the largest empire known in recorded history. Then Mongols in turn became less aggressive through years of peace. This resulted in them being driven back to their homeland and finally conquered in turn by the Chinese.

It is noticeable that women began to become liberated in Europe and Northern America during the 19th and 20th century during a time of relative peace and stability, after the Napoleonic wars. It is true in this period we did have the American Civil War, the Franco-Prussian war and the First and Second wars all fought on European and North American soil. Yet between these wars we did have years of peace, with generations of people not knowing what it was like to fight in a war. While Switzerland is one of the safest countries in the world which hasn't had a war on its soil for over a hundred years. In the USA the high rate of crime has been blamed on the freely availability of guns available. Yet in Switzerland shooting is a main national sport encouraged by all men having to do national service. In fact Switzerland has one of the most heavily armed populations in the world. Yet it also has one of the lowest crime rates.

So is it a coincide that Switzerland has also managed not to be involved in any wars for the whole of the 20th century? Also at one time Switzerland boasted that they had eliminated poverty in their country. Recently this has returned through the influx of immigrant workers doing low paid work, but it still remains low. So it means that people in Switzerland have not been brutalised by either war or poverty for a long time, which makes it possible for the male population to be armed with guns without the problem of gun crime.

This means that peace can create a feminine cycle. In times of peace men become less aggressive, their testosterone levels go down and are less likely to commit violence against women. As they are no longer being battered by men, women begin the gain confidence and self respect. This is the danger patriarchal religions understood thousands of years ago. This is why the Christian and Islamic religions made laws and customs to restrict female freedoms and encouraged men to assault women. Christian priests encourage men to dominate their wives by beating them. While in the Islamic world even today, a man is "dishonoured" if fails to beat his wife to make her obedient.

In the 19th century many wealthy women in USA campaigned against slavery. Then as they began to understand the legal position of slaves, they were shocked to find that black slaves had more legal rights than did the average women. This started the women's movement in America. Because men were becoming less aggressive and women more confident, men have little resistance to women's demands for equal rights over the next 150 years. What has been striking in the West is that the Feminist movement has been met with very little male violence. Unlike what happens in Islam countries where women who have been brave enough to fight for equal rights, have been murdered, arrested and assaulted.

As women become more free, so do men. A despotic dictatorship is only possible if the dictator can rely on a army of ruthless young men who will obey him and commit violence, murder and torture against anyone who opposes his rule. A leader who cannot find enough young men to commit violence against the people, then has to rule by consent and not violence. This means that the level of male violence in the general population has to decrease to make democracies and women's liberation possible.

So men and women have two very different strategies to gain dominance over the other sex.

The Masculine method is through violence. men simply using their superior size and strength to batter women into submission. On top of this, patriarchal institutions have created laws and customs to keep women in a condition of slavery. As well as creating competitive masculine societies that favours men and not women. The Feminine method is through co-operation. We can see this clearly with the female bonobo ape whom have created a powerful sisterhood. This has also been the battle cry of many Feminists that, THE SISTERHOOD IS POWERFUL. Unfortunately up until now, women haven't been able to put this into practise to make a noticeable difference.

Many Feminists have criticised their own sex for not making most of the opportunities that at equal opportunities legalisation gives them. This has also been a similar problem for African Americans. People like Malcolm X have complained bitterly that most black Americans have what he called, "A slave mentality". That is to say although slavery was abolished in 1863 nearly a 150 years later African Americans still find themselves the most poorest and deprived group in USA. Although one of the reasons for this, is discrimination by other ethic groups, like white people. The culture of Black people is not very helpful either. For instance there is a real problem of a anti-academic culture among young black men. Where in schools black men who try to study hard are ridiculed and physically attacked by other black men. It seems that for a black man to get ahead he has to be very secretive or very big, strong and violent, to resist bullying by other black young men.

Women have had the same problem. They also had a "slave mentality" but there are signs that they are now overcoming this. Up until the 1980s, young men were always ahead of young women academically. Girls would be ahead of boys up to about the age of puberty, then girls academic performances would drop away and boys would overtake girls in getting more places in college and universities. Yet in more recent times there has been a slow change where girls are now studying harder than boys at school right through to university. The result is that in school leaving exams in 2002 in Britain there is now a 9% gap in favour of girls and this gap is slowly growing every year. It also seems that boys are now having problems. The anti academic culture of young black men is spreading to young white boys as well. Where anti-learning laddish culture is being blamed for the poor academic results of all young men.

The result of this is that some commentators are claiming that, "the future is female". The idea is that if more women have better academic qualifications than men, they will have more of the top jobs in the future. This assumes that women will also be able to cope with the very "macho" and aggressive culture of politics and business. For this reason many women who want careers go to assertiveness classes. Which is probably what many women do need, but to go down this road too far can be self defeating for women. This can be seen in the case of the hyena. It seems that females as they develop in their mother's womb they are bathed in male hormones resulting that when they are born the young females have clitorises as large as a male penis and are even more aggressive than males. This aggression allows female hyenas to dominate the males.

The dominance by females benefits their offspring in that Hyena cubs have a far lower starvation rate than other carnivores. So it is a big help in allowing the hyena to survive difficult times. Some modern sportswomen have taken steroids to boost strength and the side effect has been to become very aggressive as well. So women don't really have to go to assertiveness classes to survive in the patriarchal market place, all they have to do is take steroids. Like female hyenas they can become as aggressive and as assertive as men. The only problem with this, is that do we want to live in a world where everyone is so aggressive? The normal patriarchal society is bad enough with 50% of the population behaving like irresponsible idiots. To have a full 100% would be even worse. Yet this doesn't have to be the only way, there is another choice.

In business there is talk about co-operation rather than competition. Business studies have shown that competition within a company can make it very inefficient. This is because if you have staff competing with each other for power and status, they are unlikely to co-operate with each other. This will result in office politics where people with attempt to undermine other members of the staff and even sabotage their efforts. So some businesses want to try to eliminate all this, and get people to co-operate rather than compete. I don't have to tell you that, it has been found that female staffs are far better at this than men.

Another quantum leap could be made in politics as we can see through the leadership of Princess Diana. The genius of Princess Diana was that she was able to portray herself in the media as a genuine caring and loving person. Something any politician or spin-doctor would give their right arm to have. Although she didn't have any political power, in the way she was able to use and manipulate the media made her a very powerful person. Which she used to further her own agenda, to create a more caring and loving world, where possible.

From the very beginning when she became a royal she responded to people in a very caring way. Now this is not unusual with famous people in the media, but she put it across in a way that no one doubted that it was genuine. To the degree not even her critics doubted this. So this made her from the start the most popular royal, and gave her worldwide fame. At first she was just content with this, but then she was to learn a trick from another royal, Princess Ann.

In the early 1980s there was a great famine in the Sudan, but the media ignored this famine so the people in the West were unaware of the millions of people dying of starvation in the Sahara desert region. Princess Ann as president of the Save The Children Fund visited Sudan and of course the media went with her, because they wanted a story on her failing marriage. Then reporters personally saw the great suffering going on in the area, and as the result of this visit the media all over the world began to report on the famine. This in turn got the Band-Aid movement off the ground. Resulting in millions of pounds being donated to try and save these people.

So likewise, Princess Diana began use her celebrity status to highlight causes she believed in. One of the most important acts she done was change people's opinions on Aids epidemic. When Aids first started to spread in the West, people greatly feared it and believed that they could catch this disease by touching people with this disease. Also as it was mostly homosexual men who got Aids, this increased homophobia, and some extreme Christians were suggesting that Aids was the way God was punishing deviant acts like homosexuality. The media in Britain encouraged these stories and I can remember reading one scare story in the British newspaper, The Sun, suggesting that people could catch Aids from public toilet seats, if a homosexual man sat there previously.

At the height of the homophobia frenzy whipped up by the British press, Princess Diana fearlessly met this hysteria head on. She visited a hospital with Aids patients inside and talked to and shook hands with patients dying of Aids. Pictures of her doing his was in the newspapers and on the TV and in one stroke she had given homosexual men Royal approval and destroyed the myth that you could catch Aids by touching someone with this disease.

She was later to do the same with leprosy as in many part of the world people still believe it is possible to catch leprosy but touching a leper. She again appeared on TV touching shaking the hand of a leper and helped overcome prejudice against lepers. Charitable organisations were finding that if Princess Diana publicly gave them support of them, she was able to generate large amounts of contributions for their cause. So they became very aware of her power to help the causes she believed in.

She also started to move into politics. In the 1980s in Britain there was high unemployment as well and an increasing number of homeless people living on the streets. The right-wing press in Britain was whipping up a hate campaign against unemployed people, claiming that they were scroungers and work-shy. Princess Diana showed the world clearly where her sympathies laid by again visiting and talking to homeless people. Though by this time the media was now wise to her tactics and wasn't so keen on reporting her doing this. So she didn't get the media coverage in this that she normally expects. The British media also tried to start a hate campaign against Princess Diana but the newspapers that attempted to attack her found that they were unable to dent her popularity with the common people.

She was to move more into politics towards the end of her life. Charitable organisations had for years campaigned again the production and use of land mines, but had never got anywhere with this. In all conflicts all over the world countless land mines were buried indiscriminately, then after the war the land mines would be left in the ground with no one knowing were they were. So the civil population living in the area would continue to be killed and maimed by treading on these mines. Princess Diana then decided to get involved, and simply by visiting a area where land mines had been buried she focused the world's media on this problem and got governments all over the world to take notice.

She was warned by conservative politicians not to get involved in politics. She herself was to claim before she died, that she feared she would be killed, and when it did happen the circumstances of her death was very suspicious, suggested a government cover up.

The great emotional effect of her death on people was immense, which was to surprise everyone. The reason for this is I believe is that in a uncaring world, where selfish and corrupt industrial and political leaders are commonplace. Princess Diana was one of the few people in establishment who showed that she genuinely cared and loved people. So in the very large numbers of people that mourned the death of Princess Diana gave a clear message to the politicians that the people wanted to live in a more caring world. This was picked up by the British Prime Minster who stated that people loved Diana because she genuinely cared. But he didn't learn from this himself and his actions have since shown he is a normal selfish and uncaring politician.

Another women was the have the same effect before Princess Diana and this was Evita Peron. It would be easy to be cynical and say that she was only a the mistress and later wife of a South American dictator. But the emotion effect she was to have on Argentina, the country where she was the first lady, shows she was more than this.

Like Princess Diana the political influence she had was very limited. Yet unlike any other Argentina politician, before or since, she was able to show to the people that she genuinely cared. The people respond greatly to her and although she was unable to do a lot for the people of Argentina she came across and a person who really believed in what she said. With her early death, people showed clearly how they felt about her at her funeral, and this gave a message to the politicians that people do want to live in a caring society. Something I'm afraid the Argentina politicians ignored.

The story of Evita Peron was given publicity by the stage musical Evita written by Andrew Lloyd Webber and Tim Rice. The genius of this musical was it portrayed clearly the emotion effect Evita had on the people of Argentina. Unfortunately when it was also make into a film the producers and directors had little understanding of what the story was about. They put a pop star in the title role who didn't have either the singing voice or acting ability to do justice to the music and lyrics.

To a lesser degree the same thing happened with Mary Robertson the first women President of Southern Ireland. Although the Irish Presidency has little political power Mary Robertson was able to present herself as a caring person. She became so popular that when she retired, nearly all the candidates to replace her were women. After Mary Robertson's performance few people were interested in voting for a male.

With the rise of Feminism in the 20th century some female politicians have risen to become leaders of countries like Margaret Thatcher and Indira Gandhi. Both of these politicians have shown clearly to the world that a woman can successfully rule a country. Unfortunately both women more or less behaved like a male ruler and didn't show the caring side of women. Though to be fair to both women, they came leaders of very patriarchal parties and had they behaved like caring women it is unlikely they would of became leaders of their parties and country.

I believe the next step for powerful women is to have a female leader of a country with the political skill of a Margaret Thatcher or Indira Gandhi. Yet also with the ability to express there caring nature in the same way Princess Diana had. So that by becoming very popular through her caring nature she is able to push forward widespread reforms to the patriarchal system.

Once we start to have compassionate and powerful women leaders of countries, very few people will want to vote for male politicians. Male political leaders have had thousands of years to demonstrate they can be compassionate and responsible leaders. Yet very few in all that time can be said to be like this. (Apart from Nelson Mandela I can't think of any genuinely caring male politician). They had their chance and completely blew it.

18

HOSTAGE TO FORTUNE

What is very apparent in a patriarchal society is the lack of love of love and compassion. The prototype of the patriarchal society comes instincts of primates like the chimpanzee or hamadryas baboon where the males threaten and batter females into submission. This is not the action of animals that are capable of loving others. The same is true for men who will rape and assault women to keep them submissive.

This attitude permeates the whole of patriarchal societies. The ruler who decides to conquer neighbouring states clearly has no love for the people in country he wants to conquer, and in fact he probably hates them. He also has no love for this own people, as he must know a war will inflict death and hardship on them as well. Likewise the rich, who exploit the poor and force people to work in sweatshops for poor wages, have no love for the people they employ.

For centuries we have been ruled by uncaring leaders who have shown very little compassion for the people they rule. It is true in the west their has been a improvement where welfare reforms have allowed unemployment pay, state pensions and free hospital care for the poor. Yet these are something the workers have had to fight for and we can see today many politician are looking for ways to do away with these benefits. Because their masters, the rich and wealthy, are complaining they are not getting enough!

Patriarchy is hell for both women and men. We can see this by the number of people who are addicted to alcohol, drugs, (both legal in illegal), gambling and even food and work. Somehow most of us are looking for ways to blot out the reality of our lives. This is because patriarchy only benefits the alpha men and even they have to watch their backs, for fear of others who want their power and wealth. Men have coped with this hell by becoming totally selfish, so he doesn't have to care for anyone but himself. This makes it possible for him to protect himself by being aggressive and even violent towards others. Women on the other hand cannot use this method because they have a maternal instinct, which makes them care for children. So many women to cope with the hell of patriarchy go to the opposite extreme and care for everyone except themselves. By not caring for themselves they are not hurt and can put up with all the physical and mental abuse metered out by men. Which means most women have had to become harden masochists to stay sane in a traditional patriarchal society.

In Jean Liedloff's Book "The Continuum Concept", she describes living among a South American jungle with a tribe where conflict, anger, hatred and violence was unknown. She contrasted this "Garden of Eden" existence with our modern world of stress, where many people need alcohol, nicotine, anti-depression tablets, as well as illegal drugs just to get them through the day. But she didn't explain fully the reason for how this "Garden of Eden" existence came into being.

She said more in a workshop she conducted in London as she explained to us that there were other tribes in the same area who did frequently have wars with other tribes. She implicated that these wars were conducted in the same spirit as we have football games, except that people did get killed. This is also confirmed in studies done on Stone-Age tribes in New Guinea. In one incident in the 1960s, anthropologists observed a battle between two tribes that was called off because it started to rain! It seems that the warriors were worried that the rain might make their war paint run! Yet this violence was enough to change the nature of the tribe so unlike the non-violent tribes they did have, hierarchical customs, laws and taboos. While the women were made second-class citizens because they weren't warriors.

This then presents a mystery. If we as human beings did once live in a stress free world of non violence that is not only shown in Jean Liedloff's book but also in the archaeology of Neolithic cities and towns. Why did we voluntary move from a stress free world of peace to that of violence and stress?

In our modern world we are unaware that it is possible to create a stress free communities where conflict and violence are unknown. But the same cannot be said of the Indian tribes studied by Jean Liedloff, where non-violence tribes live alongside violent tribes. So the people of these tribes do have a choice of living a free, non-violent and stress free existence or living in a oppressive and violent community. So why would anyone voluntary choose the latter?

The purpose of any competitive game whether it is just a game of football or a tribal war, is to be a winner. It seems that the fleeting ego boost of becoming a winner is enough for men to want to risk their lives in a tribal war. Also in this system there are other ways of gaining an ego gratification. The chief has the ego satisfaction of knowing he has power over all other members of his tribe. While all the members of the tribe align themselves in a hierarchical system where although they know other members of the tribe are above them in the pecking order. They still have the ego satisfaction of knowing others are below them. As women and children are the lowest in this system even the lowest ranking man has the ego satisfaction that he is still above them.

So it seems that the rewards of ego satisfaction is enough for men to want to move from a non-violent, stress free world to that of a stressful and violent patriarchal system. As this system developed, men began to capture other men in war and forced them to become slaves. This became another way of gain ego satisfaction because the victors had the power of life and death over their slaves and so can force them do whatever they want. Sometimes this went to the extreme and developed into sadism where the victors enjoyed the power of being able to inflict fear, pain and suffering onto their captives.

This then becomes a problem for the male slaves because they were now at the very bottom of the pecking order with no obvious way of gaining ego satisfaction. The slave then has a choice of either hating his master and seeks ways to escape. So he looks for ways to get even with those who oppress them. Sometimes this was possible like in the case of Spartacus who led the most successful slave uprising in the history of Rome, (71-73 BC), but this was only a rare success for most slaves.

The other option was for the slave to identify themselves with their masters so they could bask in the reflected glory of the success of their owners. Also the identification with their masters also encouraged the slaves to compete with each other to become the master's favourite. (Something a sensible master would encourage). So it is from slavery that masochistic behaviour starts to appear, because it was only from masochism that a slave could gain any ego gratification. This then means that the master had a even greater ego boost in that he has forced men into slavery through violence. Yet in return he receives from many of them great loyalty and devotion. While the men who don't give him this, he has the sadistic pleasure of being able to torture and murder. So the invention of slavery also created sadomasochist desires within people as the only way to stay sane in such a barbaric system.

The path of the women into sadomasochism is different because she has a maternal instinct. Nature has designed women to give unconditional love and devotion to their children, because without the commitment of females, to care and protect their offspring, most animal species would become extinct. This is very true of the human species where the newborn baby is completely helpless and can take up to 20 years before it is fully-grown. This means that the maternal instinct in human mothers has to be very strong for the human race to survive. Because of this, it is commonplace that most women find themselves spending their whole lives caring for their children, grandchildren, their aged parents and their husbands.

When men began to move out of paradise into violent competitive games like war. Women would have resisted this move because they wouldn't want their sons or lovers being injured or killed. So this would of started a battle of the sexes that for a long time women seemed to have won. We can see this in Neolithic sites all over the world. Then this changed about 5,000 years ago when suddenly in the Bronze age archaeologists were finding cities and town full of weapons of war, fortifications and images of violence and conquest.

In the Neolithic sites archaeologists have found a predominance of feminine imagery. To the degree that it is accepted that people then worshipped female deities. Which also suggests that women then were then the dominant sex.

They perhaps had to be if they were resisting men's desire for competition and war. To do this they had to find ways to control and dominate men and this was probably done through mothers brainwashing their sons. Yet in the end this failed and men began to compete with each other creating wars and dominating women through violence. Women still continued to resist and even fought back as we can see in the case of the Amazons, but in the end men won and began to dominate the world.

Women then found themselves at the bottom of the hierarchical system in a situation of slavery. So like male slaves, women they had no option but to but to adapt and become masochistic. Though the feminine masochism was different to male masochism in one important factor.

Masculine masochism was a way a man could gain ego satisfaction by identifying himself with his oppressor. While feminine masochism was simply an extension of women's maternal instinct. Through her maternal feelings she could love her children unconditionally so she leant to extend this to love all men in the same way, even if men were now taking sadistic pleasure in hurting and humiliating women.

This then meant that men were gaining a even greater ego boost because they now could abuse women as much as they liked and yet only receive unconditional love in return.

This seems to be the case over the last two thousand years where it became commonplace in all relationships between men and women, the husband became the dominant sadistic bully while the woman became the submissive and masochistic wife. While any person that didn't fit this stereotype was considered to be "unnatural". Even up to the 1960s psychologists were claiming that all women were masochists. (Something no psychologist would dare claim today).

Yet if it was hell for both men and women to begin to live in a patriarchal world, it also can be hell to come back out of patriarchy.

There is a story that the great German philosopher, Friedrich Wilhelm Nietzsche became insane when he saw a donkey being beaten by a man. On a superficial level this story sounds silly and is used by Nietzsche's detractors to make him look foolish. Yet on a deeper level it shows a problem that all men have: Most normal men, if suddenly faced with feelings that give him real distress, like seeing a animal suffer, may start to worry that he is going "soft". But someone like Nietzsche being highly intelligent, self-aware and imaginative clearly saw the implication of this. He understood that once a man begins to feel empathy with others, he is at the mercy of a bottomless pit of human suffering.

Another famous philosopher Jean-Paul Sartre had the same problem because he once commented that,

The other is hell.

Indicating that he also had difficulty with his feelings of empathy for others. The problems with empathy is brought out in the poem, *No Man Is An Island* by John Donne,(1571-1631) with his famous line,

And therefore never send to know for whom the bell tolls, It tolls for thee.

The bells were tolling for a man who was about to be executed. Now we can react to a scene of execution in two ways. We can watch it as a spectator sport, which many people have done when we had public executions, and be very glad it is happening to someone else. The understanding of why people like to witness suffering comes from a scientific theory on why people enjoy slapstick humour. It is because watching people who are foolish or have misfortune makes us feel better, to know someone else is more foolish than ourselves, or has had greater misfortune. So these people can feel better about themselves by watching another person being hanged because they know someone else is worse off than themselves. The alternative is to feel empathy with the person who has suffered misfortune and that can be very painful. Which is what John Donne wrote about in his famous poem. This is supported by a saying on love by Francis Bacon. (1561-1626) Philosophers don't normally talk much about love, but his remark about love goes to the heart of the matter.-

He that hath wife and children hath given hostages to fortune, for they are impediments to great enterprises, either of virtue or mischief.

In other words if you care nothing for others you are free to do as you like, because if you care then that freedom is gone, because you have to think about the needs of others. This is something modern women know a lot about. It they have children, the family takes priority over her career and anything else, she may want to do. The other is not hell for a man who cares only for himself, or for a woman who cares for everyone, except herself. The other can only become hell, when people begin to feel love for both themselves and others at the same time. Because the needs what you want for yourself clashes with the needs of what others want of you. This then will create inner conflict.

A man who is totally selfish and cares nothing for others can be very strong and "macho". This allows great conquerors like Alexander the Great, Napoleon Bonaparte and Hitler to start wars with other countries and be unconcerned and even unaware of the suffering they inflicting on thousands or even millions of other people. In the second world war the Germans had no problem in recruiting young men to be concentration camp guards, while the allies had no problems in recruiting airmen to bomb German cities day and night, killing millions of women and children. This behaviour is only possible by men who are not in contact with the feelings and suffering of others. I remember once reading about a famous pilot in the Battle of Britain. He had shot down many German planes and had been excited whenever he had done this. Yet in one instance he had shot down a German fighter and had got close to it while it was going down in flames and could see clearly the pilot struggling to get out of the burning plane. He was then shocked to realise there were real human beings like himself in the planes he had shot down. It may sound crazy that a man who is fighting a war didn't realise that in the process he was killing other people. Yet the reason for this would be that when men start to be aware of the feelings of others they have to go into denial to continue to enjoy "macho" pursuits like fighting wars. Once a man realises he is killing and hurting other people like himself. Then war and violence become very difficult for him. Men who enjoy watching violent films are doing exactly the same thing. The pleasure of watching say a very violent James Bond film is only possible why you don't connect this in terms of the horrendous suffering going on, if is was played out in real life. In this way the spectators in the Ancient Roman games were more honest than people today who watch violent films. At least the Roman people were not divorced from the violence they saw. Where real people were being killed and maimed. Today we watch fake violent film, yet the enjoyment of violence is still the same.

Women are less protected by the reality of the suffering around her because of her maternal instinct, which teaches her to care for others. This can make it automatic that other people's feelings become her feelings. The masculine on the other hand is individual and in its purest form. So the truly "macho" man is only aware of his own feeling and totally unaware of the feelings of others. This is why it is possible for patriarchal leaders to declare war on other countries and be unaffected by the great suffering that a war will cause.

But many men find they can learn to love and care for others and find this so difficult that they will cut off their feelings for others. Resulting in some caring and loving man suddenly turn into a cold and uncaring monster These men, in learning how to have empathy with others, discovered that empathy was very joyful and easy when they have empathy with someone who was very happy. Their happiness became his happiness. Then when they find that the person they are in love with were also able to be very unhappy then they have a problem. The other person's unhappiness immediately became their unhappiness. So the solution to this problem was is to run away from other until they have got over it.

I know personally of a young woman who became convinced that her father hated her as a child because whenever she cried he would immediately become very angry and sarcastic with her. Yet in many other ways he did show he was a caring man. Again it was clear to me the father couldn't cope with his daughter when she become distressed.

What many women are discovering today is that they find men who are a real "Dr Jekyll and Mr Hyde". These men seem to be very caring and loving and then suddenly will turn on them and become uncaring monsters. Men who begin to learn how to have empathy with others will naturally only want the joyful part of empathy. Where it becomes a nightmare is when the person he has empathy with becomes unhappy and has no control over the situation because it is another person's unhappiness. Some husbands in this situation then can become very angry with their wives and children. He is telling himself, "why should I have to be unhappy because they are unhappy". This can result in many men physically attacking wives and children simply because they express unhappiness. Certainly there have been many court cases where a man has killed his own baby because the baby was crying too much. While the wife or girlfriend protests that she cannot understand it because he is normally a very kind and caring man.

Women themselves have a similar problem. It was easy in the patriarchal age for a woman to have empathy with everyone else while she didn't care for herself. Now in recent years women are beginning to find they have real problems in empathy with others, when they begin to be aware of their own feelings. It can be wonderful for women when they become aware of their own happiness as well that of others. Before they were always happy when their husbands and children were happy. Now by being aware of their own happiness, they can become even more happy and joyful. Unfortunately when things go wrong they can also be aware of their own misery.

In the past if a woman had a husband who wanted to spend all his money on drink and gambling, she might fight him for enough money to feed and cloth their children. But if she ended up with nothing it wasn't a problem for her, because the needs of her husband and children came first. But women today find that if they end up with nothing it is a real problem for them, because they are aware of their own needs as well. So they find themselves in a "no-win" position if they live with a irresponsible man. They are able to be strong enough to say clearly to their husbands: "No, you cannot spend all our money on drink, gambling, cars and computer games". Yet she can be still be unhappy and feel guilty about denying her husband what he wants. However if she were to give in to these feeling and give him what he wants and deny herself, she would also feel unhappy. It is no wonder that heterosexual women complain today that with men, "you can't live with them and you can't live without them".

It can get even more difficult than this: What women find wonderful about having a caring husband is that she finds she can make him happy by being happy herself. So a virtuous cycle can be created, she can feed off his happiness and he can feed off her happiness. Unfortunately the opposite can be true. Also with a caring man she might find that if she is unhappy it makes him unhappy, so she can feel guilty about being unhappy. This can then create a vicious cycle where both partners feed off each other's unhappiness, making the situation worse and worse.

For this reason many women having had a relationship with a caring man, will leave him to go back to a more selfish man. She knows that with a "strong" "macho" and selfish man he will not be concerned about her unhappiness. So the relationship cannot go into a vicious cycle where the unhappiness of both partners will strongly affect the other. Unfortunately what she will find is that it is impossible to change a very selfish man. If he has a behaviour pattern that makes her unhappy, like spending all the money they have on himself or treating the children badly. She is totally unable to influence him in any way, because he doesn't care if what he wants to do will make others unhappy. But a man, who is able to feel empathy with her, knows full well that if his partner is unhappy he will be unhappy. He then has a powerful reason to do all he can to make his wife or girlfriend happy.

So heterosexual women have two choices: They can have a man who is able to love and empathy with them. But they find he has real problems if they become unhappy. Or women stick to very selfish men, who are able to cope with women becoming unhappy, and will probably be more helpful in this situation. The downside is that there is nothing a woman can do, if he wants to behave in a way that makes her unhappy. She cannot appeal to his better nature because it is unlikely that he has one.

It would be very easy if we could give a quick and easy solution, as you see with many of these "self help" books., but real life is not like this. Even today if a woman gives birth to say a mentally retarded child, it is fairly normal for that woman to devote her whole life to caring for it, even into adulthood. On the other hand it would be very unusual for a man to do this. He might help his wife look after a mentally retarded child, but he would be very unlikely to take full responsibility and back off when the going gets too tough.

So we can see that compared with women men are just beginners at learning how to love and care for others. They haven't been exposed to thousands if not millions of years of a powerful maternal instinct that makes women want to care for children, animals and men. Many men today may have strong desires to love and care for others. But when they have to put these feelings into practice and face the misery, unhappiness and sacrifice these feelings cause, they often back off.

For this reason many men have become very frightened of empathy with others. They do not want to be at the mercy of other people's feelings, so they practice being very hard "macho" men. The same time women are finding it hard to learn to love themselves while loving others. A woman who is learning to love herself finds that she is always betraying herself by putting the needs of children and men before her own. She might then choose to learn to hate men and even learn to hate children, seeing it as a way to prevent her from sacrificing herself for others.

We as a human race are standing at a crossroads. We have before us two choices; one is of a far better future than we could dream is possible for the human race. The other is a far worse future, if that is possible. In the patriarchal age we only had one half of the human race behaving totally selfishly with no regard for the feelings of others. If in the future men continue to resist empathy because they do not wish to feel the suffering of others. While at the same time women continue to learn how to love themselves by hating other people. Then it means that all men and women will be fearing and hating each other. In the patriarchal age men mostly killed each other as well as women and children in wars because they feared and hated each other. But at least it was only 50% of the population doing this. It women were to join in and learn hate and violence from men then the whole of human kind would be behaving in this insane way. In such a situation the human race would quickly become extinct.

The alternative to this is that men stop resisting their desires to give empathy with others, and women do not go down the path of learning to love themselves by hating others. That is to say they stick to learning how to love themselves and love others at the same time. The positive thing about this all is that it gives human kind a far better future. The suffering caused in the patriarchal age was caused by the dominant sex, (men) being unable to care and empathize with others. With men in the future learning how to empathize, and women not suppressing their ability to do this. It means both sexes will be motivated to create a far more loving and caring world.

19

THE DENIAL OF OUR TRUE NATURE

We also learn from primate studies is that the human race has two possible futures.

1. We can behave like the chimpanzee and live in a very violent society dominated by men
2. We can behave like the bonobo and live in a peaceful world dominated by women.

So what are the fors and againsts both types of societies?

I suppose the attraction of our present patriarchal world is that it is exciting and interesting. We can see this from the type of TV programmes, films and book that people read and watch. Many entertaining stories are about conflict and violence. This then suggests that human beings enjoy violence and conflict because this is what they find entertaining. The problem is that many people who do enjoy these things on TV do not necessary want to experience the same thing in real life.

People who enjoy violence have to some degree go into a state of denial to do this. When I was a boy I was very interested in Naval history. One of the most exciting sea battles I read about was the battle of Midway during the Second World War, and I fantasised about being a dive-bomber pilot and destroy an enemy aircraft carrier in a dive bomb attack. Yet I could only do this through ignorance and denial. If I were to think about it deeply then this would ruin the fun and excitement of the fantasy. Denial like this can come in many forms. -

1. Only think in terms of destroying an aircraft carrier as just a ship. I didn't think about the thousands of men they would die is such an attack, or for that matter the parents who will lose their sons, of the wives who will become widows or the children who will lose their fathers. Nor did I think how some of these men might die. Aircraft carriers carry large amounts of aircraft fuel so many men will die by being burnt alive when this

fuel explodes. Other men might have time to jump into the sea, but a fleet under attack cannot stop to pick up survivors, so these men will more than likely be left in the sea, to die a slow death of exposure, thirst and starvation, or to die a quicker death of being eaten by sharks. Some men might even survive and be picked up but will have to live with both the physical and mental scars of such an experience. While other men might become blind or disfigured through being burnt, or loose limbs and spend the rest of their lives as cripples. The trauma of experiencing all your friends and comrades dying terrible death can also leave a man emotionally crippled for the rest of his life.

2. If men do start to think about men dying then you can de-humanise them by saying they are the enemy and deserve to die because they are "evil". This is what happens in ALL wars the justification of war is that the other side is bad or evil. So you then have to deny that that the enemy are simply human beings like yourself.

So denial is needed to make war possible. One of my heroes as a boy was the Duke of Wellington (1769-1852) or Arthur Wellesley as he was known before coming a duke. There as many reason why even now I see him as a great general. In an age when a general would expect to lose more men through disease and exposure than battle, he looked after his men and made sure they were properly fed and sheltered. Also in was common practice then for armies to "live of the land". Which in practice means stealing food from the local population. In the Peninsular wars Wellesley made sure his men were fed by food brought from England, in this way he didn't upset the local population. He also took pride in the fact he done his best to win battles with as few causalities as possible. He was also seen to become visibly upset over the deaths of his men. Yet in spite of the way he cared for his troops he also referred to them as the, "scum of the Earth".

At first sight this seems to be a paradox. Of a general through his actions showed that he cared about his men, yet referred to them as scum. Yet a bigger paradox is a general who cared about his men at all! After all this is what war is all about, to order your men to die and to kill the enemy. To have a job of a military leader means you cannot afford to care for your troops because if did you do you wouldn't order them into battle to die.

What made Wellesley a great general was the complexity and paradox of his feelings. The caring side of Wellesley made it possible for him to ensure as few of his men didn't die of disease, exposure or in battle, while his contempt of his men allowed him to order them into battle to die. This meant he led armies, which had high morale, who inflicted greater causalities on the enemy than on themselves. Which is the way you win battles. Because a general who doesn't care about his men at all, will also not care about the causality rate and can lose battles through running out of men. While a man who was a more caring of others than Arthur Wellesley wouldn't of become a soldier in the first place, as they wouldn't of want to order men to die. In other words it is denial of any feelings for others that makes war possible. The same is true for poverty. Poverty in only a reality in our world while the majority of the people think that the very unequal societies we live in is perfectly acceptable. Or believe that there is no alternative to inequality. Because after all Communism was a total failure in creating an equal society.

Yet as we have seen through Neolithic excavations that war, violence and inequality is not inevitable for human society. It is only inevitable while we keep on allowing very competitive and aggressive men rule our world.

What needs to be questioned is the idea that the "macho" way of doing things is the only way. And for people to be aware there is an alternative to this and that is the feminine way.

When putting forward this proposal people have asked me, "so what would you do with a person like Hitler". In dealing with a dictator who wants to conquer the whole of Europe and perhaps the world, there was no choice but to go to war with him. But the question should be, how extreme political party like the Nazi came to power in a country like Germany? This happened because the Allies try to punish Germany by making it pay for the cost of the First World War. Causing widespread poverty in Germany and fuelling discontent and hatred for the Allies. In the 1930s it was a toss up whether Germany became an extreme left wing Communist country or an extreme right wing country. In the end the extreme right won out. So in was "macho" method of punishment that created an extreme "macho" leader like Hitler.

The "macho" way is to deal with violence with violence and to be fair in the short term this seems to work. In the long term it keeps on fuelling resentment. As we see in case like Northern Ireland, Israel, and the Balkans. Also the "macho" way is to deal with crime is through punishment. You deal with criminals by putting them into prison to punish them, and no one asks the question, what causes a person to become a criminal? The reason this question is not asked is because the vast majority of criminals come from people who live in poverty. This then puts into question our very competitive societies of winners and losers. Where, "the winner takes it all" and the losers get nothing.

The very competitive nature of men is what creates our world of conflict, war, poverty and suffering. And this is what both men are women need to understand.

Women in there own quiet ways are making a difference. For instance as mentioned earlier, back in the early 19th century a wealthy Quaker women Elizabeth Fry visited a women's prison in London. What she saw there horrified her, where prisoners lived in squalor and some even starved to death because they were unable to pay for food. She then used all her wealthy contacts and influence in the Quaker movement to get something done. She started to educate the prisoners and put in the minds of people that prisoners need to be reformed and not punished. This to me is a clear message of the feminine way of doing things.

The problem is that as far as the general public knows the "macho" way is the ONLY way to get things done. This is because the "macho" way is so simple and easy. "If you have a problem, you go in and kick ass", which I have said, in the short term it seems to work. The feminine way of trying to come to grips with the roots of the problem is far more complex. Because we have to see all people as human beings like ourselves and not de-humanise people we fear, by condemning them as bad or evil. In other words you nurture and care for people and not compete against them and punish them for being losers.

The feminine way was once the way human being lived their lives back in the Neolithic age. Then just just a hand full of men created a plague of violence. These men found you could get your own way through violence and intimidation. In doing so they stole from and traumatised whole communities. In the process they brutalised other men whom in turn also became violent and uncaring of others. This became a plague that swept the whole planet as brutalised men conquered peaceful matriarchal communities and brutalised the people, and taught the men to be macho. Yet we don't have to continue the make the same mistakes that were made five thousand years ago. The foundation of patriarchy is a whole list of denials.

1. The denial of men having feelings for others.
2. The denial of women respecting and caring for themselves.
3. The denial that war is total insanity.
4. The denial of the widespread poverty and injustice of our world.
5. The denial of the archaeological findings of the Neolithic age.
6. The denial of field studies of the bonobo ape.
7. The denial of the Aquatic ape theory.
8. The denial of the Gaia Hypothesis.
9. The denial of the feminine.
10. The denial of any alternative to patriarchy.
11. The denial that you cannot overcome violence with more violence.
12. The denial that you cannot reform people through punishment.
13. The denial that competition taken to the extreme leads to violence, warfare, poverty and injustice.
14. The denial that aggression leads to fear, hatred, revenge and suffering.
15. The denial that our male leaders do a really terrible job of ruling our world.
16. The denial that if women could do far better jobs, if they don't try to behave like men.
17. The denial that it is possible to live in a caring world of love and compassion.

All these denials and the propaganda that men are doing a wonderful job in ruling our planet, keeps patriarchy going. Not only that, patriarchal denials are a danger to our planet. Back in the 19th century scientists pointed out that if industry keeps on pumping greenhouse gases into the atmosphere it will warm up the Earth. This was totally ignored by businessmen and politicians. Then in the 1950s scientists had the technology to measure the gases in the atmosphere and could prove that industry was increasing the CO_2 levels in the biosphere. Again they were ignored and when environmentalist took up this cause, industry employed other scientists to refute this claim. It was only in the 1980s when there was overwhelming evidence that the Earth was warming up that politicians acknowledged there was a problem. Yet this doesn't make a lot of difference because even though they have had "Earth summits" to tackle global warming, very little has been done. Simply because, to do something about this problem would undermine the profit margins of large international corporations like oil companies, but then as capitalists will tell you, "it is the bottom line is all that counts". So it seems that profits are even more important than the future of the human race.

The mass extinction's in the last Ice Age was caused by rapid climate change. Heating up the atmosphere with Greenhouse gases will have exactly the same effect. Signs of this has been already seen with the Sahara desert marching south at a very rapid rate.

Charities like Band Aid have tried to help, but nothing has been done about the underlining cause. It is unfortunately that drought caused by global warming has first effected poor and powerless third world countries in the Sahara region where it can be ignored by the rest of the world. Years of famine in the most powerful nations in the world, namely North America or Europe would of made a big difference and you would soon see action being taken over global warming, if it happened there. Though in the near future it is more likely to be flood that will affect these countries.

The fact that the ice around Antarctica is melting at a rapid rate doesn't seem to worry anyone. Even though when the ice on the Antarctic continent itself begins to melt, we will see rapid rises in sea levels, flooding coastal towns and cities.

It seems that in our patriarchal world we have become so adapt at denial, and care so little about the suffering of others like in the Sahara region. We are not going to do anything about it until there is some worldwide catastrophe that affects us all. Then it is going to be too late to do anything.

20

THE SISTERHOOD IS POWERFUL

We are supposed to be an intelligent animal with FREE WILL. As such we are suppose to be masters or mistresses of our own destiny. If this is true, then we are capable collectively of using our intelligence and our ability to choose to create a far better future for us all.

In the past we have not used our intelligence properly and as such have made very bad choices. We have somehow allowed ourselves drift into a world of conflict, hatred, violence and suffering. The sign a intelligence animal is being able to learn from its mistakes and correct them. If we claim we cannot use our intelligence to create a better world for ALL PEOPLE, then we have to revise any idea that we are a intelligence self motivating animal.

Which might be true, after all war must be the most stupidest way to settle differences between countries. Also with all the power of technology we have today, yet we are incapable of using it to prevent millions of our own species die every year from starvation every year. This is not only criminal but shows a real lack of intelligence or our part as well.

If we want to claim we are an intelligent animal then war, crime, poverty and malnutrition cannot possibly exist in our world. As an intelligent animal we are allowed to make mistakes but the sign of intelligence is the ability to learn from them and correct them. To continue to make the same mistakes generation after generation for thousands of years is certainly not a sign of intelligence. It is only very unintelligent animals that are driven by inappropriate instincts which to do things against its own self-interest. We can see this in the case of the Cold War where we nearly went extinct, and it is possible we might still do this through global warming and rapid climate change.

This means that "mankind" cannot have it both ways. Men cannot claim that they are the most intelligent animal on this earth and yet create a world of suffering. It is not an option to say, nothing can be done about war, crime and poverty, if we want to think of ourselves as a intelligent, problem solving, animal. Clearly war, violence and poverty are caused by man's aggressive and competitive instincts. Now these bellicose instincts may be appropriate in animals like bulls, stags and lions. Where it is essential for the survival of the species that only the physically strongest males get to mate and pass on their genes, but human beings no longer needs to rely on physical strength for its survival. We are an animal that for millions of years has relied on our brains and not our brawn. We know this, because physically we are the most weakest animal for our size in the animal kingdom. Neither do human males fight each other for the right to mate with females. So man's aggressive and competitive instincts are old instincts that are no longer befitting for our survival as a species. What is more, they are certainly very inappropriate for our well-being and happiness.

Five thousand years ago our species was taken over by a plague called violent aggression. Starting off by a few men who found they could dominate others through violence. Men and women on the receiving end of this violent reacted in very different ways. Men receiving violence became violent themselves, while women lost all confidence and self respect. Even though some of them attempted to fight back as in the case of the Amazons.

As the result we now live in a world that is ruled by aggression and competition. In recent years this violence has evolved into capitalism. Now to some degree this is a step forward as it is better that men fight each other for wealth and status through competing businesses rather than on the battlefield. Yet the foundation of capitalism is that, "greed is good". The theory being that men are strongly motivated by greed and competition, which as previously stated has created a world of winners and losers.

Yet is greed the only motivation for human beings, surely it would be better is we were motivated by LOVE. Most women have no problem with this when she has a child. She is motivated by her maternal instincts to want to care and love her children the rest of their lives. Men it seems also have a maternal instinct as well. True it is not as strong that of women. We can see this in many marriage break ups where it is mostly women who are, "left holding the baby". Yet modern experience has shown men are more than capable of looking after children. We even find some men take on the role of househusband and look after the children while the wife goes to work. As well as men who will care for children fathered by another man.

So if both men and women are capable of being motivate by love to care for others. Why do we then need to be motivated by greed, competition, vengeance or hate? We are supposed to be an intelligent animal with free will and because of this, collectively and individually we have a choice. We don't have to live in a world of violence, injustice and suffering if we collectively don't want to. We are surely able to use our brains where we are motivated by love and compassion for others.

From primate studies of apes, monkeys and lemurs, we have a choice. We can behave like the aggressive chimpanzees, orang-utans and hamadryas baboons, where alpha males rule through violence. Or behave like the more placid bonobo ape, vervet monkeys, macaques, olive baboons, patas, rhesus monkeys, grey langus, capuchins, prosimians and Madagascar lemurs. Human beings like other primates have within them instincts, that they can take them in either direction.

For many primates it was just chance that pushed them into the direction of living in either a male or female dominated society. This is clearly seen in the case of baboons. Baboons that live on the open savannah tend to be male dominated. This is because in the open plane there is nowhere for baboons to hide from predators. The only defence a baboons troop has, is for the large males to band together and collectively drive carnivores away. This means the males have a very important role in baboon society and it is a big advantage for males to be very strong and aggressive. This strength and aggression is also used to dominate the females. On the other hand baboons that live in forests tend to be female dominated. This is because forest baboon males don't attempt to fight off predators as everyone climbs up the nearest tree at the approach of a predator. Because of this the male don't have such an important role, and there is no survival need for male forest baboons to be aggressive. This allows the females to come together in a strong sisterhood to dominate the community.

We can see a similar pattern in human society. Women do look to men for protection, but not protection from predators but from other men! So it is a game men play of both assaulting and "protecting" women. Even today in the 21st century a young women who gets raped because she was walking home in the early hours of the morning are condemned, even by other women for, "asking for it". The absurdity of this was brought out in the open in India during the 1960s: The Indian parliament then was pushing through a law to place a curfew on women going out at night, because so many Indian women were being assaulted and raped by men at night time. Then Indria Gandhi made a speech pointing out that as it was men who were assaulting and raping women, it would make more sense if a nighttime curfew was place on men! Faced with this logical argument that no one had a answer to, the law was quietly dropped. In Pakistan it is even worse, if a women complain to the police that she was raped it is more likely for her to go to jail. So what men have been running for thousands of years is a type of protection racket against women. In that they assault and rape women and then tell women they have to look to men for protection.

As human beings we have a choice in this, we are not slaves to our instincts like many other animals. Patriarchy is a choice that was made five thousand years ago in encouraging the chimpanzee aspects of our instincts. Which brutalises men who respond by cutting off their feelings for others and becoming very brutal themselves. While women under this reign of terror lose all confidence in themselves and become subservient to men.

In my personal experience as a child of the 1950s, it was still accepted that boys needed to be, "toughened up", by their fathers, teachers and their schoolmates. So it was all right to brutalise sensitive boys because, "in our tough world you need to learn to be a real man". I also remember at that time the police gave women who complained to the police about rape, a really hard time. They would spend hours trying to break down their stories, so only the toughest and most determined women could push forward a rape case. Even if they are strong enough to do this, the judge was still more likely to let the rapist off. It was also commonplace that the police didn't interfere in "domestic disputes" which means husbands were at liberty to beat up their wives whenever that wanted to.

The problem is that we have been taught from childhood is that, the macho way is the only way. We don't hear very much about this alternative to this, namely the feminine way. Throughout the 19th and 20th century the feminine way has slowly and quietly influenced Western society. Not only has it allowed women the vote and equal opportunity laws, as women have gained more confidence in themselves they are quietly changing society.

The result is that human society now has a real choice. We can go back to the chimpanzee model and once again brutalise our children, or we can go forward and learn from the bonobo. The problem with the bonobo model is that we have all been brainwashed by the patriarchy that sex is "dirty". Even though most people in the West today are no longer practising Christians, society is still strongly influenced by Christian attitudes. Though since the 1960s there has been a sexual revolution that is slowly undermining these rigid patriarchal beliefs.

For a powerful Sisterhood based on the bonobo model to be created, women will have to do away with marriage and pair bonding. Women's loyalty to a male partner is one of the biggest blockages to creating a powerful Sisterhood. In the 1960s many hippies attempted to create communes, many of these were failures because the males had real problems with community living. So in the end the ones that survived either done so by having strict rules about community behaviour. Or, all the men left and it ended up with only females in the communes.

For women with children communes are ideal. This is because the children then don't become the sole responsibility of one woman. This allows women to, "have their cake and eat is as well", in that women can easy led a life outside of motherhood in having some of her sisters help in the looking after of her children. Female only communes are not so good for men because they no longer have a exclusive female partner to look after his material, emotional and sexual needs.

Pair bonding gives men a big advantage in the sexual relationship between men and women. In that it allows men to have a wife and family as well as the freedom to live a live outside of the family. Female communes give women the same advantages. In that her sisters can emotionally support her. So what would be that role of men in these communes?

Women have complained that man can change when they get married. A man may be very giving and considerate while he is wooing a woman. Then once a marriage has been established he finds he doesn't have to try so hard to please her and can be selfish and even abusive towards his wife. With the breakdown of marriage in recent times men find they cannot do this anymore, because the women is free to leave the relationship. In a commune it strengths the women's power even more, because she has the immediate support of her sisters, when things go wrong in a relationship with a man.

So it means without pair bonding men cannot take any woman for granted. If he wants to have relationships with women he has to find ways he can please them, all the time. He also finds he cannot afford to upset any women because as women are good communicators and he could find himself with a bad reputation. Which will mean other women won't want to have a relationship with him.

In the few matriarchal societies that have survived up until the present day, like in Minangkabau and Keralal the reason why they have survived is because of a simple custom. In most Eastern countries they have extend families, where brothers, sisters uncles and aunts all live in the same household. In the majority patriarchal communities the wife always lives with her husband's family. So she is at a disadvantage because the family she lives in will mostly take the side of the husband. While in matriarchal communities the custom is that the husband will live with his wife's family. Where he finds himself at a disadvantage for the same reason.

So we can see how a simple change in marriage customs can make such a big differences in the power balance between men and women. What is surprising is that the men in these surviving matriarchal communities do not rise up and demand the same marriage customs as the surrounding patriarchal society. The fact that they don't do this shows us that a matriarchal community has advantages not only for women but for men as well, because any strict patriarchal society only benefits a few alpha males. This is because in a society of winners and losers only a very few males become winners most men and nearly all women end up becoming losers. So even though a matriarchal society is loaded to benefit women, the majority of men are still better off in a matriarchal society as well. Because like women they are not being oppressed by alpha men.

To create matriarchal communities women cannot like men do it through conquest and violence, they will have to do it through persuasion. This is why matriarchy has to be attractive to both men and women. Also both men and women who agree with matriarchy have to resist the type of men who want to use aggression and violence to take over and rule. It means we have to stop making heroes of violent men and stop using aggressive macho methods to solve problems.

From what we know about the bonobo ape, the Neolithic age and modern matriarchal communities that has survived to modern times we know matriarchal does work. There is an old saying that goes, "knowledge is power". People in the past have been powerless against governments of alpha males because they were unaware their was a alternative to patriarchy. Once the common people know there is a viable alternative then the people have · choice of either staying with patriarchy or moving on to a matriarchal future.

BIBLIOGRAPHY

Alam, Bilquis: 1981, *Women Members of Union Parishad, A Few Statistics*, NILG, Dhaka.

Arvind, Sharma : *Women in World Religion,* New York Press, New York, 1990.

Benjamin, J.: *Socio-religious Status of Girl Child in India*, New Delhi, Ashish Publishing, 1991.

Bhai, N.: *Harijan Women in Independent India*, Delhi, BR Publishing 1986

Calman, J.: *Toward Empowerment: Women and Politics in India*, Colorado, Westview Press, 1992.

Dak, T.M.: *Women and Work in Indian Society*, Delhi, Discovery, 1988.

Datta, V.N.: *Sati: Widow Burning in India*, New Delhi, Manohar, 1990.

De Wolk, Roland: *Introduction to Online Journalism for Women*, Boston, Allyn & Bacon, 2001.

Dikshit, D.P.: *Political History of the Chalukyas of Badami*, New Delhi, Abhinav, 1980.

Gilligan, C.: *In a Different Voice: Psychological Theory and Women's Development,* Cambridge, Harvard University Press, 1993.

Hudson, Robert V.: *Mass Media of Women,* New York, Garland Publishing, 1987.

Jain, D.: *Women's Quest for Power*, Sahibabad, Vikas, 1980.

Jordan, J. V.: *Women's Growth in Diversity,* New York, Guilford Press, 1997.

Kelles-Viitanen, A.: *Invisible Hands. Women in Home-based Production*, New Delhi, Sage, 1987.

Langman, Larry: *The Media in the Movies*, Jefferson, NC: McFarland & Company, 1997.

Mathur, B.B.: *Women and Depressed Class Population in India*, Allahabad, Chugh, 1994.

Miller, Barbara: *The Endangered Sex: Neglect of Female Children in Rural North India.* Ithaca, Cornell University Press, 1981.

Mueller, R.: *Women's Work in Third World Agriculture*, Geneva, ILO, 1985.

Rozario, Sr. R. M.: *Trafficking in Women and Children in India*, Uppal Publishing House, New Delhi, 1988.

Selliah, S.: *The Self-Employed Women's Association, Ahmedabad*, Geneva, ILO, 1989.

Sims, Norman: *Literary Journalism in the Twentieth Century*, New York, Oxford University Press, 1990.

Viitanen, A.: *Invisible Hands. Women in Home-based Production*, New Delhi, Sage, 1987.

INDEX